Day 59
Still no sign of the South Pole.

'I think the Pole is part of a giant Stealth Experiment by the Americans,' Pom said. 'I think they've buried it so it's now undetectable and we're going to walk straight past it.'

For a moment I worried we might be going in the wrong direction. Perhaps the GPS and Argos had been hit by the millennium bug – and we were nowhere near where we thought we were.

Day 60
'What's that?' I shouted, and stopped in my tracks. Was it another false alarm? We strained our eyes to the yellow haze on the horizon once more. Sure enough, there to the left was a strange rectangular shape.

'Oh, wow, that's it,' cried Ann. 'Look, there's buildings everywhere.'

Dark, square boxes and a long, low building like an aircraft hangar slowly emerged from the mist. It was an extraordinary moment. This place we had longed for for so long was suddenly upon us. The miles we had travelled all fled from my head. Now nothing mattered but the last one or two.

TO THE POLE
Five Women in Search of an Adventure

Caroline Hamilton

For
Ann, Pom, Rosie and Zoë,
my family
and Pen and Mary Hadow,
without whom none of this would have happened

This paperback edition first published in 2001 by
Virgin Publishing Ltd
Thames Wharf Studios
Rainville Road
London
W6 9HA

First published in hardback in Great Britain as *South Pole 2000* in 2000
by Virgin Publishing Ltd

All photos printed by courtesy of South Pole 2000 Ltd; Denise Martin
(page 2); Randall H Landsberg, Center for Astrophysical Research in
Antarctica (CARA); Pen Hadow and Caroline Hamilton. Map on page
viii courtesy of the Polar Travel Company; map of daily positions in
Appendix 8 courtesy of the US Defense Mapping Agency. Top front
cover picture courtesy of Peter Noble-Jones.

A catalogue record for this book is available from the British Library.

ISBN 0 7535 0507 X

Typeset by TW Typesetting, Plymouth, Devon

Printed and bound in Great Britain by
Mackays of Chatham PLC, Chatham, Kent

Contents

Let me win; but if I cannot win,
let me be brave in the attempt

Special Olympics oath

ST. JAMES'S PALACE

When I was asked to be Patron of this Expedition I accepted with alacrity. I have a particular fondness for British eccentrics and a team of ladies, none of whom was a professional explorer, walking to the South Pole struck me as being in the very best tradition of British eccentricity. But it was more than that. This was a real and dangerous challenge, just like the team's previous walk to the North Pole. I admired them and I wanted to do all I could to support them.

It has been a great pleasure for me to get to know the team since becoming their Patron. I met them on a number of occasions before they left, marvelling at their growing fitness and good humour and much enjoying hearing about the plans and arrangements for the expedition. Their enthusiasm was contagious, but I cannot say that I was not a little worried about them, especially when they told me the extreme temperatures they would be experiencing and the dangers of the ice at that time of year. So I felt that I had to do something to keep them going and sent them off with plenty of Duchy Original biscuits, some cheese made with milk from my cows and, for Christmas Day, large boxes of Highgrove fudge....

I was kept closely in touch with their progress and was delighted to be able to speak to them on Christmas Eve. Even the most courageous of explorers must feel some sense of longing to be at home with loved ones at that special time of year and I did want them to know that they were much in my thoughts. I was relieved to hear, speaking to each of them in turn, that neither their joie de vivre nor their determination to succeed had deserted them - and that the supplies I had sent with them were being enjoyed!

It was a great day when I was given word that 'my ladies' (as I have grown used to calling them) had made it. That they wanted to speak to me first on their arrival at the South Pole was deeply touching and it was a conversation I shall never forget. When they returned home they showed me some of the video footage of the trip and, without doubt, the most memorable scene was the arrival at the South Pole, the team draped with a Union Jack singing The National Anthem through furry frozen masks - it was a 'unique' rendition, but none the less special for that.

I am immensely proud of "my ladies" and their great achievement. They managed something remarkable and they did it while maintaining good health and high spirits. They have given this country cause to celebrate and I could not be more pleased than to have been their Patron.

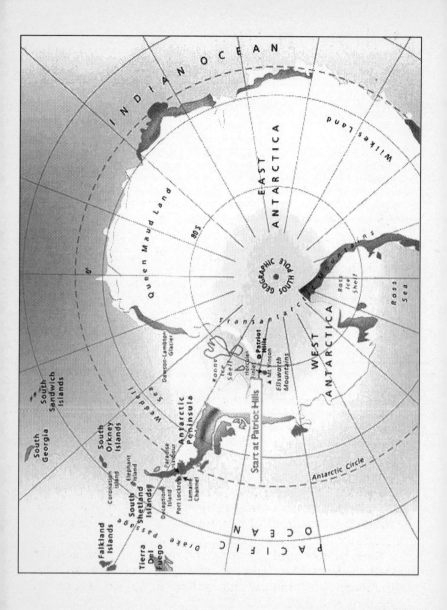

1 Ice on Sea

A T THE END OF THE EARTH, in an empty, white landscape, I tied the Union Jack to my ski pole. As I skied, the material unfurled in the wind. I felt like a modern-day Boadicea. But instead of riding a chariot, I was pulling a sledge.

This was the moment I had been waiting for. I looked at the women skiing beside me. We had trusted each other on this wild adventure. For a moment, I allowed myself to think the unthinkable: we were women battling alone against the elements, what would have happened if something had gone wrong?

In this pristine place, the sky was completely white. My emotions were swinging wildly. One moment I felt I was flying, the next every step was a trudge, head down, trying to ignore blisters and aching limbs.

For the last few days, the curve of the horizon had become more pronounced. As we skied closer and closer to our goal, thoughts filled my head. I had imagined the Pole since childhood. I had shared my idea with other women and, in so doing, realised I had struck a chord. There were hundreds of women who ached to take part in a territory formerly marked out by men.

Deep yellow sunlight appeared on the horizon and we skied towards the light. It was like entering another dimension. I felt moved and excited; filled with a sense of gratitude and awe.

Suddenly as we consulted the Global Positioning System (GPS) my stomach gave a lurch. Something was wrong. We were navigating by compass and using a GPS to confirm our position. Now, as we looked at the GPS screen I realised that, each time we took a step forward, our distance from the Pole was increasing. We were in a fantastical landscape where everything was fluid.

'We've slipped past the Pole and are heading towards Russia,' I said. 'We have to turn round.'

All attention was fixed on the task of tracking the Pole. Energised with a hunting instinct, every fibre of my being was on alert.

We moved into a fan so no one arrived before anyone else.

'Point zero three,' shouted Matty.

'Zero two over here,' Denise called back.

We had two GPSs and each showed we were a different distance from the Pole. We zigzagged in a frenzy, rushing towards whoever called out the lowest number. Eventually, by a process of elimination, we agreed on The Spot. It was just before midnight. I lifted my ski pole with the Union Jack. The flag fell behind me in a blaze of colour. I plunged it into the ice. A cheap flag bought from a souvenir shop near Victoria Station but, in that moment, it symbolised victory as well as family and all we had left behind.

We gathered round in silence. Pom started humming a familiar anthem.

'Pom that's perfect,' I said. 'We've got to sing it.'

We stood solemnly like soldiers, arms by our sides. As we sang our national anthem, our voices filled the white silence.

'Send her victorious, happy and glorious . . .'

I kept my head up. I was so full of emotion I did not dare catch anyone's eye. I felt filled with passion and possibility. Women had suffered trial by ice to make their mark. Nothing would ever be the same again.

At the end of our singing, we looked at one another. Someone let out a whoop of delight and in one instant my tears turned to laughter.

'We did it,' I said.

Then we were hugging and holding on to each other. Breathless with elation and relief.

We pitched camp that night within sight of our flag.

'Which way is the wind blowing?' Pom asked as she started unpacking the tent.

'South of course,' I replied. 'Everything is south from here.'

As I said those words, I felt a shiver. Why did 'south' suddenly have a magical ring to it? We had just conquered the North Pole and for the first time I thought of the South Pole and wondered how it would be.

That night as I snuggled into my sleeping bag in the tent which was our home, I acknowledged I was exhausted. After two years of planning and hoping, we were the first all-woman team to reach the North Pole.

A great wave of relaxation swept over me. I was literally on top of the planet. At last, I thought, I can let go. I've done it. And yet, at the edges of my consciousness, there was a sense of something, almost like hunger. Something was missing. What was it?

That night I dreamed of red, white and blue against a background of eternal white. In the dream I was puzzled by one thing, that underneath my feet there lay a solid mass of ice and rock, not frozen sea.

When we woke I wriggled out of the tent to be alone with the morning. We had reached the North Geographic Pole – the fixed point at the top of the planet. I ran in a small circle three times through every time zone in the world.

The sky was pale silver. A spectrum of grey, blue and off-white. I straightened my shoulders. My legs felt strong against the wind and I narrowed my eyes, gazing into the distance. Suddenly I knew what I had to do next. There was only one step to take. I decided I was going to the South Pole.

Here we were on a gargantuan, slowly splintering block of sea ice. At the South Pole, we would be skiing across a continent frozen solid. I remembered my dream of the previous night and the vision of a timeless land of ice. I thought of my father. I so wanted to tell the others about him but I could not speak the words. Without him, I thought, none of us would be out on the ice at all, let alone at the Pole. He always wanted to explore the frozen wastes. I hoped he was proud of me, his only daughter, fulfilling his dreams.

We drifted on shifting sea ice for seven days. We took it in turns to radio base camp at Resolute Bay with news of the weather and our spirits. The pilots of the Twin Otter aeroplanes were standing by to pick us up but, until the wind dropped and there was sun to put shadows on the ice to help them land, we knew it would be too dangerous.

There seemed no let up in the conditions. We sat or lay on our sleeping bags as the wind whipped across the ice and the tent flapped loudly. Each time someone stuck their head out to see what was happening, the skies remained determinedly grey.

I would not have chosen to be stranded at the North Pole for seven days and nights, but it was good to have time to reflect. It had been two years since we had launched the McVitie's Penguin Polar Relay and I had been living in a constant whirl. Even while we were trudging over the ice, I had reflected very little. Our world in the Arctic had become so small – we were all alone in a vast expanse of emptiness. Nothing had any meaning beyond the six of us and the boys at the end of the radio.

Occasionally I tried to think about work or friends back home, but I had no interest. My mind was totally concentrated on my immediate environment, how to get over the next ice ridge or lead, how many miles we had covered and how many more there were to go.

Now I thought about all the people who had helped us get here – the women who had come to the selection weekends, everyone who'd worked with us, as well as the other women on the relay. I felt an enormous sense of gratitude. Without them it could never have happened.

To pass the time one day, we each took a piece of spare tent fabric two inches square, a needle and thread. We laboured for hours to produce collage pictures. My badly-embroidered effort, entitled 'Pig at the Pole', consisted of two round pieces of pink birthday balloon, matchsticks for legs and a safety pin for a tail. Zoë's 'I love the North Pole' was the simplest and Pom was obviously dreaming of somewhere much warmer with her interpretation of clothes on a washing line which she called 'Arctic Dhobi'.

At other times, we played all the famous people word games we could think of. Pom and I spent a whole afternoon designing a fantasy house (complete with moat) and we all talked at length about where we would like to go for dinner and with whom. I chose Lech Walesa and the noisiest café in Soho. We all missed the sound of men's voices.

Rations were low. After two days, not knowing when we would be picked up, we split them between us to make them last as long as possible.

I had four Penguin biscuits, eight chunks of chocolate, twenty sugar lumps, a little bag of peanuts and a lump of salami. We also had one pasta dinner to share.

For Zoë and Lucy the tension was cigarettes. Zoë lasted the whole day on three-quarters of one cigarette. Every few hours she went outside to have one or two puffs, stubbed the cigarette out carefully in the snow and then brought it in to dry above the cookers. She was down to her last one and a quarter when we were finally airlifted out.

For large periods of the day, I turned myself into a parcel. I could not allow myself to worry about when and if the aeroplane would come. Instead I lay, semi-conscious, as thoughts drifted in and out of my head. I kept wondering what it would be like at the other end of the earth. Would it feel the same? I tried to picture the South

Pole but I could only see the globe and us hanging upside down.

Without noticing it, we were drifting up to five miles a day on the frozen ocean and, in places, the ice beneath us was only a few inches thick. I wondered how different Antarctica would be – in the middle of a continent which never moves and where the ice is up to two and a half miles deep.

Even as we were stranded at the North Pole, I knew I had to experience the magnificence of the polar wastes again. We had succeeded against all odds. I was filled with the power of success. I wanted to do it again. I wanted to lead another successful expedition – a journey this time to the bottom of the world. We were the first all-woman team to go to the North Pole. Now I would lead an all-woman team to the South Pole. This is my story.

2 August's Footsteps

I ALWAYS WANTED TO BE FAMOUS, or at least notorious. I never thought very far ahead and did not care what I was famous for. I just knew I wanted to be different. And that I wanted to be known.

I was a happy child, always intent on whatever I was going to do that day. I loved being outdoors – walking, fishing, roller skating. I wanted to be like my three older brothers Robert, Charles and Simon. From an early age I enjoyed boys' games but, as the only girl and the youngest, I was always outclassed.

'Unless you can keep up, you can't come out with us,' all three said.

They saw it as their duty to make things hard for me and ensure I was not spoilt.

I remember running to keep up with my brothers on walks. I remember watching them stoop to cup water from a stream with their hands on a hot summer day. I wanted a drink too and I lay on my stomach in the grass and stuck my face in the water. Cool, quenching bliss – until I heard their laughter.

'Only babies do that,' they said.

I burned with shame.

After that I always leaned and cupped my hands in streams, like them. I pretended I was drinking, but the truth was my five-year-old hands were too small and podgy to hold any water.

My youngest brother, Simon, had a smart blue bike with white mudguards. I coveted it – and the easy grace with which he could ride it up and down steps, rarely losing his balance. There were occasions when he let me ride behind him on my tricycle. Excitement, fear, adrenaline rush – I pedalled along, gathering speed and then suddenly I lost control – my tricycle, my head, my limbs, scraping along our mossy terrace. I cannot count the times Simon loosened my tricycle's wheels.

I never told our parents what my brothers did to me behind their backs. I knew telling tales would have made things worse. And, besides, my parents never took sides. They saw it for what it was: normal sibling rivalry. My parents' marriage was a real partnership and if I had to find one word to describe how they brought us up, it would be with fairness. They treated us absolutely equally at all times.

My parents married in King Henry VII's Chapel in Westminster Abbey in 1951. My mother, Jane, was the sister of one of my father's former pupils at Eton. She was nineteen and he was forty-two.

My father, Walter Hamilton, was a brilliant scholar, Headmaster of Rugby and Westminster, and Master of Magdalene College, Cambridge. At the time of his marriage, he was Headmaster of Westminster and my parents lived in the headmaster's flat immediately above the study. Being a headmaster's wife is a lonely position – made worse for my mother because she was so much younger than most of the other Westminster wives. It was also strange for her to entertain pupils at dinner who were almost her age.

My parents had three boys, two years between each. Then six years later I was born. Any shyness I might have had was soon dispelled. I learned to talk to anyone, I had no choice. My parents had such a public position the house was often filled with important people.

I remember conversations before school over big formal breakfasts. I remember academics and bishops and, once when I was very small, the Minister for Education, Margaret Thatcher. I was struck by her energy even then.

We spent all our holidays on the West Coast of Scotland at our house, Ardbeg, in Dervaig on the Island of Mull. It was at Ardbeg that we were a family (boarding schools for my brothers intervened during term time) and it was there we enjoyed a wonderful outdoor life.

The effort of transporting children and equipment from London to a Scottish island was considerable. But the rewards were great – space, rugged simplicity, the moods and changes of the sea – the perfect contrast to our lives down South. Mull was the place for having simple fun and adventure.

Our principal activities were fishing and walking. Most walks had a purpose, such as a trip to the beach to give the dogs a swim. Sometimes we took a picnic and then all bathed as well. My mother loved rushing down to the sea with her thermometer.

'Come on darlings, it's 57 degrees Fahrenheit. It's fine to swim,' she cried.

My brothers and I stripped off and stood shivering in the icy waters. Only then would Mother reveal she had no intention of bathing, at which point it was usually too late for us to turn back.

Father confined himself on such occasions to throwing his walking-stick endlessly into the sea for the dogs to retrieve, and then sending one of us out to get it when they failed to find it. Mother used to tease him that he loved our Golden Retrievers more than his children.

Most of all, I remember lobster and mackerel fishing, interspersed with the poaching of oysters. Every morning, religiously, Father set out with one or more of us to go lobster potting. As we grew up, we spent hours discussing where along the coastline the lobsters were most likely to be and then, once an unsuspecting creature had crawled into a pot, which would be the most delicious way to eat it.

On many afternoons we set out to sea again, this time in search of mackerel. Father sat in his large tomato-red jersey, pipe in mouth, one hand on the tiller of our boat and the other clasping a writhing mackerel to his stomach.

After a successful trip, we had more than enough to feed us for several days – and to use as bait for lobsters.

Ardbeg was basic, with no central heating and the minimum of furniture. It was a large, airy house and only the kitchen and sitting room ever got warm. In one was a coal-fired Aga, on which we could sit *in extremis*, and in the other was a large log-fire which Father poked from the comfort of his armchair.

No holiday was complete without the company of others. All sorts came to stay and were treated with enormous hospitality. In return, they were expected to behave as family and to participate in whatever was going on.

Sometimes we played cards, using cowrie shells as counters, but mostly indoors we read. Winter evenings in the Highlands are very long and I loved spending those hours deep in our books around the fire.

My father was the sort of man people never forgot. He had a profound influence on thousands of students over the years, many of whom went on to succeed as judges, cabinet ministers, clergymen and teachers. People often came to him for his advice – he was very wise and never judgemental.

Father's influence on me was no less profound. Behind a solemn appearance I remember him most for his sense of adventure, his charm and wit. He inspired common sense and allowed no time for pretentiousness or humbug. I will never forget the day I told him I did not want to go to university. I was seventeen.

'I'm not interested in studying,' I told him. 'Or reading books.'

His manner was often grave, his tone of voice low. His pipe was lit and the smoke curled up towards the ceiling.

'University is not just reading books,' he said. 'It is about education.'

For my father, education was paramount.

'You were born with a brain,' he said, 'you must make use of it.'

If you were good at something – no matter what – my father encouraged you to pursue it. I knew he wanted me to make use of my talents, however few they might be. He wanted me to live my life to the full.

I knew he was right. I left school and went to Cambridge University in 1982. I read a few books, made lots of friends and had a wonderful time, winning blues in hockey, athletics and cricket.

I then went on to a career as an investment banker before joining Screen Partners, a small film financing firm.

As a child, I loved reading about the Arctic and Antarctic. Father talked about Scott, Shackleton and the explorers of the past. I remember getting him to tell me about a man called August Courtauld again and again. Courtauld had been the first husband of a family friend, Mollie Butler, and he was awarded the Polar Medal in 1932.

On an expedition across Greenland, Courtauld ignored the advice of his colleagues. He chose to spend exactly five months in the winter of 1931–2 dug into a snow hole in the middle of the Greenland icecap. He was all alone, had no communication with the outside world and, for most of the time, was in total darkness underground.

'Afterwards,' Father told me, 'Courtauld said he had done it "to dispel the strange ideas of danger and risk in leaving a man in such a situation."'

Father's imagination was ignited. He always said if he had his life again he would have been a polar explorer. I never imagined it would be possible for me or that I might be the one to follow in August's footsteps.

3 An Accessible Wilderness

P EN HADOW WAS A ROMANTIC figure in my life – even before I met him. A polar explorer. A real life polar explorer – and my friend Mary was dating him. She gave me details, of course, the way friends do. But they weren't the details I wanted. He had done dangerous things in his life. He knew the meaning of adventure. What was he like?

He was an old-fashioned hero – in my imagination and, later too, when I saw him. It was 1994, I was 31. I arrived late at Mary's party to find the guests clustered in groups, the largest centred around a man about my age. I remember his strong, protective arms. And my sense of him – I instinctively trusted him.

He was talking animatedly about plans for his next expedition. He spoke of thousands of miles of frozen white sea, an endless inaccessible landscape.

It came to me effortlessly, suddenly – the thought made itself known as if it had always been there.

'I'll come with you,' I said.

'How do you do?' he replied rather formally. 'I'm Pen Hadow. Who are you?'

I felt shy, embarrassed. 'I'm Caroline,' I said.

And suddenly I was telling him how I'd always had a burning desire to see the polar wastes and stand on top of the world. Here he was: an Arctic explorer and I was suddenly filled with all the questions from my childhood.

'What do you do for water?' I asked him.

'We melt snow.'

'What do you eat?'

'The highest calorie foods you can think of – salami, butter and nuts,' he said, 'and chocolate and chocolate and chocolate.'

'What do you do in the evenings?'

'On my last expedition, I had a miniature edition of *Winnie the Pooh's Expotition to the North Pole*,' he told me. 'Do you know it?'

'Of course.' I had read it as a child.

'That's all we had,' he said. 'We used to read it out loud to each other every night.'

'For how long?'

'Thirty-six days.'

Thirty-six days in a place unimaginably cold and hostile – with cruel and sudden Arctic storms – yet Pen made it seem an environment in which I could not only survive but even snuggle down at night and read stories.

He told me a sledge-hauling expedition to the North Pole involved skiing and dragging a sledge over rough sea ice that can split open in front of you. He clearly revelled in sub-zero temperatures and, as he spoke, I did not think about the discomfort, the pain or the cold.

Pen described the way everything was pared down to the smallest, the lightest, because you had to carry it with you always.

'We even cut the ends off our toothbrushes,' he confided.

I thought of my back-packing trips through Asia, East Africa, South America, Russia and Europe – and the glee with which I always took the smallest rucksack. The joy I found in having my whole home on my back. Self-sufficiency – life pared down to basics.

Pen spoke of the emptiness and grandeur of the Arctic. He said the ice and landscape were majestic – *majestic* – his whole being seemed suffused with it. He was so alive. It was his passion for the Arctic, it was the simple details, it was the fact I was finally talking to someone who had visited the bleakest outer reaches of the planet.

'Do you think it might ever be possible,' I ventured to ask him, 'do you think one day I might be able to go?'

'Of course,' he said. 'It's just a question of putting one foot in front of the other and having a cup of tea every few hours.'

The amazing thing about Pen was that he wasn't trying to be a hero. In fact he seemed to go out of his way to make the Arctic accessible to me. He didn't tell me I had to do one hundred press-ups every day or have incredible, special talents. He didn't try to shock or scare me. Within one conversation with Pen, my vision of experiencing the white emptiness of the Arctic became a possibility.

A few months later, I had an operation to rebuild my right knee after a hockey accident. Pain, boredom, a ten-month daily grind of exercises which I undertook stoically only because I was determined to be walking again as quickly as possible.

When I was finally able to walk without crutches, I was filled with the joy of a newly healthy body. I had taken it for granted that my body would enable me to do anything I wanted. After ten months of being incapacitated, I realised how lucky, how privileged I was.

I met Pen again in 1995 a few months later and we talked a lot about the North Pole. With evangelical enthusiasm, he conveyed the magnetism and allure of the polar wastes.

'I want ordinary people to be able to experience the Arctic for themselves,' he said.

Pen wanted to capitalise on his work as a polar guide and set up a specialist travel service for the polar regions.

'The service will be called The Polar Travel Company,' he told me. 'If you want to go to the North Pole, there must be other people without polar experience who would like to as well,' he said.

I agreed. But I still did not understand how I could do it. I wanted to make the journey within normal holiday leave, did not have much money and only had limited free time to prepare.

The solution was simple and completely original.

'We'll hire guides,' Pen said, 'and make it a relay. Then lots of women can have a go without being away for too long.'

So was born the first ever all-woman expedition to the North Pole. Five teams of four, with two guides, would each travel as far as they could in up to eighteen days. At the end of each leg, the next team would be put down on the ice to continue where they left off. Gradually, over 74 days, the teams would make their way over 500 miles of Arctic Ocean to stand on the top of the world.

I was travelling to the official press opening of the Polar Travel Company when I heard a news story on the radio. An English woman, Alison Hargreaves, had been killed on K2.

'Have you heard the news?' I asked Mary glibly when I arrived at the hotel.

She was busy handing out passes and checking reporters' names as they arrived.

'Oh God,' she replied in an unusually soft voice. 'I hope this lot don't know.'

I did not understand her concern. I had never been to a press event before and was impressed with the number of reporters asking questions. I stood in the crowd, glass in hand, filled with excitement.

'Thousands of people want to go on expeditions,' Pen enthused from the stage. 'In fact,' he said looking around for me, 'I have one such person here in the room.'

Outside the photographers clamoured to get pictures of Pen drooling over a giant ice cream on a skidoo (motorised toboggan). I was convinced it must be a great success. I had no idea then that the media do not always run the stories they cover.

By the following morning, the problem was all too obvious. It was not the day to talk about a company designed to take amateurs to dangerous places. The newspapers were filled with stories of Alison Hargreaves

– her death reawakening a furious and controversial debate about motherhood, ambition and risk.

Men, it seemed, were permitted to take risks and have adventures; no one asked them to explain themselves. But women? The bottom line was we were supposed to be mothers first and people second.

The newspapers were suddenly anti-adventure. Less than six weeks earlier Alison had reached the summit of Everest, unsupported by Sherpas or other climbers, and without bottled oxygen. Her plan was to climb K2 and so become the first person to climb the world's two highest peaks in a single calendar year.

That Alison was capable of achieving this feat was not in doubt, but newspaper reports focussed only on her motherless children Tom, then aged six, and Kate, four. Two of the four women who had climbed K2 before had died during the descent, as had a number of men. By the time Alison saw K2 in 1995, there had been 113 successful ascents and 33 deaths. What right had a mother – the papers demanded – to risk her life in pursuit of sport or adventure?

I remembered Alison being quizzed by the papers about her risk-taking. I remembered her reasoning because it echoed my own. If I thought it was desperately dangerous, I wouldn't do it, she said, citing that she drove on motorways at night and did many other very risky things in her everyday life.

Pen was despondent. Because of Alison's death, the launch of his company had been ignored. A few days later Mary called me.

'Pen needs to prove he can arrange expeditions for ordinary people, not just talk about it,' she said.

'Well why doesn't The Polar Travel Company launch the relay idea with me instead?' I said, suddenly realising this was my chance.

A week later, in August 1995, I found myself at another photo-call. This time I was the centre of attention as I sat with a group of girlfriends in white clothing on a sledge by

Captain Scott's statue in Pall Mall. (Most of them did not know where the Arctic was, let alone want to go on an expedition, but they were attractive and our PR agent, Mary, said they would help get our photograph into the newspapers.)

We smiled and laughed as seven photographers jostled in front of us and took it in turns to arrange our poses. I felt strangely inanimate at first and then, when my friend Clare was singled out and asked to step forward for close-up shots, I felt I was at a dog show.

'What's going on?' we asked. 'Why is that guy taking photographs of her on her own?'

'I shouldn't worry about it, girls,' came the reply. 'He just wants pictures for his bedroom wall.'

The following day, I rushed out to the newsagent and bought all the national newspapers. I sat on the floor in my flat, desperately turning the pages until, suddenly, there we were. On page twelve of the *Daily Telegraph*, the grumpiest of all the photographers had got our picture into the national press. It was completely bizarre. I stared at the picture, trying to take it all in.

Within hours the telephone started to ring. Regional newspapers and local radio stations, as well as BBC Radio 5 Live, got hold of the story and, throughout that week, they asked for interviews. Sometimes I went into the studios but mostly I talked on the telephone. The box room at work became known as the Interview Room where I 'spoke to the nation'. At very short notice, I was booked for slots of four or five minutes and heard the show going on down the telephone as I waited my turn.

Journalists were obsessed with Alison Hargreaves. I longed to tell them that, without her death, our expedition would never have got off the ground.

'Going on a polar expedition is quite different from climbing a mountain,' I reassured them. 'There's nothing to fall off – and if you need to be rescued you're moving so slowly you're easy to find.'

The same questions were repeated. How cold will it be? What will you eat? When are you going? I soon learned there was no time for complicated answers, even if I had known enough to give them. I focussed solely on making sure I conveyed key facts.

Pen and I wanted any woman to apply for selection – no previous polar experience was required. The expedition would involve no more than four weeks' holiday and, provided we got sponsorship, it would cost only £1,500 each. Finally the number to call was the Polar Travel Company.

The response was overwhelming. I did one interview from Pen's office and, no sooner had I put the telephone down, than it rang again.

'I've just heard on the radio about this expedition to the North Pole,' a man said. 'It sounds perfect for my wife. Please could you send her details?'

The media were intrigued by the ambitiousness of the plan and so were the hundreds of women who called in an endless stream.

'You said you're looking for nineteen women to go with you.'

'Yes.'

'How do I apply?'

Mothers, students, lawyers, business women, teachers and artists all wanted to be part of the expedition. It seemed that everywhere, in all walks of life, women were looking for something more, something different – a challenge to push them to the very limits of themselves.

I was like them and had no special experience. This made the ultimate wilderness more accessible – or at least turned it into a possibility. These were women with the courage, determination and sheer bloody mindedness to leap at the opportunity of a lifetime.

We sent details to over two hundred women.

'It was simple,' one of the applicants, Rosie Stancer, said. 'It was as if a lit match had been dropped on to paraffin.'

Another, Rose Agnew, told me: 'That was it. I knew at once why I had always kept so fit and the way my life was meant to be.'

4 Wind and Rain

P EN AND I DECIDED TO HOLD two outdoor selection weekends so the twenty strongest women could emerge. In January 1996, five months after launching the Women's Polar Relay, 65 would-be explorers converged on Dartmoor in Devon for the Introductory Weekend. It was a chance for the applicants to meet Pen and me and learn more about the Arctic and the expedition. It was also a weekend in which they could meet each other and we could find out about them.

I caught the train from London at lunchtime on Friday. The morning was typically frantic – two radio interviews and two late taxis meant I flew into both studios with only seconds to spare – and it was a relief to sit still at last. I spent most of the journey preparing sponsorship packs for the women, determined to share the load of raising the finance. I had little time to think about what lay ahead.

A friend of Pen's picked me up from the station at Newton Abbott and drove me to the top of Dartmoor to Wydemeet, Pen and Mary's new house. I had not been to this part of Devon before and instantly warmed to the views. The feeling of desolation reminded me of Mull. The weather was fine and there was the same soft light soaking up the greens and browns of the moor.

Wydemeet is a large, family house set on its own in the middle of the moor. Pen and Mary had moved only weeks before and there were packing cases everywhere. The house had a warm family feel and it was a hive of activity when I arrived.

Preparations were well underway for the 60 strangers plus an unknown number of journalists and photographers soon to arrive. Pen was tidying the ramshackle barn next to the house and sweeping the yard. Mike Ewart-Smith, one of numerous friends who had been inveigled to help, was constructing portaloos and Mary was rushing about looking after journalists.

Scarcely pausing to say hello, Mary ordered me down to the river. There I found her bemused cleaning lady sloshing about in walking boots, posing as a hopeful polar explorer. It did not seem fair so, within minutes, I was in the water fully clothed, trying to look tough for a tabloid photographer.

Some women arrived early. I did not introduce myself and sent them off until the appointed time. Shy and a little apprehensive, I had a strong urge to remain anonymous.

Later, I watched from a corner as Mary checked the women into the barn like an airline stewardess. Bales of straw were piled up around her.

'Vegetarian? Blood group? Next of kin?' she asked each of them in turn.

They were given a glass of mulled wine and packed lunches for the following day. It amused me that, despite Mary's concern about dietary needs, she had provided exactly the same for everyone – a lump of cheese, an apple, chocolate bars, and a venison pie. One of the applicants, Andre Chadwick, earned points when I heard her announce:

'I'm vegetarian but I'll eat meat if that's what I need to do to get to the Arctic.'

I had no idea what most of my prospective team-mates were like. Would they be much tougher and heartier than I was? What would they think of me, their self-proclaimed leader? Would I be left stranded as they strode across the moor? Or would the expedition fail here, as they all burst into tears in a bog?

I looked them up and down without speaking. I was nervous. They came in all shapes and sizes, all ages, and from all over the UK. They had different clothes, accents, backgrounds. My friend, Pom Oliver, arrived slightly drunk off the train with her friend Ginny Rhodes, who could have been a stand-in for Patsy in *Absolutely Fabulous*.

'Has anyone seen my gold American Express Card?' Pom called across the barn.

The others looked at them nervously.

Some women had barely camped in their lives, others had never carried a rucksack or taken any strenuous exercise. Some were not very fit. As they introduced themselves, the barn was filled with excitement. Here was a unique opportunity for them to take part in a classic Arctic adventure. People said the North Pole was not for women, but why not?

The women had travelled miles to hear more about this thing we had called the Women's Polar Relay. It was a curious feeling. Pen and I stood at one end of the barn. At last it was time to speak; my voice sounded thin and quivering.

'Without me,' I said rather pompously, 'none of you would be here. I find it absolutely amazing that you not only want to go on holiday to the North Pole, but that you all want to go there with me.'

There was a hush as Pen told them more. The cold, the discomfort, the physical hardship, he could scarcely have painted a bleaker picture. But these women were not to be discouraged. The excitement was growing and, even if we had wanted to, there was no going back. Pen and I looked at each other. We were both thinking, what have we done?

When we woke at 6 a.m., it was not just raining, it was pouring. Pen told us we would walk all day across the moor, but no one knew exactly what lay ahead. We ate porridge from large steaming vats, then packed our rucksacks with sleeping bags, survival systems and all the spare clothing we could find.

Nervously, we checked what everyone else was wearing. No one wanted to be the odd one out, and we pulled on an assortment of outdoor and waterproof gear. Some had smart coordinated outfits and sturdy walking boots; others had thin soles and light jackets which might have been suitable for a stroll in the park but were sadly inadequate for Dartmoor. The wind and rain lashed down on us for fifteen hours.

A journalist from Pen's press conference was an eager applicant. Her name was Susie Fairfax and she walked in style. Her borrowed waxed coat trailed on the ground, set off perfectly by a green *Harrods* bag for a hat.

'Don't laugh,' she said when I remarked on her gold lamé gloves. 'Astronauts wear them. They're ever so warm.'

I was most wary of the tough-looking women in military fatigues and jackboots. Victoria Riches' were left over from her days in the Territorial Army, while Ann Daniels' belonged to her husband, the trousers were at least six inches too long and kept falling down.

Out in the yard, Pen gave a roll call and divided us into three groups. Each had a guide and a leader to navigate. Rob Dixon, a local rescue man, was in charge of my group. He knew every inch of the moor and I felt he could have led us over it blindfolded. A polar friend of Pen's, Oliver Shepard, was there too.

It was a bitter January weekend. Because of the mist we walked with no idea of where we were going. Visibility was down to a few yards and the rain lashed horizontally.

The three groups merged into one and we straggled along for over twenty miles. With no paths to follow, the going was slow. I stumbled over the tufts and bog, trying to talk to everyone. All I had was a few short profiles the women had provided. I could not see anyone under their waterproof hoods and instead tried to guess who they were from the way they walked.

'Isn't it brilliant?' a woman in her twenties said excitedly. 'I've never been in a bog before. When you put your foot on a green mossy bit it sinks in and then you get water over the top of your boots.'

The day wore on but the women were undaunted. We marched uphill and downhill across the bog. We waded through rivers and slipped and slithered across rocks. Drizzle turned to rain. Water seeped up from our boots and poured down from our necks. It never stopped raining. Sometimes we stopped to eat or cover our blisters.

The women talked all the time and, at every point, whether walking or standing, they encouraged each other onwards. No one would have known they were competing for places. Their spirit was overwhelming.

Only a couple dropped out through asthma and exhaustion; the rest carried on. It began to get dark. Some had torches. No one except Rob Dixon knew where we were. We were all very tired, very cold and very wet, but no one was going to admit it. We had set our hearts on the Arctic and were not going to drop out now.

'Over here,' someone called. 'I think Lisa's too cold.'

One of the women was shivering uncontrollably. We huddled around her like penguins and carried on.

Twelve hours after leaving Wydemeet, we came to a ruined farmhouse. It was now pitch black and the coldest it had been all day. We were soaked. I felt cold from the inside out. Most of the women were too tired to talk and I sensed not everyone wanted to carry on.

I squeezed next to Susie Fairfax.

'What would you give now for a baked potato washed down with a glass of ferocious red wine?' she whispered.

'Quite a lot,' was the answer.

'OK, girls. Well done,' Pen shouted above the wind and rain. 'We're abandoning the last bit of the walk. We don't think it's safe. If you make your way up the track, you should get to the road. Princetown is a few miles away and there'll be cars to take you to Wydemeet.'

So that was it. We had done it. Only a few more miles with our heavy rucksacks and we piled, steaming and sweating, into a pub for a beer. We unpeeled our dripping clothes with frozen fingers and rubbed the water out of our hair. Freed from their waterproofs, I saw people's faces for the first time.

Next morning, Pen outlined some points of navigation and gave each group map references to find. Most women had never used a compass. Everyone was tired but on a tremendous high. Pen and I asked the women if they still wanted to go to the Arctic. Only two said no. The rest were keener than ever.

By the end of the selection weekend, any doubts I might have had about the expedition were gone. I was inspired by the women's enthusiasm and the enormous energy they created. Even if I had wanted to, I could not let them down now.

I thought of the women with fondness. And admiration. They had come to hear about an expedition to the North Pole and, despite all we had done to them, they had put their trust and confidence in us.

Over the months, the spirit of the women kept me upbeat.

'All we have to do is channel that energy,' I said to Pen. 'If these women can't get sponsors, nobody can.'

We wrote letters to every company we could think of. Every day I spoke to the other women by telephone. I tried to support them and coordinate their ideas.

At the same time, I was sending out hundreds of sponsorship letters. Pen and I followed up endless ideas – and the tiniest of leads. Mary had done a fantastic job getting us media coverage. This had to help attract a sponsor. I was convinced all we had to do was contact enough companies. One of them was bound to support us.

After only a few weeks, Mary called.

'A girl from the PR agency representing Neutrogena Norwegian Formula has seen an article about one of your women, Rosie Stancer, in the *Daily Mail*,' she told me. 'She says it's the perfect opportunity.'

'What did she say?' But even as I asked I could feel it, the thrill in my blood.

Mary paused for effect.

'She said "If you don't have any other skincare sponsors, we would be very interested." '

I was thrilled and yet not surprised. Somehow I had always imagined it would be this easy.

Rosie Stancer worked at the Park Lane Hotel and we arranged to meet the PR people there. When I arrived, a smartly uniformed concierge telephoned Rosie's office. As I waited in the lobby, I suddenly realised I might not recognise her. Like everyone else on Dartmoor, she had been zipped up in her waterproofs. Even so, I would never have been prepared for the vision that swept down the stairs. Rosie was impeccably elegant in a cream silk suit and teeteringly high shoes. She saw me at once, rushed up and kissed me loudly on both cheeks. There was not a hair out of place and I had never seen such beautiful make-up. This was Hollywood, not the Arctic. I almost gasped out loud.

'That must be them over there,' Rosie whispered, pointing at two women in black. 'Let's go and knock them out.'

There in a West End hotel, four city women sat talking about the cold, exhaustion, polar bears and the need to keep our skin soft. The women from the PR agency were hooked.

That night Rosie entertained Pen, Mary and me at the Park Lane Hotel. We talked about a hundred different things and then, over dinner, the subject of the Royal Family came up. Out of pure mischief (and wine very probably) I decided to hold forth about the Queen Mother. I blamed her for the woes of society.

Pen and Mary were squirming but I would not be stopped.

'And another thing . . . No, no let me finish,' I kept saying.

Finally, after many minutes, I ran out of steam.

There was silence.

And then Pen asked, 'Caroline, you do know who Rosie's great-aunt is?'

I looked at him, bemused.

'She's the Queen Mother.'

* * *

Mary and Pen drove up for our next meeting with the PR agency and we sealed a deal. I was disappointed our total budget was way in excess of the sums Neutrogena had available. It was an important sponsorship lesson: don't raise your hopes until you know the thing is yours. We were happy to settle for a cash contribution – and several crates of hand and face cream.

The weeks and months wore on. We were still writing letters and making telephone calls. We summoned the women to two meetings in London where we discussed what to do and divided tasks between us. Several women turned out to be creative; others discovered skills they had never known they had.

Pen and I travelled all over the country to sit in front of one disbelieving marketing or PR executive after another. Even if we managed to spark their interest in a meeting, the answer was always no when our proposal went up the line.

'We decided to sponsor a local youth basketball team instead.'

'We haven't budgeted for anything like this.'

'The chairman only likes football.'

I could not understand it. Newspapers, television and radio continued to show so much interest Pen and I worried the coverage might blow itself out – yet companies refused to take us seriously.

I knew nothing about sponsorship before we began but I had soon learned the basics.

'Sponsorship is not just a source of corporate entertainment, you know. We're an asset you can buy and make work for you to raise your profile,' I complained vigorously one day.

We discussed holding the second selection weekend in July 1996 but, hoping more funding would come through, eventually fixed on a date in September. A few of the women were my friends. The rest I had got to know since January. I liked them and did not want the relationships we had built to affect the selection process. Pen and I decided to ask an experienced impartial team of outdoor selectors to run the weekend.

We deliberately told the women nothing about what the weekend would entail, to build up their worst fears, expectations and nerves. All they knew was to arrive at 6.00 p.m. on Thursday 12 September 1996 at the Adventure Centre, Kelly College in Tavistock. Dress code similar to last time and be prepared to be put through hell.

In glorious September sunshine, Dartmoor looked welcoming. So different from last time. The women greeted each other. Everyone was worried about the food and equipment they had brought with them. Was it right, too much, not enough? We were all excited. It was going to be survival of the fittest.

We put our kit on the lawn to be checked. Pen had provided us with an equipment list and anything surplus or too luxurious was removed. Wrist watches were taken away too – a trick designed to disorientate. It was interesting to see how it added to people's uncertainty.

The weekend was run by Jack Russell and his team at Kelly College. The women were briefed on navigation and map reading. Pen and I divided them into five groups, each with two selector-observers. Then we were taken on to the moor.

It was dark and each group was given a sawn-off telegraph pole, six feet long. The pole had to accompany us at all times – a test of team spirit and coping with a useless object.

We had been given a set of coordinates to aim for, but first we had to work out where we had been dropped.

'How embarrassing – I took no notice on the drive,' one woman said.

'Neither did I.'

I listened while my group debated amongst themselves, watching more than participating.

Eventually we set off through a bog. We came to a heap of enormous boulders stretching up into the sky. We clambered all the way up, carrying the pole and our fully laden rucksacks. At the top, small groups huddled, preparing themselves for the next ordeal: an abseil. Suddenly I realised I was scared of heights. It also seemed completely unnatural to me to walk backwards off the edge of a cliff.

'All you have to do is step off into the darkness and sit back and enjoy it,' Jack Russell said, fixing my climbing harness.

I looked at him as I stood on the edge chattering on to disguise my fear.

'Don't be ridiculous,' I said. 'I'm not doing that. I can't think of anything worse.'

Through careful coaxing, Jack eventually persuaded me to start. I gripped the rope as tightly as I could. I did not enjoy it at all and, two hundred feet later, was very relieved to land at the bottom.

It was fear of failure that drove me on. I would have found it hard to face the others if I had not managed it – particularly when I discovered the demons some were facing.

'The last time I abseiled it was with my boyfriend,' one of the women told me. 'He went first and didn't tie himself on properly. I stood at the top and watched him fall off and die.' Then she confided: 'That's why I went first this time. I knew if I didn't, I would never do it.'

At the bottom, we had a bidding game for tarpaulin and ropes to make a shelter. I slept with my group of ten under an enormous piece of plastic. I have no idea how long I slept. I think it was half an hour. Dawn was breaking when we arrived at a lake.

The water was freezing and reminded me of bathing in Mull. We swam across in groups of four, fully clothed and pulling our rucksacks behind us. Everyone laughed when a plastic bag shot out from Sue Riches' jacket. It was the false boob she had worn since recovering from cancer. We put on our spare (not altogether dry) clothes from our rucksacks, then set off for more miles across the moor.

I moved between groups, wanting to watch and talk to everyone. Although we had independent assessors, I had a veto. Not everyone was going to be in my relay team; even so, if I couldn't imagine sharing a tent with someone, I didn't think it was fair anyone else should have to.

We stopped at intervals for psychological tests. One of the most interesting involved looking at cartoon characters and saying which best represented the way we felt. There was laughing and joking, we were enjoying ourselves.

Everyone was desperate to be chosen. Yet they were always helping and encouraging each other. There was an incredible feeling of comradeship.

'Men would never behave like this,' one of the helpers, Hugh Bourne, commented. 'The strong ones would rush on ahead, leaving the slow ones behind. Not only that, the strong ones would point out the weak ones and try to make themselves heroes.'

Most of the women had trained hard since we last met. Halfway through, after the first few hours' sleep of the weekend, we were woken by thunder flashes for a search and rescue exercise. After carrying volunteers through the bog, Jack sent the women on a two-mile run in wet walking boots and full kit. It was 3 o'clock in the morning and a rocky track. It was too much for some and when I saw one woman collapse in tears of disappointment and exhaustion, I could not help but cry too.

The women gathered round Jack in the dark as he reallocated them. It was all getting very serious so I named the new teams Tammy Wynette, Dolly Parton and other country stars to lighten the mood.

The new teams were given wooden planks and a diagram of how to assemble them. It was a race to do it first. Some teams worked well together and improved as they repeated the exercise. Another team argued amongst themselves and never managed to assemble anything.

Finally, late on Saturday night, the selectors gathered in the dining room at Wydemeet and Pen and I listened as they hammered it out. We wanted a team of twenty which was strong enough, mentally and physically, to face the rigours of the Arctic. We also wanted women who would work as a team.

The selectors found the first ten or twelve women easy to choose but it took a long time to agree on the final eight. One of the UK's top graphologists, a close friend of Mary's, was there to help.

'I wouldn't walk to the end of the road with her,' she said of one of the women who was chosen.

In the small hours, Pen and I at last went to bed. I wrote out The List and lay, without sleeping, dreading the moment we were to read out the names.

At 7.30 a.m. the women came into the barn. It was one of the worst moments of my life. Raw emotion and tension hung in the air. Groups stood together, hardly talking. Pen and I stood at one end. All I saw was a sea of expectant faces. There was silence. Slowly, in alphabetical order, Pen read out the names.

I watched as the selected team screamed, hugged and kissed in excitement. One minute they were team mates, the next they were on either side of a divide. Elation, tears, commiseration. We had pushed these women to their absolute limits and the ones who were the most exhausted were the ones we chose to hurt. Pen and I felt guilty and sad; it did not seem fair.

Together with Dr Jacqui Smithson, the team doctor, we tried to comfort the ones who were most disappointed, but I doubt we did much good. If we could have taken them all to the North Pole, we probably would have done so.

5 Chocolate Biscuits

WE NOW HAD EXACTLY SIX MONTHS to prepare for the expedition. It was September 1996 and the first team was setting off from Ward Hunt Island in Nunavut (formerly the North West Territories) in Canada in March 1997.

This meant serious training. Pen told us to build up stamina and focus on strengthening the muscles in our hips and legs. To mimic our sledges, we dragged logs and car tyres attached with a rope to our waists across the countryside. This greatly amused passers by. Pom Oliver ran with her tyres up a hill in Majorca. The locals longed to know what terrible thing she had done to suffer such a penance.

Everyone found their own best way of training. I went running and got a cross-country skiing machine. I trained as much as I could, but found it difficult to fit it in around everything else Pen and I had to do. I hoped I would be fit enough when we got on the ice. The last thing I wanted was to let the others down.

We needed to raise most of the £300,000 budget for the expedition through donations and sponsorship. When Pen and I first talked, I had no idea how demanding or time-consuming this would be. It had all seemed so easy.

We wrote to over a thousand companies and followed up the smallest leads. There was always something to do – a telephone call, a follow-up or introduction letter, a lunch or meeting. Ninety-nine times out of a hundred it came to nothing – enthusiasm, hope maybe, but eventually a no. The team was trying hard. But time was ticking on.

I could never allow my enthusiasm to slip, never betray to the others for one moment I had doubts or fears. We had so many women counting on us now. So much was at risk. I kept busy, kept banging on doors, trying to sell the project to other people.

By Christmas 1996, Pen and I were exhausted. I got 'flu and he contracted pneumonia. For the first time, I contemplated the prospect of failure – after all, I told myself, hundreds of expeditions never happen because of lack of funds.

Then the telephone rang. It was Pen.

'I've had an idea,' he said. And he rattled off a new financing plan to make it work.

Ann Daniels was invited on to ITV's *Richard and Judy*. They persuaded her to bring her two-year-old triplets with her and sat them in the studio. Without warning, they played a video of the most dangerous places on earth. The scenes were nothing to do with the Arctic; they were used to make Ann, a mother, feel guilty.

Looking at those scenes, Ann, they seemed to say, don't you think it's irresponsible of you to leave these beautiful children behind? How would they feel if you died?

We were nervous the media might have turned against us. This would have made sponsorship impossible.

'Why can't people see it's wonderful for children to be proud of their mother?' our patron, the comedienne, Dawn French, said. 'All my daughter has got is the fact I can eat fifteen chocolate biscuits in two minutes.'

Dawn came to a fundraising party we held in January 1997.

'It's my role,' she said, 'to satisfy all the girls' husbands and boyfriends while they are away.'

It was a wonderful evening made special by Dawn. We raised money from an auction and generated the final momentum we required.

In Pen's office, the nightmare of organising equipment had already begun. Mike Ewart-Smith, who had helped at the selection weekends, was working full-time. He and Pen slaved night and day to pull it together. The expedition was expected to last over 70 days and we needed equipment and food for 25 people.

Finally sponsors came in one at a time. £10,000 here, free clothing or equipment there. There was frantic activity in Wydemeet and London.

Pen and I went out one evening to catch up on news. When we got back, there was a message from Mary on my answering machine.

'McVitie's Penguin have said yes,' she screamed. 'You've got a title sponsor.'

Pen and I looked at each other, silent with joy.

6 Echo on Water

O<small>UR BASE CAMP WAS AT A SMALL</small> isolated settlement called Resolute Bay in the far north of Canada. It is the only inhabited place in the deep tangled web of land and sea ice that has kept the Northwest Passage secret for so long.

About 120 people – some Inuit, some white – live in Resolute, either tucked behind a hill by the airport or in the village at the edge of the bay. One road connects the village to the airport. It goes nowhere else. Locals drive up and down in old diesel pick-ups.

Resolute is an access point to mining and military interests dotted along the Arctic coast. Served by commercial airlines, it is an ideal place for expeditions on the Canadian side of the Arctic to have their base camp.

For most of the year, Resolute and its surroundings are completely frozen. The sea ice melts in July or August and a few small ships arrive for the locals to collect boxes of tinned food and other dried groceries, fuel and alcohol to last the year. Vigorous negotiations take place on ships and in the dock as each person tries to get the best of the freight.

In October, perpetual daylight gives way to twilight. Then, from November onwards, the whole of Resolute is plunged into darkness. Apart from a few dim electric lights, it is black for 24 hours a day.

In winter, the temperatures fall to as low as minus 50°C. A self-imposed ban on alcohol means there are no public bars. Only a few residents are allowed to buy beer, wines and spirits for their own consumption – provided they have been approved by a special committee. There is nothing to do in winter except watch television.

In February, the sun finally pokes over the horizon and Resolute begins to get light. The relief of that moment must be overwhelming. Within a few weeks there is sunlight all day and all night. The nightmare of winter is over.

Most of the houses are made from painted wood, with corrugated iron roofs sloping out a long way from the walls. There is a health centre, a school and a church with simple wooden pews and an altar cloth in vivid colours.

When the expedition was there, everything was white, including the Arctic hares and foxes. Houses were dug out from the snow and small paths had been cleared to the doors. Polar bear skins were stretched and frozen on wooden frames.

On fine days, children roared through the icy streets on skidoos. Smaller children pulled each other on sledges and slid, giggling, down the snow-covered roofs into the drifts beneath.

Mike Ewart-Smith left the UK in February 1997 to set up our base camp at Resolute two weeks after McVitie's Penguin came on board as our title sponsor. All the teams would spend up to two weeks training in Resolute with Geoff Somers, a giant amongst polar explorers. Geoff's achievements include sledge-hauling across Greenland and being part of the longest dog-sledding journey across Antarctica – 4,000 miles in seven months. I felt privileged when Pen told me Geoff had agreed to train us.

'Wrap up warm now,' I said rather meanly to Mike as he set off with no idea of what he'd find. A highly experienced sailor and a leader for Operation Raleigh though he was, Mike had never been to the Arctic.

I imagined him in the aeroplane enjoying time on his own at last. Since arriving at Wydemeet two months previously, he had worked with Pen to coordinate equipment and supplies. They had been on the telephone constantly, persuading people to do things cheaply and quickly. They were also discussing everything with our guides, Matty McNair and Denise Martin, who both lived in Canada.

'How's Mike getting on?' I asked Pen who was finishing things off in England.

'We've lost the house we were going to use as base camp,' he said. 'Morag called just before Mike left to say we couldn't have it after all.'

Morag Howell was Base Manager for First Air, the airline taking us on and off the ice. I had met her at the first selection weekend.

'Why didn't you tell me?' I asked.

'I didn't want to worry you. Anyway, I think we've got somewhere else. Morag's friends, Gary and Diane Guy, have lent us their garage,' Pen said. 'All poor Mike and Geoff have to do now is convert it.'

He explained that Gary ran the electricity generating station (or Powerhouse as it was known). The garage-cum-workshop was filled with heavy machinery, car and skidoo parts, furniture and knick-knacks – even a hundred boxes of Christmas decorations. Mike and Geoff had three days to convert it before Matty and Denise arrived. They cleared all Gary's gear out, put up partition walls, built a small kitchen, two bedrooms with bunk beds and an office. They then fitted it with e-mail, a fax machine and all the radio equipment we needed.

'I've named it the Rookery,' Mike said, 'in honour of you Penguin girls.'

The temperature was below minus 40°C and none of Mike's thermal clothing had arrived. He borrowed a jacket and long johns from Geoff (several sizes too small) but made light of it on the telephone.

Penguin Alpha

The Rookery, up near the airport, was not big enough to house everyone. Mike arranged for the guides and each team of girls (known as Penguin Alpha to Echo) to stay in a house in the village before they went on to the ice.

There was friction between Matty and base camp, and there was a lot to do before Alpha and the guides could set off. The girls – Ann Daniels, Claire Fletcher, Sue Fullilove and Jan McCormac – needed to train with Geoff and get used to conditions. Pen needed to teach Matty how to use a GPS and the teams' clothing needed alterations. We had given Matty a prototype suit to test at her home on Baffin Island but, unfortunately, her ideas had not worked out.

'I'm worried about some of the equipment too, Caro,' Pen told me. 'I'm afraid not everything she's ordered is going to work.'

At last, on schedule, the first team were off. They flew to Ward Hunt Island at the northern tip of Canada, landing on a patch of ice marked by a couple of filled bin liners.

A yellow Post-it note on my desk at work said it all:

'Mike Ewart-Smith called. The aeroplane has left.'

After all we had been through, this was it. The expedition had started at last. Nothing else mattered.

Penguin Alpha was extremely well focussed. Their progress was slow but Pen had warned us not to expect too much too soon.

'Great blocks of broken ice are piled into walls, or pressure ridges, for mile after mile across the frozen ocean,' he said. 'Some pressure ridges at the beginning are as tall as houses.'

The girls formed chains to haul and shove their sledges over them.

It was exhausting work. Matty found it difficult to move her sledge and, after a couple of days, Alpha divided most of her sledge-load between them. Then Matty suggested a rest day, explaining that she and Denise were travelling 500 miles to the Pole. The girls spent a restless few hours in the tent, desperate to get going again.

* * *

Other expeditions had set off from Ward Hunt Island at about the same time and it was a tremendous boost when Alpha overtook a couple of unsupported efforts early on. Then one evening as they were cooking, the girls heard a noise.

'What if it's a polar bear?'

The tent door opened and three bearded faces poked in.

'Hello,' the girls said, politely. 'Do come in. We've just put all our food in the pan and we're making chocolate chip cookies.'

Back in London, hearing the stories, I felt odd. I rushed into the office each day for news of distance travelled – unbelievably Alpha was managing up to six nautical miles a day. I spoke to Mike or Pen regularly for other news. There was still so much to do – preparing the later teams and raising more money. Yet I felt strangely disorientated and found it hard to concentrate.

At Easter, I decided to fly out to Resolute to see things for myself. With only a few days' notice, I arranged a Canadian business trip. I stayed the night in Edmonton, in a truckers' motel, then caught a flight north through Yellowknife to Resolute Bay.

Before long, we were crossing the tree line and there was nothing but white below. I had seen landscape like this when I met Matty and Denise on Baffin Island in January with Pen. But this time I felt apprehensive. What if I did not like it at Resolute? What if I was frightened? Would I want to come back and do my leg of the relay?

Nobby met me at Resolute airport. He was at base camp and in charge of filming.

'What a drama we've had,' he said, giving me a big hug. 'We lost radio contact with the girls for three days and then Bravo couldn't set off. But it's all right now, Alpha are on their way back.'

The cold was overwhelming. More than a second without gloves and my hands were colder than I had ever known them. Agony to warm up. I went outside in the wind wearing a hat but my forehead was exposed and I ran back to the Rookery with a searing headache.

'How on earth can the girls be managing in this?' I wondered out loud to Mike.

They not only managed, they were doing brilliantly. On their last night on the ice, Alpha crossed the 84th parallel – their own private goal. When Bravo arrived on the ice, they ran to meet them.

When I saw Penguin Alpha they looked so well it was hard to believe they had travelled nearly sixty miles through the most extreme conditions on earth. They were jubilant.

Diane invited us over that evening. The girls ate enormous platefuls of ham and mashed potato and chattered and fell over each other with stories. We heard how Sue got her feet wet and how Ann fell into the water up to her neck and no one noticed.

'What did you do? Why didn't you shout?' I asked her, incredulous.

'Well, I didn't see much point,' she said, 'I just thought I'd better get out.'

The girls also told us about the broken radio.

'Sue remembered her physics O-level, and she and Claire rebuilt it.'

Jan showed us the finished article and told us proudly, 'The hair grips that hold it together were my contribution.'

I was filled with excitement. If Alpha could do it, so could the rest of us. We were going to get there. We were going to prove the cynics wrong.

'The buzz is back,' I wrote in a note to Pen.

Ironically, my biggest worry was that Matty was not up to it. She was clearly not as fit as Alpha and she had a very long journey ahead.

'Could Denise guide on her own?' I asked Ann, as we dried the tent for Penguin Charlie's training.

'Oh, yes, definitely,' she and the rest of the team agreed.

But Pen was not keen to change arrangements. He had guided many people across the Arctic sea ice and knew far more about its hazards. I knew that neither he nor anyone else at base camp was prepared to compromise safety. Besides, even if we wanted to express doubts, an open radio line with the girls in the tent was hardly the place for a private conversation.

The other major worry, as always, was money. The need to order and test equipment quickly at base camp before Alpha set off meant we had overspent considerably. Mike sat me down to go through the numbers. He hoped for a refund on some of the kit but other things were clearly wasted.

'Unless you raise another £15,000, Caroline, the expedition will end with Penguin Delta.'

I held my breath.

'Your team, Echo, won't have enough money for its flights and all your hard work will have been for nothing . . .'

Mike's great talent as Operations Manager was his straight-talking. But just at that moment, I wished he was a little less blunt.

Penguin Bravo

Gary and Diane told us that when the expedition arrived in Resolute, the locals laughed.

'Most people don't take any notice of expeditions coming through here. But you should've heard the gossip about you lot. Girls going to the Pole? No one thought you stood a chance, especially when they saw how small you were,' Diane said.

With Alpha back, the locals began to take notice. I was walking with them one day when the policeman stopped in his car.

'You girls have done awesome,' he said.

I felt very proud. It meant a lot that people were now following our progress. Diane sewed a Penguin logo on the back of her parka and popped into the Rookery several times a day for news.

Penguin Bravo was a less obvious team than Alpha. It comprised the youngest, Emma Scott, and the oldest, Rose Agnew – as well as Catherine Clubb and Karen Bradburn. They referred to themselves sometimes as 'Boring Bravo' but that did not stop them giggling. Karen's speciality was extremely crude jokes.

When I arrived in Resolute, Bravo were on their way on to the ice. Mike and Nobby told me they had hardly seen them while training with Geoff. Pen was away with other clients and they were concentrating on keeping everything under control. Sue Self, our reserve who came out later, was a valuable extra pair of hands.

There was always something for Mike or Nobby to do. Something to wash, mend or sew sponsorship badges on to. There were two sets of equipment to organise – one for the team out on the ice and one for the team training at Resolute – then there was food and other supplies to prepare for team changeovers.

Nobby bought tampons for Matty and Denise. Faced with a choice at the Resolute Co-op between Regular and Super, he asked the check-out girl for advice.

'One of the women is about your height with quite narrow hips, and the other one is slightly taller,' he said. 'Which size do you think they'll need?'

It was still very cold and there were lots of pressure ridges to climb over. Bravo made good mileage and, by the time I got back to England, I was feeling confident. I was sure it was only a matter of time before we reached the Pole.

Back home, I met Serena Chance who had moved to Wydemeet to help organise the teams. I knuckled down to the funding crisis. I wrote letters, made telephone calls and became increasingly frustrated.

Penguin Charlie
Victoria Riches was on this leg with her mother, Sue. I asked them if they would prefer to be in different teams

41

but they did not think they would enjoy the expedition as much if they were apart. That made it difficult to choose who to put with them; I hoped Paula Power and Lynne Clarke would be all right.

As with all the teams, the Arctic ice pack was constantly moving under Charlie's feet. As the weather gets warmer, the sea ice starts to melt and move with the ocean currents. This makes it break up, opening leads of open water and leaving big lumps of floating ice.

I knew from Mike's progress reports that conditions were bad for Charlie. For the first week, they covered seven or eight nautical miles most days, but then they reported that the wind was increasing rapidly and there was severe drift to the east. The ice was groaning and lumps of ice were being pushed up and sucked into the water around them. It was minus 20°C, the wind was gusting at 40 miles an hour. They had to pick their way through a maze of leads and rubble.

Pen and Geoff said the ocean currents would be worse if they went further east than 74°W. But there was not much Charlie could do about it. They drifted 22 miles east in one 24-hour period and, over the next seven days, the ice took them all the way over to 61°W.

The drift was also taking Charlie backwards. This meant they were in danger of losing all the good mileage they had made at the start of their leg. Over one three-day period, despite travelling continuously, they found they had gone no further north at all.

On 21 April 1997, I thought it was all over. I walked into the office at 8.30 a.m. and Mary was on the telephone.

'I don't know how to tell you this,' she said in a very flat voice. 'They've all fallen in.'

I felt my heart hammering.

'Are they okay?'

'Yes, I think so. But I don't know what's going to happen.'

Suddenly it hit me – the dangers we had taken on. I wondered whether Echo, my team, would ever leave the UK.

I met Charlie at Resolute airport when I arrived with Echo to train. Bad weather had delayed their changeover with Delta and they had had less than an hour to wash and get ready. Nothing betrayed the dramas they had been through. Only Victoria and Paula looked as if they had lost weight. Otherwise they all looked almost as well as Alpha had done. I wanted to talk about the day they fell in and check they were all right. We exchanged a few knowing looks but otherwise we had to keep quiet. There were a lot of people around, including David Hempleman-Adams, waiting to go home. We had agreed we did not want anyone to get hold of the story. We did not want the guides or anyone else criticised. It was crucial to avoid adverse publicity for the sponsors, especially as we still needed to raise money.

Pen and I did not want to worry the friends and families of the fourth and fifth teams who were still to go out on the ice. I did not tell anyone, not even my team-mates in Penguin Echo. They first heard about it in Resolute when Pen sat us down and tried to interpret what Charlie had told him.

Pen moved salt and pepper pots across the table as people to explain what had happened. First Sue had gone in up to her neck, then Victoria had tried to rescue her. Then the ice had broken up and Victoria had fallen in too. With Denise's help they managed to climb out of the water and balance themselves on loose, floating ice.

Sue lost a boot and their sledges were in the water. With Lynne and Paula holding on to a rope, Denise jumped in several times and swam to rescue the equipment. The water was so cold she was exhausted within a few strokes. Lynne and Paula pulled her out and put the tent up to stop her freezing. Meantime, Sue and Victoria paddled towards Matty on the other side. She wrapped them in spare clothing and they set off to find a way back to the others.

'Then a miracle happened,' said Pen. 'The ice closed up before their eyes. They were back together again, thank God.

'That's what I think happened, anyway,' he said. 'There wasn't long to talk to the team before their flight and they all remembered it slightly differently. The one thing they did all say, though, was that Denise was a hero. If it wasn't for her, the expedition might well be over.'

Penguin Delta

Penguin Delta were out on the ice while we were training. They radioed in to Mike and Nobby every two days and we often listened in at the Rookery. There were 220 nautical miles still to go and we anxiously watched their mileage. Whatever they left undone was up to us.

Penguin Charlie had drifted a long way east, so Delta were travelling in a diagonal line to make up for it. This affected their mileage north, which was frustrating – for us as well as them. We spent a lot of time calculating our 'batting average' as Zoë called it. We knew we had to get to the Pole by the end of May because, after that, the ice would be melting and it might be too dangerous for an aeroplane to pick us up.

We talked about it endlessly in the evenings – working out how many days, how many hours, how many miles. We felt a weight of responsibility for the other women. Everyone had done so well; we could not let them down.

Rosie Stancer, Andre Chadwick, Juliette May and Sarah Jones were all strong characters. They admitted there were times when they did not get on very well. But it did not affect their performance on the ice. They took full advantage of improving weather and ice conditions and travelled 110 nautical miles north. The relay was back on track.

Penguin Echo

Gradually, through selling various rights, we continued to raise money. When I and the rest of Penguin Echo left the

UK, there was still a shortfall. But after all we had been through, I was determined. I knew somehow it would turn out all right.

Seven days before our departure, I had a heavy cold and my neck was in a brace – the result of a farewell night out clubbing. I hobbled on to the aeroplane with Lucy Roberts, Pom Oliver and Zoë Hudson.

I began to contemplate all we had done. The relay had worked and twenty total amateurs – all women – would shortly have participated in an historic expedition. Whatever happened now, I felt proud.

It was great to be back at the Rookery with its familiar diesel fumes. There was Mike's little office, with the radio, computer, telephone and fax, there were the charts and the polar bear posters – and there were the bunk beds just as I had left them at Easter. We looked at the charts to see how far the expedition had got – we still had a very long way to go.

Geoff was a fountain of knowledge and we trusted him implicitly. Before we set off on our leg, we trained with him for ten days. The ridges on the sea ice were melting and getting too easy, so he took us pulling our pulks [sledges] up into the hills around Resolute. We learned to camp and navigate with the sun. He also taught us how to recognise and treat frostnip and frostbite.

Geoff showed us how Matty and Denise did things without saying whether he agreed. Above all, as with the other teams, he gave us confidence that we could survive on the ice.

I knew Zoë well. She had been my physiotherapist when I injured my knee and we had become friends. I knew Pom too; the wife of Kent Walwin, with whom I worked. Lucy, by contrast, felt slightly left out to begin with and we worked hard to include her. At first, we were competitive, each trying to prove we could ski fastest. This was largely due to nerves.

Before I left home, I spoke to Rose Agnew: 'I've had the most marvellous time, I really have,' she enthused. 'But, please Caroline, just make sure you get there, won't you?'

The other teams had got us to within 110 nautical miles of our goal. The North Pole was potentially within our grasp and even when we were exhausted, we knew we would have to keep going.

'If Captain Scott's expedition had done 100 yards more every day,' Geoff said. 'They would have made it.'

Clearly, the less weight we pulled, the faster we could go. Therefore during a radio call with Delta, I asked to go through a kit list with Denise. It was less cold than it had been. Some additional layers of clothing were no longer needed.

I told Denise Echo would be coming out with the very minimum personal kit. I could not say it over an open line (the whole of Resolute was usually listening), but I hoped the guides would leave some of their extra kit behind on the aeroplane at changeover.

Eventually, the day came when we were to leave Resolute and fly on to the ice to take over from Delta.

I wrote my diary in the Twin Otter: 'Since breakfast, I have been getting progressively more nervous. Desperate not to leave anything behind – made worse because I seem to have spent my entire time at Resolute mislaying my possessions – and so anxious to reach the Pole . . . For a long time now I have not allowed failure to enter my head. The pressure is intense and I haven't felt as nervous as this for a very long time. It's like the time before an exam in which I am expected to do well. All the preparations are over and everyone associated with the expedition is desperate for us to succeed.'

We refuelled at Eureka, a godforsaken weather station at 80°N, and said goodbye to Pen who had flown that far with us. I wrote in my diary: 'It was very odd leaving him behind and a few tears rolled down my cheeks as I waved goodbye through the window . . . We have come so far together, it is not fair that he has to be left behind at the final hurdle.'

It was not goodbye for long. After three hours' flying (one hour away from the girls on the ice), the clouds came down. Without shadow to show the surface below, the aeroplane was unable to land and we had to turn round. Emotionally spent, we arrived back at Eureka at 4.30 a.m.

We spent three days waiting for the sun to reappear, mostly as guests of the Canadian military based at 'Fort Eureka' – a prefabricated station straight out of *M*A*S*H*. We watched *Trainspotting* one morning as Hercules aeroplanes flew in and out. Finally, after several false alarms, the pilots decided we could set off again.

I wrote, 'we fly high in the sky across the pack ice. Below is a patchwork of fields, flat bits surrounded by hedges and walls of ice rubble, and leads cut at angles, as if the ice has been slashed with a Stanley knife. Then just as I am invited to sit in the cockpit, clouds appear on the horizon. A horrible *déjà vu* looms. Within minutes there is no shadow at all and it seems impossible that we will be able to land. We see the tent and little red figures jumping up and down, waving madly. The Twin Otter passes over the runway the girls have marked out, but each time we hit the ice the aeroplane pulls away. My heart sinks – I know we cannot afford the cost of another aborted flight. But then we come back a third time, hit the ice and bounce along to a halt. This is it. We're here. Sarah and Andre, Rosie and Juliette come running from the tent to meet us.

'"I'm fucking glad to see you," said Sarah. Hugs and almost tears.'

When we landed, it was so familiar being amongst friends, I forgot we were just specks on the Arctic Ocean. But eventually the changeover was complete and we were left in the middle of nowhere.

We headed north immediately and started to warm up. After six hours skiing, it was 9 p.m. and the GPS said we had done eight nautical miles. A good start to our leg. We called it a day.

Matty and Denise seemed impressed with our first day's performance. That evening we told them we wanted to go as fast as possible because we were frightened the ice would melt before we got to the Pole.

It was a beautiful morning and I was having a good day. The sky was a cloudless blue and the snow was bright white. For the first time, the air was still and sunlight caught in the crystals of snow. As we moved, the whole place sparkled.

I went in front and we settled into an easy rhythm. The ice seemed strong and stable. It was easy to forget I was skiing over a deep black ocean. Behind me, I could hear wafts of conversation as Zoë and Pom talked. I did not want to chat. I wanted to be alone with my thoughts. I thought about the colours I could see around me. How strange it was that there were so many blues and greys, even pinks.

Six women and thousands of miles of continuously moving ice. Denise said she had seen a seal a couple of weeks previously but, apart from that, as far as we knew we were the only living beings on the planet.

Abruptly, the scenery changed. We were no longer weaving our way through strange boulders of ice on soft snow. We were up against a series of ridges and walls. The ridges were made of large blue blocks of ice, cut neatly into cubes and piled on top of each other. The ice must have cracked in a myriad straight lines and then, as the currents forced huge pieces back together, it had broken to form great natural obstacles. In places the ridges were thirty feet high.

We took off our skis and began the laborious business of clambering up and over the walls. Lifting the sledges on to each ledge and sliding them up between us in a chain had become a routine. We worked efficiently together, without stopping. But it was depressing that our initial rapid progress north had now dropped to about one mile an hour.

I found it difficult to balance on the uneven blocks of ice; they were five or six feet square and I did not want to fall. It was very hard work hauling the fully laden sledges. My shoulders ached and I was thirsty.

'How long till our next break?' I shouted to Lucy, who was our daily timekeeper and who told us when each hour and a quarter was up, and we could rest for five minutes.

'Not long,' she shouted back. 'Let's stop over there, on that nice flat bit.'

As we approached the last wall of rubble, the wind started to whistle. I heard a rumbling and a creaking. Then the cubes of ice began to shake almost imperceptibly.

'Quick. It's moving,' someone shouted behind me.

I looked down to see water slopping around my boots. The ice on which I stood was beginning to sink. Hastily I jumped on to firmer ice. Just ahead of me, Matty and Zoë scrambled quickly and turned round to help. I threw two sledges as hard as I could towards them, then hurled myself and my skis over the top.

I fell on to the flat pan beyond, and saw Pom, Denise and Lucy performing the same assault course trick. Sledges and skis came raining down. We gathered them up as fast as we could and ran further on to the firmer ice. It felt like solid ground at last and I slumped thankfully on to my sledge.

The temperature was dropping and we were getting cold. My wet fingers had turned into ice blocks. I dreaded the ache I knew would follow as they warmed up again.

As we skied on, the sky was grey and the wind was getting stronger. Something strange appeared on the horizon. At first I thought it was a mirage – we had seen a few while training at Resolute. But this was different. As it came into view, I realised why the air had turned so cold: the wind was wet. There was open water ahead.

There in front of us was a vast expanse of Arctic Ocean. It lapped gently at the icy shoreline and the wind ruffled the waves. In the far distance, perhaps a kilometre away, we could see the other side. Somehow, we had to get over.

We clambered up on to boulders to look east and west, squinting to the horizon and trying to see a place where the lead might be narrower. But it was a vain hope. As far as we could tell, the water stretched at least five kilometres from left to right. There was no way of knowing which way to head for the best.

I had no ideas. I was happy to go with someone else's intuition and, in the end, Matty suggested turning right and going east. It was not easy. The drift was forming little leads out of the big one and there was a lot of thin grey ice to get over.

We followed Matty's ski tracks as she skirted her way round. The grey ice was no more than a few inches thick. It sagged under our weight and felt as if it might sink at any moment. Careful not to concentrate weight on too small an area, we tried not to get too close to the sledge in front.

Tentatively, we inched our way forward for nearly a mile until Denise said it didn't feel right. Reluctantly, by a majority decision, we turned round and retraced our steps.

It did not seem so far going back but, as we headed west, it became clear our prospects of finding a way over the big lead were no better. In fact, they were worse.

We soon came across an open lead about eight feet across. The ice was slashed in a clean break with steep, thick sides. I pointed the ends of my skis over the edge and looked straight down to the water five feet below. The water was a sharp azure blue. I could see several feet of ice beneath the surface before the water turned darker below.

How many fathoms lie under there? I wondered. No one wanted to turn round again. Even though it meant heading south, we decided we must find a way over this lead.

We went quickly, trying not to waste too much time. At our next snack break, the others went ahead to see if there was a way across. I stayed behind to take a photograph. I was on the exact spot where, an hour earlier, the ice had been moving. Our ski and sledge tracks showed clearly. Yet where the ice had been solid before, there was now a gap of about ten feet. It occurred to me we might be bounded on all sides by water; that we were on an island we would never get off.

Denise reappeared. 'There may be a place down here. We need to move fast,' she called.

Hurriedly, we skied over the small rise and saw a place where the gap was wider. Large lumps of ice seemed to have formed a bridge. Each lump was big enough for one person to stand on. It all depended whether they were packed together or 'floaters'.

If we could make our way over and then find some more stable ice, we might be back with a chance of getting over the huge lead. We took off our skis so we could jump if necessary but, learning from Charlie's experiences, we stayed attached to our sledges in case we needed life rafts.

Matty went first, I followed. The lumps of ice wobbled in the water and were extremely unstable. I needed to study each piece to find a good foothold without losing momentum. I tried not to feel too frightened; the thought of going back was worse than going forward. With one last long step, I pulled myself up on to the other side.

Pom was just behind and she helped shove my sledge towards me. Its nose went straight in the water, but I pulled it up and out, hoping the contents had stayed dry. Then it was Pom's turn. I tried to explain the sequence of steps I had used to get over and where I had put each foot.

Pom teetered on the final lump and I held out my hands to encourage her. She leaned forward and stepped bravely towards me. But before she reached me, her feet slipped back and down. The last piece of ice must have come free when I went across. Now, as Pom stepped on to it, it floated away from under her.

'My worst fear about falling through the ice, is being sucked under, like in *The Omen*,' Pom had told me before we set off.

I saw the panic in her eyes and then I grabbed her. I grabbed her by the harness and pulled her towards me, dragging her legs and chest through the water. Adrenaline pumped through me and, in one movement, I swung her up on to the solid ground where I stood.

Pom crashed into a hard, sharp piece of ice next to me. I fell over backwards and heard her yelp with pain. She lay, half-winded, on the ice at my side.

Finally, after what seemed an eternity, Pom slowly got up. She was grimacing and holding her shoulder. Her eyes filled with tears as she tried to tell me she was all right.

'Thanks, Caro,' she smiled weakly.

Then her face crumpled and her fear and pain were obvious. I almost cried too. All I could do was fling my arms round her hoping to hug it better.

Zoë and Lucy did not see what happened to Pom. All they knew was the lumps of ice they were waiting on in the lead were moving too. With Pom's piece dislodged from the bridge formation, there was nothing to bind the rest together and the lumps were floating apart.

Zoë and Lucy turned round as fast as they could, jumping across the open water. They fell over each other as they slithered and scrambled back to Denise on the firmer ice.

'I think I've dislocated my left shoulder,' Pom finally managed to say. 'It hurts like fuck and I felt it pop out.'

'Does it still feel out?' I asked anxiously.

'No, I think I felt it go back in again,' Pom replied, this time managing a better smile.

The sharp pain Pom felt at the moment of impact had eased slightly. But now the whole of her left side was on fire. She clutched at her shoulder with her right hand, pressing it with her fingers and desperately willing the pain away.

I tried to dry her by rubbing snow into her suit to absorb the water. As I did so, Pom began gingerly to move the joint. She knew the shoulder must have dislocated but, from the sickening clunk which followed almost instantly, she hoped it was now back in place.

Without really knowing what she was looking for, Pom fumbled around in her suit to see if her shoulder was broken. At least there was no blood.

Pom told me later she wondered how she was going to pull her sledge. She did not want to tell me how bad it was, in case we radioed for an airlift and ended her expedition. Besides, we were all in a race against time; the team could not afford to wait for a rescue. I won't ask Caro for too much help, she told herself.

I knew Pom was putting a brave face on it, but I could not tell to what degree. I took her at her word about getting her skis back on. Together, we adjusted her harness so it pulled as little as possible on her damaged shoulder.

Our party was now split in two, three on one side of the lead and three on the other. Zoë, Denise and Lucy had the tent in one of their sledges, we had the cookers. There was nothing to be done but move off once more, hoping for another place to cross and reunite.

On our side Matty went first, and Pom and I stayed together moving as fast as Pom could manage. There were fewer bumps and cracks than there had been and it was easier than on the other side. We could see the others across the water. At times we were within easy speaking distance but then, if our ice undulated or the others had to go round further leads or obstacles, we lost sight of each other.

After an hour, I stopped.

'I've had enough of this game, Pom. The time has come for an emergency peanut.'

I waved my snack bag defiantly and passed it to her.

Or at least I tried to pass it to her. We dropped the bag and the nuts went everywhere.

'Well that's torn it,' said Pom, mimicking my solemn tone. Then, in the voice of a 30s' film actor, she announced, 'I'm afraid the expedition is at an end. When they dropped the peanuts, Pom and Caroline knew they could go no further.'

It was such a relief Pom could still laugh that we giggled together in the snow. A few tears even rolled down our cheeks for the second time that day.

I had visions of us hurling equipment at each other across the lead and something vital sinking to the bottom. Surely, if we just kept going far enough, the lead would end. I began to believe that every corner we skied to would be the last, but the lead kept winding on. It was very discouraging, we were not even moving in the right direction. We were travelling south-west, further and further away from our target. With each step, we were wasting valuable energy.

Then I heard Zoë shout, 'Over here. You can jump over here.'

My heart leaped. Six feet of water lay between us. With a run up, we should be able to make it across.

'You go first this time, Pom,' I said. 'Watch out for her shoulder, whoever is catching her.'

I unclipped Pom's sledge from her harness and waited as, without a word, she took a few running steps and a big leap. The ice crumbled where she landed on the other side. She winced badly as she fell into Denise's arms, but I knew then we would be all right.

Matty and I jumped over and the others all helped with our sledges. The unspoken tension of our separation turned into hugs of relief and we collapsed on the sledges for a quick drink and some food. This time it was celebratory peanuts all round.

I realised then how tired I was. Looking at the others I could see we were all exhausted. We had a choice. Either we could give up on the day and camp where we were – or we could attempt to make up lost ground and get back to Lake Tahoe, as Zoë had christened the huge original lead.

I thought Pom should decide and told the others about her shoulder. But she was adamant.

'We must keep going. It would be much too depressing to stop here,' she said.

We were a ramshackle group making our way slowly north again. I chatted to Zoë for the first time that day and she told me how worried she had been when we were split up. In front of us, Pom was trying feebly to use a ski pole with her bad arm. Zoë asked what had happened to Pom and I knew her well enough to realise she was very concerned medically.

Finally, six and half hours after we had first seen it, we reached the shores of Lake Tahoe once more. It was quite unchanged except we were a little further east than we had been and the sun was lower in the sky.

Silently we put up the tent. It took much longer than usual to tighten the guy ropes and fix them into the ice with our skis and poles. My back ached badly as I dug and heaped snow on to the tent valances to keep the walls in place. Each time I bent over, I thought I would never stand up again.

Inside the tent, Pom lay on her side on top of her sleeping bag. All she could think about was the incessant throbbing that stretched from her neck, over both shoulders and down her left arm. Three fingers on her left hand had been numb for hours and she had tried to revive them by using her ski pole as she trudged along. With each jarring movement the burning returned and she preferred to let the arm hang loose, (even though that made skiing and jumping over cracks so much harder).

I must not tell them how bad it is, Pom kept on at herself. All that matters is I don't hold them up. I'm not giving up. If they're getting to the Pole, I'm going with them.

Outside, I sat for a moment while Lucy and Denise strung up the radio aerial. I had time to take in the view. Perhaps because I was so tired, the waves on the lead seemed gentler and more serene, unaware of the trouble they had caused. Below me, our tent was nestled in a sheltered dip.

With luck the lead might freeze or even close up over night. But I wondered what we should do if it did not. Should we just sit here and wait? Or should we try going east again? I worried that we might never get round this lead. But most of all I worried about Pom and whether it was safe for her to go on.

We could help her over difficult bits but I doubted she could cope with only one arm. If only she was not left-handed – or had damaged the other shoulder. These were negative thoughts I did not want. I stood up to join the others in the tent and decided to think about dinner instead.

'Lucy,' I whispered, 'would you mind cooking tonight? It's supposed to be Pom's turn and I offered to do it for her. But you know how I always upset the pans. Pom said she couldn't bear the strain of watching me – do you think you could do it instead? Sorry.'

By morning Lake Tahoe had frozen. Thin grey with a sprinkling of snow. Over the next days Pen flew a 'boat' out in case we met too much open water; I walked without skis for a day because of broken bindings and the ice rumbled and cracked.

Sometimes, with a bright blue sky and the sun catching the snow, it was a mystical fairyland. At other times, when the light was grey and great shapes of ice were scattered all around, it looked more like a nuclear wasteland. The snow could have been radioactive dust.

'What if the whole world looks like this now? How would we know?' Pom and I wondered.

We travelled across 'pans' – flat areas of ice surrounded by spectacular walls of ice rubble we had to get over. The blue chunks of ice looked as if they had been cut into cubes with a knife, like Turkish Delight.

It was very difficult to clamber through the rubble and balance across ice bridges; all the time hauling a 120 lb pulk which insisted on nose-diving into every available cranny and snagging on the smallest bit of ice. We helped Pom with her sledge and sometimes we could step over ditches, at other times we had to take our skis off to scrabble over boulders.

On our penultimate day I wrote in my diary: 'Another Penguin record SMASHED. 16.5 miles travelled, leaving just under 16 to go. We could go much faster today because the ice suddenly became incredibly flat. It almost looks like a frozen ocean. Before, the flat bits have had lumps of ice littered all through them, a scrapheap of smooth and twisted shapes, but now the flatness stretches to the horizon.'

The excitement was mounting. We knew the Arctic could throw anything at us at any time – just as we got into a rhythm, suddenly a lead or an obstacle would appear – but at each stop, the Pole was becoming a reality. We talked about what we would do and how we would feel when we got there. How were we going to film it? Should we sing 'God save the Queen', and what were the words to 'I'm on Top of the World'?

We finished that night at 10.30 p.m. and everyone's feet hurt. I felt exhausted but I did not want to sleep.

The following day, we set off in bright sunshine – a good omen for reaching the Pole today, I thought. I began to think how proud I was, how much we owed the teams who had gone before us, the guides, how wonderful the back-up team and sponsors had been.

As on previous days, my emotions rushed up and down. We did five miles in the first two marches but then slowed down. The previous day's euphoria seemed to have gone. I took a turn at the front and tried to pick up the pace again. It was cloudy by now and the snow conditions tiring. Lots of drifting meant that one moment our skis slid smoothly and the next they disappeared in the snow.

Despite Pom's shoulder, we went much more quickly than anyone expected. We covered 109 nautical miles in just ten days. As arranged, we radioed base camp at 7.00 p.m. – only three miles to go and lots of excited noises at the other end. We were still navigating by compass but using a GPS to confirm our direction. Deep yellow sunlight opened up on the horizon and, in almost biblical fashion, we followed it, confident it must be the Pole.

But then the GPS said we were moving further away again.

Using the GPS tracking, we had to pin the Pole down. But then, with 0.03 miles left, where was the Pole? Each time we stepped forward, it seemed the distance increased.

Matty and Denise whizzed past each other, heads down intent upon their GPS screens.

Eventually at 10.45 p.m. after 13 hours' skiing, I stepped forward momentously to plant the Union Jack. This was the moment I had been dreaming of. This was what the last two years' planning had all been about.

We flung our arms round each other, exhausted but thrilled. For me, it was a mixture of elation and relief. We'd done it. Here was a piece of ice that looked like every other piece of ice. It was my North Pole. And no one else's North Pole because, by the morning, this piece of ice, with us camped upon it, would have moved with the current.

We drifted for seven days. We measured the days by radio calls. The high spot was *Family Favourites* at 11 o'clock every morning. The star of this show was my mother, who, after being so worried about me for so long, had suddenly announced before I left England that she wanted to come out to the Arctic to meet us. I was thrilled but never quite believed she would do it until, crackling over the air waves one day, I heard her voice.

'It's only me darling. Ovaaaar.'

It was so exciting, I felt almost more emotional than when we reached the Pole.

Finally, the weather improved. A Twin Otter arrived to pick us up. It was flown by Amy, First Air's only female Arctic pilot. It seemed a fitting end for the first all-woman expedition to the North Pole.

Before I left I went to look for the last time at the place we had marked as the Pole. I cried. I had come to think of it as my home. Where my North Pole has gone now, no one knows. But wherever it is, it will always be My North Pole.

7 Facing South

THROUGHOUT ALL THE CELEBRATIONS and publicity following our return, the thought of going to the South Pole was always in my mind. In March 1998, a year after we had set off for the North Pole, I could bear it no longer. I called Jan McCormac from Penguin Alpha, and she and her husband Andy came to my home in Brick Lane in London for a curry. I was wondering how to broach the subject when Jan beat me to it.

'When are we going on another expedition, Caroline?' she asked. 'I'm absolutely bursting to do something, you know.'

'North or South?' I asked her.

'Don't mind,' she said instantly. 'Which would you prefer?'

With all my heart I wanted to go to the South Pole, but I decided to try to keep an open mind.

'All I know,' I said, 'is that I want to go all the way this time.'

'Yes,' she said.

'None of this relay business.'

Jan's face lit up.

'Definitely,' she said. 'Not that I didn't enjoy it last time. It's just I knew we could have done more.'

There was a pause.

'The thing is Caroline,' she said at last 'who's going to be in the team?'

I already had ideas about which of the North Pole girls would be good team-members. They needed to be strong, and we had to be sure to get on for over two months on the ice.

'You tell me who you think for a change, Jan,' I said and reached for a paper and pen. 'Let's go through them one by one.'

That was it. Suddenly, bubbling with excitement, Jan – the most discreet person I know – turned into a ruthless assassin of character.

'Oh God no, I couldn't go with her, I'd kill her,' she said about one. And of another: 'The trouble is, she's mad. Nice but mad. I don't know what you think, Caroline, but I always worried she might leave me behind.'

'All I know about the South Pole is we need to do it in the Antarctic spring while it's light,' said Jan.

'That means travelling between November and January. Maybe we could get there for the millennium,' I said excitedly, 'then we would be able to celebrate it simultaneously in every time zone in the world.'

In the weeks that followed, Jan and I began to sound people out.

Ann Daniels, who was in Penguin Alpha with Jan, was quite matter-of-fact at first.

'Yes please,' she said. 'Jan called yesterday and my parents have agreed to look after the triplets.' But then a few sentences later, she interrupted me. 'Oh I'm so excited, I can't really think of anything else. Can we go this year? I don't think I can wait until next.'

Pom Oliver gave an instant yes.

'Thank Heaven,' she said. 'I've been worrying about what to do for the millennium. It's the perfect solution. But we must take champagne.'

Others were more contemplative.

Out of earshot of her husband, one confided sadly: 'Of course I want to come. But the trouble is, I want to have babies too and I think if I don't have them now I never will.'

Another said: 'I don't know. I'm not sure it's fair on my partner. I know if I say yes, I've got to commit myself one hundred per cent and we have so little time together as it is.'

If there was one person I was absolutely sure of it was Rosie Stancer from Penguin Delta. It was always clear that for Rosie the North Pole was a warm-up for the South.

'Definitely count me in,' she said instantly.

Zoë Hudson, from Echo, was typically thoughtful and the idea of another expedition anywhere took some weeks to take hold.

Within two weeks, I had my team-mates:

- **Ann Daniels**, 32, from Yorkshire; a civil servant working in Yeovil in Somerset and mother of pre-school triplets
- **Zoë Hudson**, 32, from Leeds; a chartered physiotherapist specialising in Sports Medicine and senior lecturer at the University of East London
- **Jan McCormac**, 30, from Middlesex; one of only two women in the Metropolitan Police Royal Protection Squad, the highly-trained group of police officers who travel the world as bodyguards for the Royal Family
- **Pom Oliver**, 46, from Sussex; a former film producer, now developing and refurbishing property
- **Rosie Stancer**, 38, from London, a freelance journalist living in Prague

The question still remained: North or South Pole? I kept asking the others but no one would make a choice.

Zoë said: 'I think the others should choose where we go, Caroline. I was in the final team last year with you and I've been to the North Pole. They didn't have that chance, so it doesn't make any difference which I would prefer. If they want to go North again, I'd like to go North too.'

Like Zoë, I wanted the others to choose. The difference was I did care where we went and I passionately wanted them to agree on the South Pole. They were all so polite, it was frustrating.

Except Rosie who called frequently and faxed memos about why the Antarctic was best.

In the end, it was a combination of Rosie, the millennium and my desire for the South Pole that won the day.

We talked to Pen and he agreed to help us.

'No one wants you to succeed more than I do,' he said.

We then went to see Geoff Somers in his cottage in Keswick. Discreet memorabilia filled the place – a team of miniature wooden dogs pulled a sledge across a shelf – and Geoff's lead huskie from the Trans-Antarctica expedition of 1990 was chained up outside the front door.

We crowded into Geoff's kitchen and pored over maps. He told us about Antarctica and the hazards we faced. We listened intently.

'The big question is, Geoff,' I finally plucked up the courage to ask. 'Do you think we're up to it? And, if so, will you help train us?'

Geoff smiled his shy smile. 'Well, I suppose so,' he said. 'If you really want me to.'

We were thrilled. Our back-up team was coming together.

Next we needed a base camp manager. Our plan was to have the base in England but we knew from the North what an onerous and time-consuming job it was likely to be.

'Why don't you ask Julian Mills?' said my new polar friend, Steve Martin. I had met Steve at a Foreign Office party a few months earlier where we had both felt out of place amongst an extraordinary assortment of distinguished people.

'Julian looked after us when Dave Mitchell and I went unsupported to the North Pole,' Steve said. 'He was brilliant.'

I called Julian and went to see him. I liked him instantly. He had a strong, dependable presence and I felt nothing would ruffle him. He had valuable business and marketing experience and, most important of all, had no doubts he was the right man for the job.

* * *

By the end of summer 1998 our plans were set. In October 1999, we would fly to a tented camp at Patriot Hills on the edge of Antarctica. Then we would ski 604 nautical miles (695 statute miles) from Hercules Inlet across the frozen wastelands in temperatures as low as minus 50°C, dragging sledges up to twice our own body weight.

This was a much bigger adventure than the North Pole relay and we did not know what lay ahead. All I knew was what I had known as a child – Antarctica would push me to new physical and emotional limits.

8 Highgrove

DARTMOOR WAS WHERE OUR POLAR adventures began and we were drawn back there in September 1998 for our first big planning weekend. We stayed at The Plume of Feathers in Princetown – the place we had trudged to through wind and rain on the first selection weekend.

This time, unbelievably, the weather was worse. As intrepid explorers, we spent the whole weekend indoors. Even I grew slightly tired of scampi and chips but it was useful to talk through ideas, without the wind snatching our words and our waterproofs flapping so loudly it was impossible to hear. On one foray up on to the moor, my waterproof poncho was shredded.

Playing to our respective strengths, we divided ourselves into a Marketing and Technical Department. The Technical Department comprised of Ann, Jan and Zoë. Their first task was to write to suppliers to try to get as much equipment sponsored as possible. This would help considerably, even though we would still need about £250,000 in cash, principally to pay for the charter flights to, from and across Antarctica. We expected the flight from the South Pole to Patriot Hills alone to cost over £100,000.

We knew from experience how difficult it was to raise cash. This time, we were determined to lay the foundations for our success as early as possible. But it was with trepidation that Pom, Rosie and I agreed to be the principal marketeers.

'If we learned one thing from the last expedition,' I reminded the others, 'it was cold-calling companies for cash is a complete waste of time. With the exception of one, every single corporate sponsor we had came on board because of a personal contact.'

'It's true,' Rosie said. 'It would be nice to think that a marketing executive would come into the office, see a sponsorship proposal and think: "that's a good idea". But they don't.'

'The way round it is for each of us to think of everyone we know who could introduce us to important people in companies,' I said. 'Ideally, we want to be introduced to top people, such as chief executives, so they can enthuse their marketing departments.'

We racked our brains, made lists and, by evening, were all talked out. We slept in the pub's little bunk house. When we woke, the weather had cleared a little and we spent a blustery few hours retracing our steps of the day before in search of Pom's car keys. Miraculously I spotted them by the side of the road and, since it was now too late to walk, we drove over to Wydemeet to see Pen and Mary and their new baby, Wilf.

'I do hope she doesn't tell us *everything* about the birth,' Jan said on the way. 'I'll be sick if she does.'

Mary did, of course. Propped on pillows like an Edwardian duchess, she spared us no detail.

'The epidural was marvellous, I didn't feel a thing,' she said. 'But you wouldn't believe the size of the mediaeval torture instruments they shoved in and out. There was blood everywhere. The doctors and nurses were sweating.'

After an hour or more of detail, we finally turned to our expedition and Pen and Mary asked how we were getting on. They wanted to know whether the team was finalised and whether there was a chance another friend of ours might come.

'The problem is,' Mary said grandly. 'It's either the expedition or her husband. I know which I would choose –' she paused for definition – 'the expedition.'

It was not the truth, of course, but in typically blunt fashion Mary had summed up the situation perfectly. We had taken on an enormous project; it was vital we all pulled in the same direction. Unless we devoted ourselves wholeheartedly to the expedition, resentments would build and we would be much less likely to succeed.

Christmas 1998 in Costa Rica was the first Christmas I ever spent abroad. Two wonderful weeks driving all over the country in a hired Daihatsu jeep. I climbed volcanoes and waterfalls, lounged in hot pools and trekked through rainforests amongst the most colourful wildlife on earth.

I thought what a contrast it was to the endless shades of polar pale. Standing in a tropical rainstorm for Midnight Mass, it was hard to believe that, at the same time next year, I would be cramped in a windswept tent at minus 40°C.

I returned to London completely refreshed. Sleeping twelve hours a night, my batteries had slowly recharged and I felt ready to face the work ahead.

'If we give ourselves a big push in the media, it will get people talking about us again,' I said. 'I think we need to remind potential sponsors just how much coverage we got last time and how much we can get for them again.'

It soon became a question of how, rather than whether, we should announce the expedition. We needed a dramatic image. In February 1999, after considerable debate, we agreed we would launch ourselves off a high building. I rang Mary to ask if she would act as our agent again, to organise the press to turn up for the show.

'We'll all be abseiling,' I promised. 'In beautiful down jackets given to us by Rab Carrington. Three yellow, three blue and some nice red helmets. All we need now is a venue but Jan says she may be able to sort that out.'

Jan was a police officer and member of the Metropolitan Police Royal Protection Squad.

'I can't talk now,' she often said if I called on her mobile telephone. 'I've got shooting practice this morning and then I'm off to the hairdressers with the Crown Princess of Sweden.'

Inevitably, Jan's time was rarely her own but, even so, I did not take much notice when she told me she was finding it difficult to take unpaid leave for the expedition. I simply assumed it would come right somehow, until Ann called me at work a week before the date for the photo-call. Breathless, and without saying hello, she told me:

'Sit down. Take a deep breath. Jan's just telephoned me. She can't come.'

'Oh damn,' I said. 'That's a shame. Oh well, I don't suppose it matters too much. No one will really notice if there are only five of us in the photos.'

'No, you don't understand, Caroline,' Ann interrupted. 'She can't come on the expedition. They won't let her have time off work.'

Up until that moment I had had flashes of panic about sponsorship. But with the potential loss of Jan the bottom fell out of my world. There was so much to do: we were in the middle of arranging the launch, there were only a few frantic weeks before we were going to Norway to test our equipment, and we still had not raised the money or even thought everything we needed to do for the Antarctic.

In short, we were miles from even setting off for the Pole, let alone reaching it, and I felt a surge of doubt as to whether we could manage it without Jan's steadying hand. For the first time, too, the thought of what we were doing frightened me.

Ann said Jan was too upset to speak to me. So we rang the rest of the team as well as Julian, Pen and Mary and, together, we discussed what on earth we should do. No one dared articulate it, but it was clear they all shared my view of Jan's importance. I wished there was something I could do.

When I did get to speak to Jan, she was devastated and still wanted desperately to be part of the team. Ironically, I felt the biggest problem was her professionalism.

'I'll tell you what I'm worried about Ann,' I said on one of our late night telephone conversations. 'Jan is so good at doing what she's told I can't see her fighting the decision. I can hear in her voice that her training's kicking in. She's gradually putting her own feelings to the back of her mind.'

But I refused to believe there was no hope.

'Surely there must be a way of changing their minds,' I kept saying. I tried to tell Jan how essential she was to the entire team. One particularly emotional evening, I wrote her an e-mail.

My very dear Jan,

There are several things I want to say which you might not believe if I said them over the telephone and that is why I am writing. You, Jan, are the most important person in our expedition. We laugh about how the team was 'selected' and maybe some people are only there because we get on and understand each other well. With you there is one essential difference. There has never been any doubt in my mind that you are the rock upon which the whole team relies. Your strength is colossal and, particularly when the team has been together on Dartmoor etc, it is obvious how much support everyone derives from you.

My exact words yesterday were that the whole expedition was 'severely rattled' by the possibility that you were not part of it. I meant it and it was an understatement. I may have sounded calm to you over the last week but I am really worried. I have very severe doubts that the expedition can succeed without you and I am also genuinely frightened personally about landing at Patriot Hills and setting off into the unknown without you.

Please send me a message back to say that you have got this one. And then let us speak tomorrow about how we are going to make it all work. It will be all right if we keep positive and together we are going to reach the South Pole.

All my love, Caro.

Of course, the other minor problem now was we had no building to abseil from. There were only a few days left to go and, with Rosie on holiday and Pom in bed with 'flu, Ann, Zoë and I spent the weekend wondering whether we should postpone the launch. But on Monday morning, Ann rang again.

'What about the First Aid Nursing Yeomanry (FANY) Headquarters at the Duke of York's Barracks?' she said. 'They're pioneering women and so are we. My friend is a FANY. I'll ask her now.'

By the end of the day, Ann had arranged it all. With her customary contempt for red tape, she not only lined up the building but also persuaded Navy instructors to stage manage the abseil as well.

In the meantime, Mary was doing her bit and news of the expedition was getting around.

'Please can we do an interview with you on the radio in half an hour?'

'Could you spare a few minutes so I can write something for the *Mail*?'

I took lots of calls, I loved the buzz. Being in demand was so much more fun than working.

On the evening before the launch, we had a strange little gathering. Julian was there with copies of the press pack and details of journalists and photographers due to turn up. Ann and Zoë looked as drained as I felt and I did not know where to start with the traumas of the week before.

Rosie was back, dazed from her holiday. Pom sat, white as a sheet, a silk scarf round her throat and with a large pair of sunglasses to avoid the glare of the subdued lighting. With her head in her hands, she bravely agreed to go through with the abseil.

At 5.30 the next morning, the telephone rang. It was the *Today* programme on Radio 4.

'Sorry to wake you so early, but we're doing the Kurds all morning and I'm afraid we won't have time for your interview. Sorry about that, but at least you can go back to sleep.'

There was far too much to do to sleep. Everyone was staying at my flat and half-clad women rushed about preparing for interviews. Pom was on *Sky* – miraculously managing to speak – and Zoë and Rosie were taken by taxi to television studios. I packed the car with our gear and then, with Ann bubbling on the telephone to a radio station beside me, I tuned in to Zoë and (extra small) Rosie, who looked like a down-filled maggot in her (extra large) jacket on the *Big Breakfast*.

I still did not like abseiling but, with a dozen photographers and television cameras below, I had no choice but to climb over the parapet and lean horizontally with my big polar boots on the wall. On my right, Zoë squealed with delight as she bounced and I slid in a line with the others on the end of our ropes. Just keep concentrating Caroline, I thought grimly. And don't look down.

Curiously, it was only when my feet touched the ground I felt my heart pound. At that precise moment, my mobile telephone rang. I apologised and fumbled in my pocket, wondering who wanted to interview us now.

'Have you got a moment, Ms Hamilton?' a woman's voice asked in a nasal tone. 'I got your number from a central register. Can I interest you in private health and accident insurance?'

Even now, I think it was one of my friends having a laugh.

'Over here. Look at me love. This one's got film in.'

It was the same as it had been for the North Pole, with photographers jostling and clicking in front of us. We smiled and laughed and smiled again. There were lots of journalists asking questions about the South Pole and we were all on a high when the FANYs invited us in for a drink.

Their commanding officer, a delightfully stylish woman called Lynda Rose showed us around. She had greying hair, full army fatigues and impeccable scarlet lipstick.

The walls were lined with pictures of independent, strong-willed women and, in one small frame, there were the three George Crosses they had been awarded for Special Operations in the Second World War. The citations describing their bravery were absurdly understated. I felt a fraud when the women who ran the headquarters told us how courageous they thought we were.

I could have stayed all day listening to the FANYs' stories but, before long, we were on the move again. This time, it was a quick change into our best clothes, into Pom's and Ann's cars and off down the motorway.

'Where is Highgrove, anyway?' I asked, as I drove Pom's car.

'Who knows?' Pom said. 'Just follow the others.'

It was an amazing feeling; no sooner had the cameras stopped flashing, than we were off to meet our new patron, Prince Charles. We did not know whether Jan would be allowed to come and I was thrilled when I saw her car in the car park. Apart from anything else, I did not think she would be comfortable being there if she was not on the expedition.

Highgrove was much smaller and more intimate than I had expected. We saw Prince Charles first at a distance, strolling on his own in the grounds. His Assistant Private Secretary, Elizabeth Buchanan, then invited us into the house by a back door through the wellies and waterproofs. She showed us into a small room lined with Prince Charles' watercolours. I was struck by the variety of subjects.

We were waiting in the room to be summoned when Jan appeared with another Protection Squad officer. She looked rather awkward on the other side of the fence as a guest. I remembered how difficult she had found it to screw up the courage to ask Prince Charles to be our patron.

Elizabeth Buchanan soon told us the Prince was ready and we shuffled through, on our best behaviour, to his private sitting room. We shook hands and mumbled our names, then sat in armchairs for a cup of tea and Duchy Original biscuits.

Instantly, Prince Charles put us at our ease. He was utterly charming and relaxed. I was very impressed by how much he knew about us and polar travel in general. As I looked at him, I could hear my grandmother telling me he had an artist's hands.

Prince Charles appeared genuinely interested in what we were doing and, perhaps with the exception of Jan, we all found him easy to talk to. He asked a lot of questions and told us about some of his own experiences in the Canadian Arctic, laughing loudly as he recounted misadventures.

'Did your bogies freeze in your nose when you were there?' I asked, rather cheekily.

There was a shocked hush from my team-mates, but Prince Charles was unfazed.

'Oh yes,' he said. 'Didn't yours?'

When he told us he was going to the Falkland Islands on an official visit, this was the opportunity we had been hoping for. In view of the costs of the service offered by the flight company Adventure Network International (ANI), Julian was researching the Falklands, the British Antarctic Survey and the RAF as possible alternatives. We thought this would be easier than asking the American scientists based at the South Pole for a lift on one of their flights.

We had heard the United States National Science Foundation was likely to be unfriendly and unwilling to allow us to use the airstrip at the South Pole. Our only hope, we thought, was to obtain official British backing before we approached them.

'I don't suppose you're likely to meet anyone in the Falklands who would like to fly to the Pole to pick us up, are you?' I asked Prince Charles.

He looked at me quizzically and paused.

'But that would have to be the RAF.'

'Ye-es,' we all responded together and looked straight at him.

'It's either that, or we could all get pregnant and marry Americans when we get there so we can be repatriated as US nationals,' I explained.

'Oh, right,' the Prince said at once, obviously fearing for the future of his subjects. 'In that case, I'd better see what I can do.'

In the early stages, Jan took charge of the Technical Department. She called and wrote to equipment and clothing manufacturers and researched the different products available. Early in my polar education, Pen told me polar explorers have never agreed on what should be taken on an expedition to ensure success. Ever since Scott and Amundsen, when one favoured ponies and manhauling and the other chose dogs to pull their sledges, the tiniest piece of equipment can arouse the fiercest debates.

'Let's try to think about the big things first,' I said.

As an initial step, we talked to Sue Fullilove who, together with Ann and Jan, played such an important part in Alpha's success at the North Pole. The first leg was the coldest and, therefore, the one most like Antarctica.

'I'd certainly get a better clothing system this time,' Sue said instantly.

Sue, Jan and Ann suffered in the North with fabrics which did not wick their sweat away properly. As we talked I realised there were many things I still did not know about their leg of the trip.

Typically, Ann looked on the bright side.

'Actually, I quite enjoyed having to take my suit off and dry it above the cookers. It was so nice to go to sleep in dry clothes.'

But even Ann admitted it was pretty unpleasant putting frozen ones back on in the morning.

On a polar expedition, dampness needs to be avoided. If clothes or sleeping bags get wet, they lose their insulating properties, get heavier to carry and ultimately freeze. Drying them above the cookers involves burning extra fuel, but extra fuel means extra weight, and warmth in the tent also creates condensation which can make equipment even wetter.

As part of Penguin Echo, Pom, Zoë and I had different memories. For us, the bindings holding our boots to our skis were the biggest problem. After 300 nautical miles (and being used for training at Resolute Bay), the uniflex plastic design was just not strong enough.

'It should be better this time, though,' Zoë said, 'because rather than having to clamber over all those awkward pressure ridges and boulders of ice, isn't it going to be much flatter?'

I nodded. 'It should be. But I still don't want to have to keep mending them. Apart from anything else, it was such a waste of time, stopping and screwing new ones in. Do you remember the day the glue wouldn't stick and I took my skis off? I was exhausted.'

Zoë laughed and, without any sympathy, told the others how funny I looked stomping along without any skis. Every few steps one or both feet went through the thin crust of snow and I fell in up to my chest. After nearly a day of pulling myself up and out, I really did not find it funny at all – but there was nothing to be done until we pitched camp and could make more repairs.

In view of the potentially smoother Antarctic conditions, we decided to try more conventional Nordic bindings. This meant abandoning the comforting big white Sorel boots we wore before. Instead, we thought about a smaller, racier version made by Alfa in Norway. Three small metal pins on the binding slotted into holes at the front of the boot and then the whole toe was clamped to the ski by a metal spring.

The best news was that Jan was back on board. After the initial trauma, she kept things very close to her chest so I don't know what eventually swung the balance. All I cared about was that she was part of the team once more.

9 Any Colour Skin but Pink

I HAVE NEVER LIKED THE PROCESS of getting fit and found it all too easy to let training slip to the lowest priority. There was so much to do, I often decided to stay an extra hour at work or write one more letter to a prospective sponsor instead.

In London, the best I could do was run for an hour a few times a week and sweat it out on the old Nordicsport skiing machine in my flat. I hadn't touched the dreaded thing since the North Pole, except for use as a clothes horse, and I was very reluctant to bring it out of retirement. I had to admit it was an extremely effective way to get fit and exercised all the right muscles for hauling a sledge.

Its great disadvantage was that, even with television (at full volume to drown the clatter) it was incredibly boring. I marvelled that anyone could use it if they were not preparing for a polar expedition. Another disadvantage appeared to be that, while it was good for my triceps and ski poling action, the skiing machine was doing nothing for the look of my arms.

'Gosh, look at your biceps,' I remarked to Pom as she took off her jumper one day. 'What have you been doing? I've never seen you with arms as big as that.'

'I know, not bad eh?' she retorted. Then: 'I don't understand what it is about you, Caro. Most women's chests go completely flat as they get fitter. But yours just seems to explode.'

I laughed. 'Well thank heaven for my under-wired sports bra,' I said. 'Otherwise I'd be all over the place.'

I had thought I had an ally in Pom as the other 'weakling' – neither of us rated our chances of hauling the others out of an Antarctic crevasse. Now suddenly, she had deserted me. How smug she looked in her little white T-shirt – without saying a word she had obviously been working out big time with weights.

I thought about joining a gym but, as soon as I walked in, I remembered why I could not do it. For me a gym is like church – it is a place for very private business. I hate the excessive chumminess of aerobics instructors. I did not want anyone to monitor my progress or know what I was training for. I scowled at the manager as she tried to approach me.

In February 1999 we went to Norway to train and test equipment. Before leaving I was very nervous. I worried I might not like the cold and hardship and, for some reason, I kept thinking about going to the lavatory.

'Perhaps if I don't eat too much, I won't have to poo,' I tried to console myself.

I have never liked performing outdoors and knew I found it even more difficult in the biting cold.

Going to Norway for ten days' training was a mini-expedition. For the first time, we were taking complete responsibility for ourselves. Geoff was coming out after a couple of days, but there was no Pen or Mike to help with equipment.

Jan had not been able to concentrate properly on the expedition for some time and this made me very anxious. Ann and Zoë tried to make up for her absence in the Technical Department but, maybe because they weren't involved with organising equipment for the North Pole, I worried they might not appreciate the complexities of getting everything ready on time.

I shared my concern when we were training one weekend.

'I think we should go through all the kit we need to take and then make a list of who is doing what,' I said. 'I know it's difficult because we don't necessarily know everything

Jan has done but no one can organise it all on their own. We've all got to help. It's absolutely vital we don't screw up Norway.'

I felt better for having got that off my chest and we put our heads together to make a plan. We had some clothing left over from last time, we also had offers from manufacturers to test their kit.

Rosie volunteered to pick up six climbing harnesses and plastic toboggans she had seen Czech children playing with. Pom agreed to sort out food and Ann said she would chase up clothing and borrow equipment from people she knew in the navy. My role was to fill in the gaps and run around London to pick up rope, dried dinners and other last-minute essentials.

Skis and bindings were a complicated decision. As we talked I grew worried that, because it was difficult, the Technical Department had put it to the back of their minds. Zoë said she would try to sort it out, but it was Helge Hoflandsdal of Åsnes Skis in Norway, who really saved our lives. Pen suggested we called and, by some fluke, Zoë caught him in early one morning, a few days before we set off.

Even better, after Zoë worked her charms, Helge offered to drive for three hours with a selection of skis and bindings to meet us at our destination: Geilo. (The car hire woman at Oslo airport told us to pronounce it 'Yay-lo' – a word I found easiest to say if I stood on tiptoes and then sank down to my heels on the second syllable).

On our way from the airport, we called in on Sjur Mørdre, one of Norway's leading polar explorers.

'Oh there's nothing modern about these,' he told us, holding up the Alfa boot we were keen to try. 'I designed these boots for my own expeditions. The heavy felt linings are no different from Amundsen's.'

We asked Sjur technical questions about the North and South Poles but he did not seem interested in having his brains picked by us. As we climbed back into our minibus, I voiced my thoughts to the others.

'Maybe it's because we're no longer complete novices, just comparative ones,' I said. 'Surely he can't have felt threatened by us?'

'I don't think our experience has anything to do with it,' Ann replied. 'Remember David Hempleman-Adams in Resolute Bay?'

I did not need reminding; he and Rune Gjeldnes were attempting the North Pole at the same time we were. Hempleman-Adams laughed at our chances.

'Don't worry, Matty,' he said within earshot of the rest of the team. 'If you fail, you'll know that it's only because you were with a bunch of amateur women.'

I could not help smiling when the rumour went round that they were delayed at the start on Ward Hunt Island because Gjeldnes had forgotten his cigarettes. After failing with a broken sledge, his expedition was leaving Resolute's tiny airport as we arrived. I was not wholly surprised when he ignored us.

'I suspect some people don't want us to succeed,' I said.

We dropped a 'flu-stricken Rosie at a hotel in Oslo. Then, with five of us and all our equipment somehow squeezed into a 'people mover' designed for a neat little family of four, Pom drove and I sat in the front while the rest slept on top of each other in the back.

We drove up into the mountains along winding roads and past beautiful fjords. The scenery was uniformly grey and white and, every now and then, a light sprinkling of snow came down. It was dark when we arrived in Geilo. There were banks of ice fifteen feet high at the side of the snow-packed road. Lights twinkled from the town and I realised that, far from the frozen hardship of a polar expedition, we were approaching a perfectly civilised ski resort.

There were familiar Alpine-style chalets, ski-hire shops and even a few bars and restaurants with rubber floors. But the place was almost deserted – just a few locals going about their business on stand-up toboggans. Some had shopping or children on the front; they reminded me of

Cambridge ladies on old-fashioned bicycles with large wicker baskets.

Geilo, like the rest of Norway, was extremely expensive by British standards and we stayed the night at a youth hostel with roaming teenagers who similarly could not afford to go out. In the morning, while we filled our pockets with free processed food from the breakfast room, Zoë went to collect her new friend Helge from the railway café as arranged.

Helge was a tall, well-built middle-aged man wearing a Norwegian patterned jumper. He jumped out of his car, apparently oblivious to the freezing temperature or the icy drive, and greeted us with a big smile. Quietly we helped him unload and set up a workshop in the youth hostel cellar.

Helge spent a whole day with Zoë and me, patiently explaining the merits of different bindings and showing us how to screw and glue them into the skis. He also gave us skins to experiment with on the bottom of our skis (to stop us slipping backwards). As he went through everything, I realised how little any of us had known about the choices made on our behalf for the North Pole.

'Don't worry about giving anything back until you get home to England and decide what you want,' Helge said when we had eventually fixed up as many combinations of equipment to try as possible. 'I'm sure you will like the skis and at least one type of skin and binding. They have been used on lots of expeditions.'

That was, of course, what we wanted to hear but it was even more useful when Helge told us about problems other expeditions had encountered with equipment. Most manufacturers are proud to tell you that something 'has been tested at minus 50°C' or 'was used on a successful Everest expedition'. What they never say in their advertising is how the equipment performed in those conditions or whether the mountaineers enjoyed their experience. We hoped to learn from other people's comments and to find out what repair kit we needed in case things went wrong.

* * *

The night after the youth hostel experience we were braver. We pitched a three-man tent in the snow (on concrete, as we discovered when we tried to put the pegs in) and lay head to toe like sardines. I was shocked to find Pom's face just three inches from mine. If one person turned, we all had to turn. There were complaints about snoring but at least we kept warm in our giant sleeping bags.

We rose early, intending to catch the first train up to Finse where our training was to begin. But we had all forgotten how much longer things take in the cold and, by the time we had packed up the tent, had breakfast and changed into our expedition clothing in an underground car park, it was nearly midday.

We skied around town with our sledges a little, much to the amusement of the boy in the ski shop who had helped to adjust Helge's bindings, and waited for the next train. We were all quite tense and there was much less banter between us than usual. I sensed we had all found it frustrating to spend so long getting organised, and I tried to reassure myself as well as the others that learning about equipment and how we worked together was not time wasted.

Then the train arrived and we had only a minute in which to load ourselves and everything on. I sat next to Zoë and we watched in silence as the scenery outside grew whiter and whiter. We passed houses buried in snow with chimneys puffing defiantly.

It was a beautiful day with a bright blue sky. I had never seen anything like it – long, deep valleys and steep rocky mountains covered in a thick, sparkling blanket – and this was just the regular train from Oslo to Bergen. I looked at the other passengers. No wonder the Norwegians are such good polar travellers, I thought, they do it every day.

Every now and then the train stopped and, even with no obvious station outside, a few people jumped on or off into the snow. When after a few hours we reached Finse, there were a few buildings and even a platform to mark the spot.

We piled out of the train as hastily as we had boarded. The station could have been from *Thomas The Tank Engine*. I half expected the Big Fat Controller to appear. Instead we were left alone with our belongings, a few oil drums and the post bag, as the train slid slowly away and into another long tunnel through the mountains.

'Right, where are we going to camp?' Jan asked as if one of us should know.

'God knows,' I said. 'Let's go and look over there.'

I waved aimlessly over to the other side of the station and, after tying ourselves to our sledges, we shuffled off in that direction.

At that moment, a man in a designer cross-country suit appeared on fluorescent skis. He told us there was only one place to camp and that was on the other side of the lake.

'Oh, *tak*,' we thanked him, using our only Norwegian word.

Then we looked at each other, puzzled. There were a few mountain huts in view and a nice warm hotel bar right next to the station, but where was the lake? It all looked the same, a landscape of white surrounded by white.

'I reckon that's the lake,' said Zoë, pointing. 'Remember how the bay at Resolute looked. When you stood on top of the hill behind the village, the frozen sea looked like that flat bit over there.'

We set off. Pom and I fell down the first slope, knocked in the back of the legs by our sledges. Then we settled into single file, trudging along in that familiar way and dragging our equipment in dustbin bags on little red sledges behind.

The sun was setting and the temperature had dropped quite substantially by the time we reached the other side. I felt a numbness in my cheeks and, as I reached inside my sledge for another pair of outer gloves, I glanced at the thermometer I had brought with me.

'Guess what the temperature is,' I called out, reminding myself of my mother on family holidays in Mull.

'Minus ten?' Jan shouted.

'No, minus twenty-five.'

'Oh, goodie,' Pom sounded relieved. 'It doesn't feel as bad as I remembered.'

Once the tents were up and our belongings safely inside, it was time to go back to the station to meet Geoff and Rosie. Feeling rather too much like a girl guide, I took a compass bearing from the tent, so we could find our way back, and we set off again on our skis. Zoë led the way and no one was surprised when, this time, she took us into the bar by the station platform.

The bar was part of a small hotel built like a mountain hut. It was spacious and had large picture windows overlooking the lake. Stuffed mountain animals, old wooden skis and snow shoes adorned the walls. We sat at one end of a long bench table carved from a single piece of wood. There were black-and-white photographs showing the history of the single-track railway and nineteenth century ladies in long woollen skirts enjoying their holidays in snow and ice.

A photograph caught my eye. It was a picture of the members of Captain Scott's expedition of 1911–12 when they came to train, like us, in the mountains nearby. The woeful inadequacy of their tweed clothing struck me. They looked so confident and hopeful.

Just next to this image was the shattered dream – the famous photograph of an exhausted Scott and his four team mates taken at the South Pole when they knew they had been beaten by Amundsen. Not one of them is smiling. I remembered seeing the same picture for the first time as a child. I could not understand then how, having reached their goal, they could look so glum.

Before long, another train arrived and Rosie and Geoff appeared through the darkness. Rosie was even thinner than usual as a result of her 'flu, but they both strode in with heavy bags. We all felt we had been apart much longer than two days. There was lots to tell and we chattered on quickly, often interrupting each other with news.

'You'll be proud of us, Geoff,' I said after a while. 'I think we've remembered just about everything. Rosie picked up some stray Helly Hansen stuff they sent us in Oslo and we've got all sorts of different kit to try. Now all we need is white gas so we can cook you a delicious dinner in our tents. You did manage to pick up some white gas in Oslo, didn't you?'

'No,' Geoff said. 'Didn't you?'

'No.'

I was irritated by our inefficiency but there was no point showing it.

'Is there any other type of fuel we can use in those cookers you lent us?' Pom asked Geoff.

'Well, I suppose we could use unleaded petrol,' he said. 'But it won't do the cookers much good.'

'If we have to buy new ones afterwards, we will,' I replied. 'But there aren't likely to be many petrol pumps around here.'

'No, but I expect we could get some in Geilo. I'll go back there in the morning on the train,' Pom volunteered.

This seemed harsh but Pom would not accept our protestations.

'Don't be stupid,' she said. 'There's no point in us all going back. It's fine, you lot can ski and I'll see you later in the day.'

Back in the tent that night I was frozen. Besides our sleeping bags, we only had thin insulating mats between us and the snow. I fell asleep easily but then woke in the small hours, my whole body aching with cold. I tried to ignore it and, with my eyes tight shut, lay still, not wanting to roll into another cold part of my sleeping bag. I pulled my hat down lower over my ears, curled up deeper inside and cursed Ann's happy snuffling as she slept beside me.

Finally, after what seemed an age of waiting, it was morning. We waved goodbye to Pom and organised ourselves for a day's trek up on to a glacier above the tents. With the sun out, it was much warmer, the air was still and the weather looked fair. We packed our sledges with plenty of food and spare clothing and set off in pairs towards the mountain.

It was hard work skiing uphill through the snow and no one wanted to be seen out of breath. We stopped occasionally for something to eat and our progress slowed as it got steeper approaching the glacier. Geoff paused near different snow formations to show what was happening to the ice underneath.

'You must get used to concentrating all the time on what's going on around you,' he said. 'Even when the wind is blowing and you're tired, you must keep your heads up and think about the conditions. Look over there for instance, you can see the snow is sitting differently on the ice. That might mean there's about to be an avalanche.'

'What about crevasses, Geoff?' Ann asked.

We were all worried about crevasses in the Antarctic and I was hoping to see some in Norway so we could at least visualise the hazards that lay ahead.

'The trouble with crevasses,' Geoff replied, 'is that you often can't see them. They form when the glacial ice is moving over a sloping bit of rock and the ice has to split in parallel lines at the top to bend. The problem is the snow can form bridges over the gaps and then you may not know there is nothing underneath until you fall through.'

I had heard this before from Geoff and it was not reassuring.

'So how do you know if you're approaching a crevasse field?' Jan asked.

Geoff pointed up at the glacier.

'You see where the ice looks as if it's falling over the edge like a giant waterfall? And where it joins the rock at the sides? There could be crevasses there.'

But it was not the day for crevasse hunting. It was a day for getting used to our skis and hauling our sledges again – and I did not like the fact I was finding it difficult. Everyone seemed much fitter than I was and I noticed they seemed to glide better and get further with each stride.

Finally, after five hours of straight uphill, we were up on the glacier and Geoff agreed we should turn round. The sun was lower and the air was colder. I was looking forward to some Alpine racing down to the bottom.

But going down was even worse. The skins on the bottom of my skis meant I could point straight down the hill at impossible angles and still not move an inch. Now I was taking three or four strides to only one of Rosie's and, unless my legs moved extremely fast, I was bashed from behind by my sledge or pulled over by it as it whizzed past.

I could not understand it and hated being left behind. Ann stayed with me and encouraged me with chocolate stops. Unlike me, she had the excuse of never having skied downhill before. As we stumbled together, I did my best not to show how frustrated I was.

Eventually, over a rise, we saw Geoff waiting and pointing the direction down. I relaxed a little and reconciled myself to plodding slowly to the tent. Ann and I skied side by side, tired and in silence, until Ann suddenly commented on how pretty my bright pink skins were. In the fading light, they cast a sharp reflection on the snow and in a moment I remembered Helge's words:

'I'm only going to give you one pair of these man-made skins,' he said. 'I think they're dreadful because they're so resistant, it's impossible to ski with them, even downhill . . .'

So that was it. I was not incompetent after all. I did not say anything but the following day, when we swapped kit to test, I carefully chose another pair of skis. This time, I shot off at quite a pace and even managed to glide a little. I was so relieved. Possibly, my efforts of the day before had improved my technique, but I did not care. All that mattered was I could keep up. I could even look around and enjoy the scenery.

And I did not have to ask who had the dreaded pink skins. It was obvious. There was poor Jan, sweating it out, lifting her skis with every step and almost running rather than sliding across the snow. From then on, each day, it was any colour skin but pink for me.

It was always good to get back to the tents at the end of the day. We lit the cookers inside as soon as we got there, melted snow for water and usually made soup as an aperitif before an early dinner of rehydrated food. Then, after dinner, we skied off again in the dark to a nearby hostel to have lessons with Geoff in the light and warmth.

I am normally lazy about practical tasks but I concentrated hard when we took our cookers to pieces and Geoff showed how to mend them. I carried on practising with the parts while we asked him questions about clothing and equipment. In Antarctica, there would be no one to help us and I wanted to understand how the vital equipment worked.

Geoff reminded us how to navigate. We picked his brains about how he did things and asked how the South would differ from the North.

'This is like Antarctica,' he shouted through a howling gale. We were huddled in two bothy (survival) bags with the wind racing over us and blowing snow horizontally. 'You wait until we turn round and go back. This is what it's like. Huge winds against you, all day, every day. Are you sure you still want to go?'

A few miles further on we did turn round. It was like turning to face an oncoming lorry. The freezing wind scythed across our faces and knocked us backwards. We struggled to do up our hoods and fill the gaps where the wind whipped through. A few yards away, Rosie crouched down taking the longest to sort herself out.

Next to me, Pom's arms were going like windmills. I knew what that meant: her hands had gone and she was desperately trying to warm them.

We moved off eventually, with our heads down, and battled to make ground against the wind.

Later Geoff asked us quietly, 'Who was looking to check what was happening behind you this afternoon? I bet none of you saw that great big avalanche. No one had more than a couple of inches open under those hoods. Remember what I told you?'

As usual with Geoff, none of us knew how much he was joking.

His point was well made.

Each day we skied and stopped every few hours for a break as we had in the Arctic. We had an assortment of unfamiliar clothing. It took a long time to undo zips and velcro and, in the cold, it was easy to become impatient.

'I'm getting cold. I've got to keep moving,' Jan said suddenly at one of our breaks.

She skied off at once before I had even taken a bite of chocolate.

'Wait for us,' Zoë called out. 'I've got to put my food back in and do up my sledge.'

But, because of the noise of the wind, Jan could not hear and we had to get going as best we could. Rosie's boots came out of their bindings and, after Zoë and I bent over to help, we were a long straggling group making our way to the tents.

'I don't think we should ever leave people stranded like we did today,' I ventured to say in the evening. 'When it's blowing like that you can't hear if someone's in trouble behind you. I'm sure we mustn't split up.'

'I agree,' said Zoë. 'But that will only work if no one faffs. That's the problem. There's too much fiddling about.'

'Yes,' said Jan, 'and if you get cold, it takes too long to warm up. Ann and I hardly stopped at all in the Arctic.'

Alpha's time on the ice was much colder than Echo's. We used to stop skiing on the dot every hour or hour and a quarter, sit down on our sledges and snack for five minutes. Even though it was too cold to stop for long, it was a good way to break up the day and I enjoyed our chats and laughs.

'We've got to eat, though,' I said. 'How do you do it if you're always moving?'

'Easy,' said Ann. 'I never stop eating. My pockets are filled with food. I chomp as I go along.'

We slept in two three-man tents and, after our night in Geilo, Jan and Pom decided that Ann, Zoë and I snored the loudest and must share together. (Geoff had brought his own tent and kept to himself).

'That's not fair,' I joked. 'Rosie makes a huge noise. It's only because she wears those ridiculous ear-muffs that she doesn't wake herself up all night.'

But it did not make any difference to me. A tent is like anywhere else I have lived: a place to be untidy. As long as my tent-mates did not mind me littering the floor with my few possessions, I was happy to share with anyone.

'I still don't understand it,' I complained every morning. 'Someone must have stolen my hat. I can't have lost it *again* in such a small space.'

Zoë sighed but Ann was sweet.

'It's okay Caroline, I don't care what you do in here,' she said. 'Remember, I'm used to camping with toddlers. At least you can be useful. You can light the cooker occasionally.'

During random inspections of the tents, Geoff delighted in showing us our mistakes. Fortunately, I do not think he noticed the night I left the fly sheet open and the wind filled our boots and provisions with snow. But there was no hiding from him when my sledge went missing in a snow drift, or when the bamboo sticks and snow holding the tent down blew away.

We settled into a routine. Ann was in charge of our tent, organising where we put what and making sure we dried our clothes properly. She also did most of the cooking and melting snow, with Zoë and me as her helpers. We cut the snow into bricks, held on to boiling saucepans and, in my case, tried to keep to only one part of the tent.

At the North Pole, it took three hours to get packed up and started every morning. From the moment we woke up, there was so much to do – melting snow and making hot cereal and coffee for all of us. We knew how important it was not to waste time.

In some ways, it was easier to be efficient with only three people in each group. The trouble was that, with the noise of the wind, we often did not know what was happening in the other tent.

'We're ready,' we sang out to the others one morning.

'Oh, piss off, "B" team,' Pom's voice came back at once. 'We've only just lit our cooker. You'll have to wait until we've had breakfast.'

On another occasion, when Geoff suggested we practise taking the tents down and putting them up again in the wind, it really was the 'A' team versus the 'B' team. We clung on to the wildly flapping fabric, desperately trying to thread the long tent poles through, and I was very aware how we tended only to look out for the people we shared with.

'I think two tents are divisive,' I said later. 'We must go in one if we possibly can. Otherwise there's a real danger we will only concentrate on the people we're sharing with rather than making sure the whole team is all right.'

Pom's face lit up. She was brimming with ideas for tent designs – not all of them necessarily very practical.

'We need to be together to share ideas if things go wrong,' Ann agreed. 'We'll be able to support each other much better if we are all under one roof.'

There was silence.

Then I heard Zoë whisper to Ann, 'That's all very well. But what's going to happen when Caroline shares with Jan?'

'What do you mean, Zo? Are you saying you find me difficult?'

Even before she answered, I knew what she meant. Jan was so tidy – her rucksack was always neatly packed and she had plastic bags for everything. I, too, wondered whether we might drive each other up the wall. I did not want to fall out with anyone and suspected I irritated Lucy at the North Pole when I lost my things and borrowed hers without asking.

'Well, why don't we try different tent combinations before we decide on one tent,' Ann suggested diplomatically.

'Okay Captain Chaos, it's you, me and Rosie sleeping together tonight,' Jan said later as she settled in to the 'A' Team tent. 'Now before you come in Caro, hand me your hat, gloves and goggles and I'll look after them overnight. When you want them in the morning, just ask. All right?'

Dutifully, I handed everything over to Jan the Police Officer. It was the perfect arrangement.

'This way, Zo,' I told her proudly, 'Jan puts all my possessions in a stuff sack and everything I don't give her I wear in bed. Then I don't have to worry about losing anything and Jan can organise the tent as she likes. So, contrary to what you may think, Jan and I actually get on jolly well together, thank you.'

Before we left Finse, Ann telephoned Liv Arneson. In 1994, Liv was one of very few women ever to ski to the South Pole – and she did it solo and unsupported. We were all keen to meet her.

When we telephoned, she could not have been more friendly.

'Sjur Mørdre said he'd given you my number,' Liv said. 'Please come and visit. I'd love to meet you.'

We spent several hours at her house outside Oslo before we caught our aeroplane home. We deluged her with questions and she answered them all. I was struck by how incredibly normal she was. Seven hundred miles on her own, without a radio (it broke early on). And yet, like Pen, she did not say it was difficult, that she had been tired or cold or that there had been any major dramas.

Above all, I remember her saying: 'I enjoyed every minute of it. When I saw the scientific base at the South Pole from a distance, I didn't want to get there. I didn't want my expedition to end because I was having such a wonderful time.'

Meeting Liv encouraged us enormously and we learned a lot from our trip to Norway. We learned how to get on with each other as a team in harsh conditions. We discovered some of the equipment we liked and disliked. Most of all we realised that expeditions are not always successful. For Antarctica we were going to have to be much better organised and prepared.

10 Prusik Loops

I FIRST MET ANNE KERSHAW in March 1999. Everything we heard about her made her a force to be reckoned with. Her husband, Giles, was a distinguished Antarctic pilot. When he was killed in a microlight accident, Anne took over the running of his company, Adventure Network International (ANI).

ANI is the only company with a commercial licence to fly in Antarctica. Its business is exclusively in Antarctica where it is an airline, a tour operator and a provider of support services to expeditions like ours. Its prices are notoriously high.

Almost without exception, people sucked their teeth and spoke with awe about Anne Kershaw. Otherwise fearless polar explorers were terrified.

'She's an extremely tough business woman, you know,' they all said very quickly. 'You'll find she drives a very hard bargain.'

I was intrigued.

'Maybe it's because all these men are so used to charming people and getting things for free, they don't like it when a woman stands up to them,' I suggested to Pom.

'No, I don't think it's that. She probably is very tough,' she replied, 'but that's OK, so are we. I'm sure she can't be any harder than those film producers you deal with every day.'

'Just be completely straight with her,' Julian advised. 'You've got nothing to hide. Like anyone else, I'm sure Anne will respond well if you're honest with her. Most of all, don't try to pretend you've got the money to pay her when you haven't.'

Anne told Pen ANI was getting booked up and we knew we needed to see her to make arrangements. In some trepidation, Pom, Zoë, Julian and I went for a meeting soon after we returned from Norway.

In the middle of Beaconsfield, the ANI office was incongruous. A small plaque on a terrace of Georgian cottages marked its existence and we went through to a yard at the back.

Anne was nothing like the ogre we had expected. A slight, well-dressed blonde, she greeted us warmly. Then, in a few precise steps, she took us into her office.

'So,' she said in a soft Scottish accent, 'first of all let me tell you a bit about ANI. Then you can tell me about your team and what you want to do. Most importantly, I have to tell you now that we won't take anyone to Antarctica unless we think they're up to it. I know you had guides on your trip to the North Pole, so you're going to have to convince us you'll be safe setting off on your own this time.'

With that, Anne poured coffee and, for the next three hours, she grilled us. What kind of training were we doing and who was supplying our kit? Did anyone have any medical skills, and would the others carry on if one of the team was evacuated? What kind of precautions were we planning for the wind and crevasses?

We took it in turns to answer, all on our best behaviour. Gradually, I felt she relaxed. Each time we responded well, she smiled more and her shoulders dropped. She told us stories about other expeditions. We even risked a few light-hearted comments and she seemed to enjoy our sense of humour.

'We're very busy this year with the millennium,' Anne said. 'I only have a few places left. In order to secure your flights, you'll need to pay a deposit in the next few weeks. I'll work out the exact amount, but the deposit won't be less than a hundred and fifty thousand dollars. How are you getting on with sponsorship?'

'Oh, awfully well,' I said at once, and we bubbled to reassure her.

The marketing department was in overdrive. Julian had helped us produce a brochure and we were talking to different companies. We had reached the North Pole and generated a lot of media coverage; we had a proven track record. I was hopeful it would be easier this time. But the months wore on and still sponsorship was not forthcoming.

So began a cat and mouse game with ANI. Throughout the summer, Anne called to say she was holding our places but she could not hold them for long without money. Every time we spoke to her, I apologised profusely and told her about our progress with potential sponsors.

'Obviously, we're trying to raise the funds as soon as possible,' I told her. 'We do understand if you can't keep waiting and have to take other people instead.'

Each time I said this, I cringed with worry. I remembered being told about Pen's difficult telephone conversations when he was holding things together for the North Pole. He used to crouch lower and lower, sometimes screwing himself into a ball, to exert his maximum charm.

In July, we felt we had to show ANI some progress. I telephoned their office to make an announcement.

'We will have our funding in place by the end of the month,' I said. It was not an unreasonable hope.

But then our latest potential sponsor stopped answering my calls and the end of July came and went.

On 1 September, I got a message Anne had called. I did not dare call back and waited a day for the courage. I woke with dread – I really thought she was going to tell us we were too late.

'Anne,' I spluttered, 'we've been horribly let down. We were going to be sponsored by a mobile-phone company but they pulled out. And we've just discovered that they're going bust.'

'Och, I am sorry,' Anne said.

I kept gushing desperately, trying to persuade her everything was still on track.

'What do you think your chances are of raising the money?' she asked.

'One hundred per cent,' I answered without hesitation.

I flushed with the confident sound of my own voice. Then I went into overdrive.

'Lots of other doors are open and there are many other opportunities,' I told her.

Sweat poured down my back.

'I'm terribly sorry we still can't pay you. I can't understand why it's taking so long. I'm never going to do this sponsorship thing again. I wake every morning at six o'clock, so angry we've not raised the money. But then I think of you, Anne, and how much worse it must be for you, how awful it must be trying to run a company with customers like us.'

There was silence.

'Thank you for telling me,' she finally said, sweetly. 'Very good luck and please do keep me informed.'

I could not believe it. Nothing about how we had to pay by the end of the week, or a deadline we had to meet otherwise we could not go. I thanked her profusely and got off the telephone as fast as I could. My heart was pumping. I felt I could conquer the world.

We tried everything to get around ANI and their exorbitant prices. If we could only arrange a free lift from the South Pole, we could reduce our budget substantially. The RAF was our first port of call and Prince Charles's office made sure our request was considered by the Chief of Air Staff. In the middle of the Kosovo crisis, his personal staff officer wrote a charming letter, but regretted they did not have any suitable aeroplanes.

'Never mind, I think I can penetrate the Pentagon,' Rosie said, brightly.

And so she did, through a convoluted route starting with the British Ambassador in Prague. This time the head of the US Air Force cited US Government regulations as the reason why they could not help us.

The only other option was the British Antarctic Survey, but clearly not all scientists approve of expeditions.

Every approach we tried got us nowhere.

In the midst of this we had to train. One of the difficulties was that nothing could replicate the demands of hauling a sledge for ten hours every day for two months. The best we could do was have relatively short bursts of intense activity, then weekends away to put in longer hours.

Through spring and summer we spent many days pulling motor tyres or logs across the countryside to simulate our sledges. One or two tyres, combined with friction, require a similar force to a sledge to pull. They also have the same irritating habit of getting snagged on rocks and heather as our sledges would on sastrugi (irregular ridges on the snow).

It became routine and really quite normal to trudge along like this. I did enjoy people's reactions as we passed. On one occasion, when Pom and I were covered in mud, whole families stopped with their mouths open as we made our way through Berkshire villages.

'What's wrong?' I wanted to ask them. 'Have you never seen anyone with a log tied on a rope round their waist before?'

As well as the physical aspects of training, Geoff strongly advised us to continue to get used to living with each other in a tent. I did not know whether this was because he thought we were especially difficult to get on with or whether, with his usual thoroughness, he was leaving nothing to chance.

A few days before we went to the Lake District in May, I said to Ann solemnly, 'I think we should practise camping this weekend.'

'No, Caroline,' came her swift reply, '*we* don't have to practise camping. You do.'

She was right. Why would anyone want to stay in a tent when they could stay in a hotel? I thought.

The weekend was a beautiful bank holiday and we pitched our tent in a campsite outside Keswick. We had two long days tramping up and down hills with heavy rucksacks, taking care to choose the boggiest and most arduous routes.

Then we moved on to the Peak District.

As arranged, we met Dave Cummings in a pub. He was a friend of Ann's and had helped us abseil at the launch. As we chatted, I wolfed down an enormous plate of chicken and chips. It reminded me how much I needed to eat when taking strenuous exercise compared to my sedentary life in London.

'Okay girls,' Dave said after we settled in. 'I want you up early in the morning and then we'll learn some basic rope and rescue techniques.'

This was just what we needed. Dave was an excellent and reassuring teacher. He laid out the ropes at the top of a fifty foot crag and we pretended one of us had fallen in a crevasse. We took it in turns to be the victim, fixing a dangled rope to our harness, and then waiting while the others at the top struggled to tie clove hitches and prusik knots for a pulley system to haul us out.

I remembered some of the knots from fishing and boating in Mull. I was pleased I found the pulleys relatively easy to grasp. At least that makes up for my lack of strength, I thought to myself, conveniently ignoring what would happen if I fell down a crevasse and had to rely on the others to fix the ropes to pull me out.

I was also much less frightened than before. Now I understood the system of knots and saw why they did not slip, I did not mind the height and was much more confident. Ann and I even had a race up the ropes using a prusik loop as a foothold and another fixed to our harness.

Dave showed us how, by sliding the loops up the rope and pushing ourselves up with one foot a few inches at a time, we could, if necessary, climb all the way out on our own. The hardest part came when I tried to clamber over the edge at the top and, pathetically, I resorted to Dave's outstretched hand for help.

Predictably, Ann won our race. Then, as I stood at the top congratulating myself for having made it at all, I heard Zoë chuckling as she climbed up after us. Just as she had at the launch, she shinned up the rope in half the time I took, as if she had been doing it all her life.

'It's not fair, Zo,' I complained. 'My legs are twice as long as yours. Why can't I bend them up to my chin like you?'

'Well, you could do those stretching exercises I showed you in the mornings for a start,' she replied, in a rather too formal physiotherapy kind of way, I thought.

I was sure Zoë must get tired of being presented with minor injuries by people she met at parties. But, as an international sports physiotherapist and university lecturer, she had the valuable gift of being able to explain what was wrong at the same time as making people better. We all consulted her about various problems – including my stiffness – and, even on the telephone, she was usually able to sort things out.

Sometimes, too, if I was really lucky, Zoë told me to rest from training for a few days, although I noticed she never suggested I might have 'overtrained' like she did the others. Ann, Jan and Rosie were incorrigible enthusiasts and I sometimes felt quite sick just listening to what they got up to in the gym.

Ann was a relatively new convert, which probably made her worse. Her ex-husband, Jez, was in the Navy and, although he went on a number of adventures which she quite envied, Ann herself never took any physical exercise until the first selection weekend for the North Pole.

Jez had heard me on the radio one morning and come home and told her, 'Right, Ann, this is your chance.'

'Don't be stupid. They don't want people like me,' was her blunt reply.

But she was wrong. We did want people like her. Jez bought her some walking boots and packed her off to Dartmoor in his camouflage jacket and trousers, and with a huge, heavy rucksack. She knew nobody; the environment was completely alien. She told me much later how much she had hated it.

'I burst into tears halfway round, I was so wet and cold and miserable. But then I thought to myself, Pull yourself together, Ann, you're no different to anyone else here. You're going to do it. So I did and now I can't imagine ever not being fit again.'

'Do you want to do the London marathon with me next month?' Ann asked. 'I think it will be really good fun.'

'Don't be ridiculous Ann,' I responded. 'I did it once and it was absolutely horrific. But what do you mean, you're doing it? Last time I spoke to you, you had fallen over jogging, had a bandaged ankle and were hobbling about on crutches.'

'I know. I still am. Don't tell Zoë, but I'm going to start running again soon and I'm sure I'll be better by then. Anyway, if you don't want to do the marathon, would you mind looking after the triplets?'

I could hardly say no. Anyway I like children and thought it could be fun. Rachel, Lucy and Joseph (aged 5) stayed the night and at 6.30 a.m. our marathon day began. I persuaded Zoë to help and, after a brisk game of football in the flat, we slumped gratefully together in front of *Match of the Day* as the children ate their cereal.

Then the BBC coverage of the marathon began.

'Look kids, Mummy's on telly,' we called, forgetting for a moment they were celebrity children, well used to seeing their polar mother interviewed. They rushed to the screen as 30,000 people swarmed across it.

Joseph turned away in disgust. 'That's no use. We like it when Mummy is on her own. We'll never see her with all those other people. Is she going to win?'

A short time later, we made our way to Tower Bridge to scour the crowd of runners. Zoë and I had a child each on our shoulders to act as flags, and the third took it in turns to stand on a post, as we waited patiently for Ann to appear.

She gave the children an emotional hug, then we rushed off. We leaped on tubes and squeezed the children on to every form of public transport, desperately hoping to see Ann again along the route. Crisps and chocolate kept the triplets' spirits up and I must have told them, 'Mummy's coming soon' a hundred times. Despite all our efforts, we didn't see Mummy again until we arrived, shattered, at the finish.

Zoë and I were completely exhausted. I bathed the children and gave them supper and then, as Ann drove the children happily home to Somerset, she and I stared at each other over a pint in disbelief.

'How does Ann look after the kids every day?' Zoë asked. 'It's unrelenting. She's on her own with them and has her job to do as well. I always knew she was amazing but I would have opted to run the marathon if I'd known.'

I agreed with everything, except the bit about the marathon. The children were incredibly well behaved but, even so, my mind was treacle.

'I think that plan to get pregnant at the Pole may be a mistake, don't you?' was all I had the energy to say.

11 Outer Reaches

O NE COMPANY AFTER ANOTHER turned us down for sponsorship. We were increasingly worried about funding. Occasionally, I found myself in a state of paralysis, unable to think or do anything, but most of the time, it helped to keep busy. Each time I followed up an idea or lead, no matter how unlikely, my hopes were raised.

Often I got up at 6 a.m. to write letters before work, and there were always things to catch up on at weekends. Everyone was trying as hard as they could and we talked every few days, encouraging each other and trying to keep ourselves going after each rejection. I always wanted to move on to the next idea and make sure we had other options.

Ideally, we were looking for a title sponsor – a company to contribute most or all of the funds we needed and put its name to the expedition. By including its name in the title, a sponsor would stand a good chance of being mentioned in media coverage.

The key was to identify companies whose brand values and corporate culture fitted with those of the expedition. We were all women, we were breaking new ground and, as an expedition, we were relying on each other totally as a team. Planning and preparation were essential to our success. This must appeal to plenty of companies, we thought.

Some companies had already agreed to sponsor equipment and became official suppliers. But from a cash sponsor's point of view – the title sponsor or any other – we did not believe it mattered whether the company had products or equipment we needed.

The most important thing to any sponsor or supplier was that we got good media coverage. They would be using us as part of their marketing strategy and it was essential that the expedition – and the companies supporting us – were featured in newspapers and on radio and television as much as possible.

We continued to talk to the press throughout 1999, explaining our plans and generating interest. We kept telling journalists we were definitely going, even though the main purpose in talking to them was to impress potential sponsors to enable us to go.

Our lives were controlled by journalists. They were always looking for stories and angles. What is it like to leave children behind? How do you think you'll survive as women? What will you miss most?

Then came the big one. It emerged that another expedition was being planned for the end of the year – and it contained two women. This was exactly what the press wanted: rivalry between two women's teams, each vying to become the first British women to reach the South Pole on foot. We were hounded by newspapers wanting us to tell them we were desperate to win.

The other expedition was a commercial trip organised by ANI. As well as the women, it contained five men and two highly experienced guides, including Geoff Somers. The press rarely mentioned this, but we did not worry too much. At this stage, we thought all publicity was good publicity.

In July 1999, I went away for the weekend and came back to fifteen messages on my answering machine from friends telling me about a feature in a Sunday tabloid.

I rang Jan and she said, 'It's terrible. I'm so cross about it. How dare they?' Jan read the words unemotionally. I listened in silence. It was a feature about the North Pole relay. It was as if my character was being ripped to shreds. I felt punched in the stomach.

The expedition was getting closer, it was becoming a reality. Yet none of us knew whether it was going to happen. The newspaper article made it harder. For a few weeks, I felt empty and numb, and did not want to talk to anyone about the expedition. Valuable time was slipping by.

I sensed Jan disliked the uncertainty even more than the rest of us. She was finding it hard to keep going as if all was well. One day in July she rang me.

'I know you don't want to go in two tents, Caro, but I'm afraid we're just going to have to,' she said. 'I spoke to the manufacturers today, and they can't make us a single big one after all.'

'Maybe we should try another company then,' I suggested, feeling frustrated, but knowing there was no point pushing it.

Jan was due to go on holiday shortly with her family and I hoped that would reinvigorate her.

The day she was leaving, the telephone rang very early. I answered it half asleep.

'It's me, Caro. I'm in hospital,' came a muffled voice sounding only just like Jan.

I woke up fast. 'What's happened to you? Are you OK?'

'My face is all bashed up. That's why I can't speak properly. I came off my bike and they've spent all night setting my wrist. It's a really bad break, apparently.' Her voice was choked. 'And now we can't go on holiday and I feel so guilty about letting Andy and my parents down.'

'Don't worry about that, Jan. You didn't do it on purpose,' I said, trying to make reassuring noises. But I could not concentrate. It was 24 July and we planned to set off at the end of October. Fourteen weeks, I thought to myself, desperately calculating how long she had to get better. Surely that must be enough time.

Zoë and I went to see Jan in Kingston Hospital. Her face was distorted and bruised and her arm was in plaster, hanging from a sling overhead. She tried to smile but her mouth was swollen.

'What do you reckon, then, Zoë?' I asked her afterwards.

'It all depends on how quickly the bones can mend and how it responds to treatment. Unfortunately, we won't know that until the plaster comes off in a few weeks' time.'

Zoë was too non-committal for me. I so wanted Jan to be all right. If professional footballers could play after a major injury, then surely Jan could recover from a broken wrist. I tried to encourage her to start treatment with Zoë at once, but all the time I felt there was something holding Jan back.

Jan's wrist had smashed through her hand and broken the bones like a jigsaw. Major surgery, two metal plates and several pins were required. The team was in limbo. None of us dared say we had given up hope of Jan coming with us, yet it was on all our minds.

It was almost a relief when Jan made the decision herself. It was 12 September when she telephoned. No matter how much she wanted to come, Jan could not get better in time. She had to pull out.

We went to Swanage to practise ropes again with Dave Cummings. We talked a lot about Jan and we were desperately sorry. Tentatively, we began to discuss how we would manage without her. Did we need a replacement? In which case, who?

In the end, we were all agreed. We had spent a lot of time together since Norway, talking and getting to know one another. Gradually we had taken control of the expedition. We knew so much more than when we started.

As a team, we were much more confident and focussed, less reliant perhaps on single people. We did not want to change things. We had set our sights on our goal and no one questioned whether we should carry on. It was clear that this was just another hurdle we had to get over.

It was September 1999 and we were leaving on 31 October. We still had no money and we needed to raise

£250,000 in cash. We had offers of equipment but everything needed to be thought through and finalised. We had had so many leads and followed up countless ideas.

We had met Michael Holmes, a PR agent who had given us a fresh push in the media. He was a director of the charity Special Olympics, and I thought of a way we could raise money for us both.

'It's a perfect fit,' I said. 'Special Olympics is about giving people with learning disabilities a focus and confidence through sport. About changing people's lives. Those are the same things we say about ourselves.'

Michael fixed a meeting with Paul Anderson, the head of Special Olympics in the UK. His enthusiasm gave me fresh hope, especially when he agreed to introduce us to Independent Insurance. We met them together and a week later they confirmed their sponsorship. Not the whole amount, but a significant contribution. They would also insure us.

It was a great moment. A turning point. At last something had happened about which we could get excited.

It was now or never. It was only a month to go before we left and we were far from fully funded. We had to start ordering equipment. Zoë began her leave as a lecturer and moved into Screen Partners' office, where I worked. She was on the telephone continuously. Every few hours large packages arrived, some sponsored, some not. I tried not to think of the money we were spending – money we did not have.

I was frantically busy. It was holiday packing and planning from hell, a thousand times worse than any trip I had been on before. Our equipment list was several pages of minute detail. I was helping Zoë with decisions and errands, trying to raise thousands of pounds, finish off my proper work and organise my life all at the same time. We were going to the outer reaches of the earth for three months and everything had to be sorted out before we went. I was in the office by 7 a.m., leaving at 10.30 p.m., last orders at The Pride of Spitalfields, then bed at midnight. Same clothes day after day.

I was always on the telephone. I found the tension put an authority in my voice and I could get things done immediately. I spoke to everyone who had tried to help us with sponsorship, including a man called Martin Booth who worked for an agency.

'I've got the Marketing Director of the M&G investment group interested. We should get a meeting next week,' he said. I had heard that kind of thing before and I did not get excited. Yet I knew this could be our last chance.

A friend of Pom's had produced a new CD Rom presentation for us and Zoë stayed up through the night to customise it for M&G. Ann came to London for the meeting. I did not have time to prepare. I was on my mobile telephone all the way to M&G's office in the City. However, I gave the performance of a lifetime. I looked the Marketing Director, Gary Shaughnessy, straight in the eye and told him how the expedition was a perfect fit. 'M&G is a pioneer, and so are we,' I said.

Then it was back for a meeting with ANI and the customary dance about money. We nodded sagely and said everything was under control.

It did not feel that way.

There was still an unimaginable number of things to do. As well as sponsorship, lots of equipment had still not arrived or been decided upon, we had to apply for Antarctic permits from the Foreign Office, rent an Argos satellite transmitter from the USA and sort out how to freight everything to Chile in time for our flight to Antarctica.

Martin Booth rang. Gary had approval from some of his colleagues but had to speak to more. We were getting tense. If M&G came in, they would be the title sponsor. The stress was infectious and everyone in the office was caught up in it.

'Quick, it's Martin Booth on the telephone.'

'More approvals, I'm afraid,' Martin said. 'We'll have to wait another day.'

It was torture.

Zoë and I were in a meeting with Martin when the telephone rang. It was Gary. Zoë left the room and hid; she could not bear the suspense. Martin gave nothing away. He put down the telephone and said, 'No news, I'm afraid.'

I had no time to think about anything. No time to think about the enormity of what we had taken on. Or the dangers that lay ahead in Antarctica. All I could do was move as fast as I could from one task to the next – one call to another – desperately trying to get everything organised in time.

Marks & Spencer agreed to sponsor our food and Pom came round with bulging carrier bags. Assorted nuts, cereals, biscuits, fudge – all the highest calorie foods she could find in the store. We tasted everything. Some was impossibly sweet, but we knew food tasted different in the cold. Also when your body needs more to eat, you crave fattening things. We created a diet of 5,200 calories in 1077 grams. It was all about packing the highest number of calories into the lowest weight.

Rosie rang, very excited. 'Mars want to sponsor us,' she said. 'I'm not sure how much money yet. Expect a call from their Head of Marketing.'

Then a PR agent for BT called out of the blue.

'Our client has heard about your expedition and is thinking about sponsoring you. Could you provide us with some information?' he asked.

I could hardly believe it. Surely one of these big companies must come through. Surely we must be on our way at last.

It was frantic. And all the time, I was supposed to be doing my normal work. Calls from film producers and lawyers, negotiating contracts, all this had to be fitted in around organising sponsorship. There was so much going on. It was impossible to keep everyone informed. Time telling the others was time not spent making decisions. I was on the telephone all day every day.

There were three weeks to go until we were due to leave at the end of October.

I had another meeting with Martin and Gary at M&G. Gary sat us down. He was very po-faced and I did not know what he was going to say.

'I think it's all right,' he said slowly. 'I think I've got all the approvals. Now, I'd like to hear what you think our overall strategy should be, Martin.'

I could hardly believe it. Everyone else was so straight and serious. They wanted to call us the M&G ISA Challenge.

I tried to stop grinning. I did not listen to what they said. I could feel my heart beating and I wanted to hurl myself out of the window with joy.

'We've done it,' I shouted down the telephone to everyone I knew.

'I'm so glad, darling.' Mother sounded excited as well. 'I'm so pleased the uncertainty's over. I don't really want you to go, but I've decided that I'd much rather you went than I had to live with you being disappointed.'

But we had not done it yet. We still had to sign contracts and make media plans. At the same time, the equipment list was getting longer and longer.

Julian had asked Lawrence Howell to help with our communications. Known as Flo, we knew him as the ex-husband of Morag, who had managed First Air while we were in the Arctic. Flo's reputation went before him. For over twenty years, he had designed batteries and communications systems for countless expeditions all over the world. His experience of polar expeditions was unparalleled.

I was fascinated. 'Do you do it all from home?' I asked when we met him.

'Just about,' he said. 'I've got seven acres of radio masts in my back garden near Aberdeen.'

Zoë was at her best. 'Would you be able to make us a solar panel? We need to recharge batteries for the video and telephone, and run the GPS off it as well if necessary,' she said.

'Yeah, I can do that,' Flo said confidently. 'It will take me a while though because I'll have to adapt your equipment and test it at very low temperatures. How long have you got?'

'Two weeks,' we said.

Flo sighed and nodded his agreement. It was amazing what dinner with four girls could achieve, I thought.

Back to the endless cycle of telephone calls. Things were not finalised yet with M&G. We were in discussion with the newspaper who had published the article I had been so upset by. M&G wanted issues to be resolved with the newspaper before we could go ahead. I wanted to rest and get away from it all. I did not even have time to be tired.

In the middle of this, dinner with the eminent glaciologist, Charles Swithinbank, was an evening of surreal calm. We went to see him near Cambridge. We asked him about routes from Hercules Inlet to the South Pole and he entertained us with stories of his forty years studying Antarctica.

Then it was back to London and a friendly meeting with the newspaper. Finally, please, let it be all right, I thought.

Zoë was sending Pom on shopping missions from morning to night. Ann was concentrating on her children and Rosie was getting ready to come over from Prague. I was still trying to do my normal work and organise the business side of things.

A week before we left, everyone came to my warehouse flat and we started packing food. Not having to think was a welcome relief. I almost relaxed. Pom was in charge and I just did what she told me.

Everything came out of its packaging and we made up our rations in plastic bags. Seventy bags of breakfast and dinner and 350 bags of snacks – one for each person, for each one of 70 days. We chopped 350 Mars bars into bitesize pieces and put them with nuts, biscuits and family size bars of chocolate. Jan and Andre Chadwick helped as well.

Pen came to London to help finalise equipment. He was coming with us to Punta Arenas in Chile and from there on to Patriot Hills on Antarctica.

We finished packing food at 1 a.m. and, the following day, Monday, I went to work. I returned to organised chaos. Equipment had been arriving all day and was being unpacked. The whole place was littered. A power drill lay buried in one and a half kilograms of loose tampons, and unwrapped bars of Swiss chocolate were stacked next to ski bindings and duct tape.

Every available inch was taken up with activity. Zoë and Ann were drilling skis on the floor. Pom's friend Judy was making gaiters, wristlets and stuff sacks with her sewing machine. Nobody took any notice of me. They only reacted when I told them that I had signed the contract with M&G.

'Well done,' they said. Then they went back to their tasks.

In the evening we started packing boxes. Great big packing boxes from a removal firm. The contents of each box were written on tatty pieces of A4 paper and were taped on top. We finished at 2 a.m. and started again at 7 a.m. the next day. We had 21 boxes, all of which had to be taped and labelled, then carted down stairs to a van we had hired to take them to the airport.

At 9.45 a.m. we changed into our sponsored clothes and ran down the road to M&G's offices. We met the Chief Executive and the PR people. Very nonchalantly they gave us the cheque.

I was utterly exhausted. For months, I had been unable to sleep properly. I woke every morning at 5 a.m., my mind buzzing with the thoughts I had gone to bed with. There was so much to remember, I never dwelt on the responsibility.

We were on the final countdown. We still had to talk to the sponsors' PR agents and agree contracts – but at least the end was in sight. I dreamed about getting on the aeroplane and not having to think or do any more. All we had to do now was keep going and concentrating for the last three days.

I set a day aside to try to finish my proper work, but I did not succeed. I had lunch with my brother Charles, and Robert and Simon called to wish me luck. For the first time, I thought about what it would mean to be so far away for three months. Away from the frenzy of life in London. The simplicity of Antarctica appealed to me more and more.

'Happy Christmas,' I said. It was only October.

Finally, we got to the last day. It was a Saturday and no less hectic. I spent a few hours shopping with Pom and Zoë and then the whole day and evening in the office once more.

'I should be finished by lunchtime,' I had said to Pom hopefully. But, needless to say, it took hours to write to the sponsors and PR agents, photocopy contracts and write last-minute notes to Julian. I finished my last bit of Screen Partners work at 10 p.m. and thought about my packing.

Then it dawned on me – I didn't actually have any packing to do. Everything I needed was in those boxes. I didn't need any clothes except the Rab Carrington kit and my red Marks & Spencer fleece and leggings for travelling in. It was such a relief only to think about luxury items – a pair of pink nail scissors and photographs of my little godchildren I wanted to take with me to the Pole.

I fell into bed at 2.30 a.m. and woke again at 5.15 a.m. with the alarm. No time to think or even feel I had ever been asleep. I scurried back to the office to clear up with Pom, and went back with her to my flat. There were another seventeen boxes to finish filling and taping up. We were very tired and it was taking much longer to do things. The A4 paper with lists became old envelopes and the numbers on the boxes gave way to arbitrary letters: A B C D E G M T X.

The flat was still in chaos. We were all convinced we would leave something behind. At the last minute, I found sponsors' stickers amongst the waste paper and a GPS lying on the floor by the bath.

I rang Julian at what I thought was a decent hour.

'Hello, how are you?' came his bleary voice half asleep. 'Didn't you know the clocks went back?'

It was fantastic news. A whole extra hour in which to get ready.

The doorbell rang and there was a clatter up the stairs. Two hours early Pom's husband, Kent, her brother, Mike, and Mike's wife, Sally, crashed in with champagne and croissants to celebrate our departure and take us to the airport.

'Poor Kent,' I said to Mike and Sally. 'It is pretty hard to lose your business partner and your wife at the same time. You will look after him, won't you?'

I told them how Kent had nervously addressed my long-suffering colleagues at work a few days before: 'Now, I want you to know that it's going to be fine. We boys are going to be absolutely fine without the girls, aren't we?'

I had one last look around the flat. Discarded clothing and expedition kit was everywhere. I had never left the flat for such a long time and my principal thought was of the mice infesting the building – the smell of chocolate and cheese from our packing still filled the place – and I imagined their chums throughout the East End flocking here for a massive millennium celebration.

The journey to the airport by van seemed to take forever. I relaxed and switched my mind off completely, enjoying the first peace I had had for weeks.

At Gatwick, we went inside the terminal to find the others. There was Julian, calm as ever, then Rosie rushed up, and so did Ann with the triplets.

'Here, take these, before I forget,' I said, thrusting their little M&G T-shirts into her hands.

Ann's parents were there, sitting quietly.

I introduced myself, marvelling at their willingness to move into Ann's house to look after the children while she was away.

We piled all our boxes and baggage on to trolleys. Then we posed outside with two athletes from Special Olympics and kept smiling for a couple of press photographers. A few friends arrived to see us off and as a gaggle we made our way to the check-in desk across the terminal.

I expected tears from at least one person. But, after all we had been through over the last few weeks, there was only relief. Our excitement was quiet. I felt no fear or trepidation. I did not even care whether we got to the South Pole or not. If nothing else happens, I thought, we've achieved something huge in just setting off.

12 Punta Arenas

W E FLEW TO PUNTA ARENAS in Chile, where we were scheduled to stay for three days before flying approximately 2,000 miles by Hercules to Patriot Hills. On arrival, it was a shock to learn that all flights were delayed. Worse still, there was no information or assurances when we could leave. All we knew was that we were in a strict queuing system and would have to wait our turn.

'The weather's bad at Patriot Hills. Wind, snow. All flights are delayed. You'll be here at least a week,' ANI's doctor told us bluntly. 'We need cloud cover at least 7,700 feet high,' we were informed. 'The wind has to be under fifteen knots, we need good contrast on the ice and good visibility on the horizon.'

Bad weather in Antarctica clearly meant delays were the norm. ANI's policy was to keep everyone booked on flights in the same order. We found out there was a passenger flight scheduled to leave ahead of us, and then a fuel flight (it would just take drums of aircraft fuel to Patriot Hills).

A week with no chance of moving or getting started. The sky was blue, the sun was shining and the birds were singing; Antarctica seemed a world away. I felt strangely calm. My grandmother used to talk about people 'getting away' when they died and that was exactly how Punta Arenas felt. I was in a curious twilight place, waiting. Just waiting.

On the minibus into town from the airport, I started chatting to another of ANI's customers, Ginny Michaux. She asked me what we were doing.

'We are skiing to the South Pole,' I said.

'Pardon me?'

I repeated our plans.

'I'm amazed,' she said at last. 'You look like regular people – fit, regular people. Given away,' she added, 'by an incredible energy.'

Ginny was a delightful woman whose sparkling blue eyes and big smile belied her years. She had travelled for twenty-four hours from Virginia and was on her own, none of her friends had arrived. We all adored her and ended up drinking or having dinner with her every night.

Punta Arenas is a major starting point for journeys to Antarctica. It is sheltered in a large squiggle of coastline at the very bottom of Chile. Both Punta Arenas and Tierra del Fuego (which we could see clearly across the Magellan Strait) are places inextricably linked with my childhood.

At last I was here: the place my father had visited in 1961 and talked about with such passion. He was visiting schools in South America for the British Council and he went all the way to Tierra del Fuego.

Father always spoke about his flight to Tierra del Fuego as one of the great adventures of his life. Looking around the hotel I saw black-and-white photographs of airmen and aeroplanes from that time. When Mother joined Father in Santiago on his way back through Chile, her flight to Santiago from London took three days alone.

These had been magical places in my imagination. But, as I looked at Tierra del Fuego across the Magellan Strait, I felt a pang of disappointment. From where we were, it was an uninteresting lump of land across a few miles of flat grey sea. Neither place looked anywhere near as romantic as they sounded.

When the Portuguese explorer, Hernando Magellan, came through the straits, we were told, the local inhabitants were burning fires on the beaches of Tierra del Fuego. That's why Magellan gave the island its name. There was romance here after all.

Punta Arenas has a population of about 100,000 and is built on a grid system. In the more central area where we were staying, there were large colonial-style Spanish houses. Elsewhere the buildings were mainly concrete with long, sloping corrugated iron roofs. The smarter roofs were painted in vivid reds, yellows, greens and light blues.

The bars and cafés varied from the dirty and dingy near the port to more stylish Spanish bars. We had a drink in the Union Club underneath the José Neguira Hotel where Ernest Shackleton gave a talk before setting off for the Antarctic.

Sitting there, I thought of the astonishing journey of Shackleton in 1914. His ship, *Endurance*, became trapped in the pack ice and the expedition never reached the Antarctic coast. They spent the winter on board and, when *Endurance* was crushed and they watched it sink slowly beneath the ice, they took lifeboats and managed to carry them across the ice. Then a few of them rowed 800 miles across the Southern Ocean to get help – one of the longest journeys ever undertaken in an open boat – and somehow found their way to South Georgia. Shackleton and two friends crossed the mountains and glaciers without ropes or proper equipment in only three days.

The Union Club bar was built like the inside of an old wooden ship with portholes and highly varnished walls. I could imagine Shackleton leaning over charts as *Endurance* crashed through the ocean that we would be flying over to Patriot Hills. So much had changed, and yet the adventure – the buzz – must surely be the same.

'I wonder' I wrote in my diary, 'what it must have been like in the early days when explorers sailed into Antarctica in the spring, built themselves a hut and then spent the whole winter huddled indoors eating, getting unfit and on each other's nerves. They had no communication with the outside world and never knew whether their ship would get back through the pack ice to pick them up the following year. And that was before they had taken even one step towards the Pole.'

They must have had moments when they felt trapped and desperate. I felt tremendous respect for them. By comparison, I knew, our journey was easy.

Sitting at the table, we drank Chilean Pisco Sours (tequila, egg white and lemon juice). There was an unspoken tension in the air. I knew we felt Rosie had let us down before leaving London (to us it seemed as if her priorities had been askew – particularly the last weekend, when we were all rushing around madly, and she chose to go shooting).

I felt responsible. I knew how important it was that we all got on. We needed each other. We were a team. *En route* to Chile, Rosie had apologised to me and I had said, 'Don't give it another thought. It's all done. We need to move on.'

But Zoë found it much harder to let the tensions and bad feelings go. For the first few days in Chile she kept jumping down Rosie's throat; other times she just ignored her.

One night Zoë stomped out of the restaurant where we were having dinner. Ann was clearly upset by the atmosphere and followed her outside. I don't know what Ann said to Zoë, except that it was probably similar to what she had said once before when we were training and Zoë was being difficult: 'Fuck off. You're out of order. Now what's the problem?'

They ended up getting very drunk together.

I was relieved Rosie was being human again, but I still felt frustrated with Zoë. At the same time I knew I must not lose patience with her.

I reminded her, 'We've got to work together. It's not fair what you're doing. Unless you sort yourself out and make things right with Rosie you're going to blow it for all of us.'

Zoë nodded. I knew she realised how important it was and I hoped I hadn't been too harsh.

'You've got to sort it before we go on the ice,' I insisted. 'If I was Rosie I would be in tears by now. She is not herself. It's obvious how on edge she is and that only makes things worse. You say you're worried about what she brings to the team, Zo, but the answer is she brings nothing if you make her nervous and don't allow her to bring anything.'

I reminded Zoë what I thought Rosie did bring to the team: unfailing optimism, great humour and a determination never to give up. I thought of all those telephone calls to Prague; Rosie had bubbled with ideas and enthusiasm every time.

'Over the last eighteen months, knocking on one potential sponsor's door after another and following up all those leads that have come to nothing,' I said, 'it's been Rosie, more than anyone else, who has kept me going.'

The following day Zoë was more relaxed and talked to Rosie too. 'I don't know what's been going wrong with me. I turned into some sort of monster,' she said.

Tensions relaxed a great deal after that. The three or four weeks before we set off had been so frantic that, as a group, we had more or less split into two. In Punta Arenas we came together again as a team. It was a great relief.

'You're all very different and yet you work so well together,' Ginny told us. 'You're one of the most cohesive groups of people I have ever met.'

Cohesive. I liked that word.

A week later we were still in Punta Arenas.

'In all practical senses,' I said despairingly, 'we are actually no closer to Antarctica than we were when we left London.'

We were hideously aware that the ANI trip to the Pole, guided by Geoff, had managed to leave on 3 November. We were all intrigued how the seven punters would get on. As far as we knew, they had paid about US$50,000 each, never done any polar skiing before and didn't know each other. They were staying in separate tents and even separate hotels in Punta Arenas.

'The team dynamics could be a triumph or a complete disaster,' I said to Zoë.

'Not a trip I'd like to be a guide on,' she agreed.

* * *

In some ways, the wait was a good thing. Not only did it give us the vital opportunity to bond again before we went on the ice, it also gave us time to refine and modify our equipment. The tasks seemed endless and they filled our days.

We divided ourselves into a boys' team: Pen, Zoë and Ann, and a girls' team: Rosie, Pom and myself. The boys went downstairs, squashed into the room I shared with Pen and Zoë. They pushed the three beds together, leaving a small strip of space on the floor and a desk at which Pen played on his new computer. Their Blue Peter-type tasks were drilling bindings on skis, fixing up batteries and finishing off boards for the cookers to sit on. (Many of these tasks we had deliberately not done in London so we could transport our kit more easily and with less risk of it getting damaged.)

I worked in the girls' team in the others' room upstairs. Most of our clothing was sponsored by Rab Carrington and Helly Hansen. It was identical, so we sewed coloured ribbon into each item to identify it.

'We know you, Caroline,' Rosie said. 'If we don't label everything, you'll lose a glove and nick one of ours.'

After sewing duties, I was allowed to join the boys' team. Pen was giving Rosie and Pom a GPS lesson which I listened to while making a protective house for one of our new cameras out of an old green camping mat and some thick tape. By the time I had finished it looked like an evening clutch bag tied with a white bungee cord bow and I minced in to see the others, who were suitably impressed.

'Actually, Caro is surprisingly good at that sort of thing,' Pom said rather flatteringly. 'I remember her sewing at the North Pole.'

After that I was in charge of foam houses. I made one for both the stills cameras and the video camera, and then Zoë even let me make one for the precious aerial for the BT Iridium telephone. Ann made a fitted carpet out of 3mm black closed cell foam to help keep the tent warm. This was stiff competition for the Stanley knife and tape.

Mostly we worked quietly, concentrating on our tasks and every now and then asking for coffee to be brought up. The maid spoke very little until, one morning, there were wild shrieks as she flicked through the newspaper and then ran leaping through the hotel.

Via pidgin Spanish we grasped that she had won a big house on the lottery. From then on, she continued to work, but her perpetual enormous smile overwhelmed her and she could remember nothing. Our refreshments grew noticeably fewer.

Pen was invaluable. He had list after list of equipment modifications and preparations, including cutting and sticking parts of charts and equipment manuals into log books and calling the United Kingdom to set our watches to correct GMT. At least once every day, he went to a cyber café to send digital photographs and video back to the UK. He had a sexy computer in a silver briefcase and, with the help back home of Julian and a boffin called Peter Bierdo, he laboured long and hard to make it work.

It seemed to me that the new technology Pen had was too sophisticated for other machinery, including the Chilean telephone system. The cyber café felt like 'daddy's office' does to a small child – somewhere Pen went every day and where none of us understood what he was doing. (Ann and Zoë were braver and went to the cyber café one morning to watch England play Scotland in the European Championship play-offs.)

Pen was clearly determined we should succeed. He filled us with as much advice and information as he could. Nothing was particularly difficult or clever; just a ton of common sense which he had gathered over the last ten years on lots of expeditions, both successful and unsuccessful.

He was full of ideas and suggestions as to how we should do things. He was particularly good at raising issues for us to resolve through discussion. I was so glad he was there. I had always hoped he would be – to give us that last bit of confidence. But I don't think any of us had an idea quite how much there would be to do and how fantastic it would be to have someone so completely dedicated to helping and telling us everything he knew. Provided we concentrated as hard as he was concentrating on us, I knew we would learn so much.

The delay also allowed us to forget home and focus on what lay ahead. Kent rang wanting information about work and, suddenly, I was back in real time – documents, negotiations. Somehow it was easier to piece it together in our hotel room than it had been in the chaos of the Screen Partners/expedition office before I left.

'It's amazing. We've only been away a week, but England seems a million miles away and, already, I don't care what's going on there,' I confided to Pom.

The equipment took a starring role. To some people a cooker or a tent may seem like a boring piece of equipment but to us they were imbued with sacredness – they were all we had between us and the risk of death. Lots of expeditions fail because of equipment failure and we had to think hard about spare parts and tools for fixing. Once we were on the ice, we could not go shopping. We either had to mend something which was broken or fashion an alternative. We tried to think of every eventuality. We had to get it right.

We made most of our calls on our Iridium telephone, provided by BT. It worked brilliantly in our tent at minus 30°C but, because it used satellites, it did not work indoors. This meant we had to take it in turns, standing on the grass in the middle of Avenue Colon outside our hotel with its chunky twelve-inch aerial pointing into the sky. I felt playful. The whole scene was so absurd. 'It looks as if we're calling ET,' I said.

Sometimes, if communications were bad, Julian at base camp in his office in Berkshire moved into 'over' and 'roger' on the telephone which made me laugh even more. He already had an excellent matter-of-fact radio/ telephone voice.

I spoke to Julian most days, finalising sponsorship and money. He was extremely efficient and seemed to have things very much under control. He was solid and reassuring. Soon he would be the only voice connecting our wildnerness with the world; it was essential we all felt we could rely on him.

We had arrived in Punta Arenas with seventeen boxes and fourteen bags of equipment. I felt very important travelling with our cardboard boxes, especially as the tape said: fragile, fragile, fragile all along.

After we had been there a few days, 21 more boxes of cargo arrived – much to the horror of the man who owned the hotel. Most went to ANI's warehouse a few miles out of town, leaving the rest piled up in our rooms.

The date for our departure to Patriot Hills crept further and further into the distance. One morning at breakfast, Pen said ANI had rung to say the weather at Patriot Hills was absolutely horrid: big winds, snow, zero visibility. Geoff's expedition was stuck in their tents five miles outside Patriot Hills unable to move.

'Thank heaven we're nicely tucked up in this warm hotel then,' we said.

We were at the mercy not only of the weather, but also of ANI. It made me cross. Staying in hotels was costing us a fortune – money we did not have. Seven hundred miles was a long way to ski. Didn't they know how much we needed to get started?

I had been ready to love ANI who, initially, I saw as pioneers working in an outpost to help people to realise their dreams. I felt let down. I knew unhelpful officials often came with airline jobs, but I expected the people who worked here to share at least some of our passion. But I guess, as the only outfit, we weren't so unusual to them.

With time to kill, the corner bar at Pub 1900 was our favourite: curved wooden chairs with red leather backs and seats, gold curtain rails, wooden panelling, large windows. It served a vicious vodka and tonic and was a good place to sit, write and watch the world go by.

Four seasons passed in every day. One minute it was bright blue sky with hot sun, then an icy wind followed by grey skies and rain. Not that it made much difference to us, we only had one outfit: Marks & Spencer's black leggings, a white M&G ISA polo shirt and red fleecy jacket (also branded). We all had trainers with identical white socks, except Rosie who had little black boots with heels.

I liked wearing the same clothes every day. I relished not having to think about what to put on. Thanks probably to the fact that we all wandered around town every day in identical outfits plastered with M&G ISA, we became minor celebrities. One evening a reporter from the local newspaper interviewed us in his very limited English. His principal concern was that we only had two husbands between us. A photographer came and took a group shot in the dark on the pavement. The article and photograph appeared in the local newspaper the following day. Lots of people saw it and complete strangers came up to us in bars and shops to say hello.

This notoriety was taken to a ridiculous level when, sitting in the Corner Bar, as we called it, a good-looking man leaped from his seat and accosted me.

'Hello, my name is Flavio,' he said. 'I am a producer with ITV Patagonia.'

From then on, my limited Spanish meant he lost me. But it was clear he knew we were going to the South Pole and I assumed he was asking if we would go on his television show.

'I think we've got a television appearance coming up,' I whispered to the others.

They looked bemused as Flavio continued.

'Ten o'clock. In the night. *Sabado*. *Si?*'

When we arrived at ITV Patagonia, a security guard showed us up a long flight of stone stairs and, waiting at the top, was a troop of boy scouts.

'We've come to see Flavio,' we announced.

And then, out of the crush of people, Flavio appeared, white teeth flashing. He was caked in theatrical make-up. We started to laugh uncontrollably.

We were ushered through some tiny studios. A live band was playing and we stood crushed in a corridor, trying to keep quiet and out of the camera shot. Pen was gone in a flash and, almost before we noticed, he was back, draped in cameras, ready to record the event for us as well.

This was live television, although not necessarily as highly polished as some UK shows. Flavio was the presenter and, after a few brief questions (to get our names and occupations right), there was a loud roll of drums and we ran into a little room in front of the cameras.

A brightly coloured sofa and a fake oil painting – it was a typical talk show set. Except this was a talk show in Spanish and Flavio spoke at an impossible pace. Pom had had a few vodkas and most of her Spanish deserted her. I understood perhaps one word in a hundred.

Flavio started with Pom and then turned to me. I heard the word *hombre* and guessed that, like the news reporter, he was asking if I was married.

'*Non,*' I replied and pulled a long face. That seemed boring so I turned to the camera and made an appeal. '*Hombres, hombres por favor,*' I cried out, carried away by it all.

Cheers went up amongst the studio crew (there wasn't an audience) and then it was back to Flavio. He was sweating profusely and desperately trying to keep things going.

'Are you the ice girls?' he asked.

'No, the Spice Girls,' I said.

'Oh, really. Sing us a song.'

More cheers and we all stood up, arm in arm.

'What are we going to do? I can only remember the National Anthem,' I whispered to Pom.

'Try Abba,' said Ann and then we were off. Ann and I are both tone deaf but we were the only ones who knew the words.

'Money, money, money,' we shouted at the top of our voices as the others joined in for the chorus.

Eventually we slumped back exhausted. Flavio probably thought he was safe when he asked whether we wanted to dance. But Zoë leapt from her armchair, hurled herself across the studio and flung her arms round his neck. Hip clamped to hip, Flavio was lost for words and the camera panned elsewhere.

Within moments, the band struck up again and we were off on a cancan round the room. Finally, amidst much clapping and shouting, we fell in a heap on the sofa on top of him. Poor Flavio had probably never been more grateful for a commercial break.

We were ushered out of the studios and down the stairs, giggling all the way. And then it was back to the Corner Bar to celebrate with chips and vodka.

My father used to tell the story of how, one day, while he was in Punta Arenas, walking past the Anglican Church, he saw his name on a board outside: WALTER HAMILTON, HEADMASTER OF RUGBY, PREACHING TOMORROW. No one had told him anything about it – obviously the Anglican community was so thrilled to have someone new in town they thought that he must give a sermon.

Father loved telling us how he stayed up all night composing. He could not give one of his normal school sermons because his talk was scheduled for Easter Sunday.

We found the Anglican Church (next to the British School) and Pom, Rosie and I went to communion there at 10.30 a.m. It was a beautifully kept school and church – whitewashed with bright blue paintwork on the windows and roof. It was a little wooden church with a wooden clock and bell tower, fifteen polished wooden pews on either side of a simple aisle, stained glass over the altar and a typical English altar cloth and board holding the hymn numbers.

There were seven other people in the congregation: five women in their 70s, one husband of a similar age and a younger blonde woman. The vicar was young too and spoke English with a continental accent. The old ladies could have lived anywhere in middle England, with their coiffed and set hair, silk scarves and sensible mackintoshes, stockings and smart shoes.

The hymns, from *Ancient and Modern*, were ones not usually sung in England, but we did our best to join in, backed by an electric organ. The vicar preached – presumably from the same simple teak pulpit as my father – all about the need to avoid self pity and how God was always there to give us hope, providing strength to the weary. 'However bleak things look as you walk along,' he told us, 'God is looking after you.'

It was very poignant and not difficult to guess that Pom and Rosie were praying exactly the same things I was.

'Can we trust in God?' the vicar asked.

'Yes,' answered a woman's strong voice at the front, instantly and with complete conviction.

It was a special moment.

After the service, the vicar, Sammy Morrison, asked us into a side room to have coffee with the congregation. Despite their colonial and expatriate appearance, it turned out that all of them were born as Chileans and had lived in or around Punta Arenas all their lives. Most were born of Scottish or Australian parents and had romantic Highland names.

I went to tea with the vicar. I wanted to look through the church ledger to see if I could find Father's name. It was raining when I arrived and the house was very simply furnished and strangely European.

'You've been getting your skis adapted,' the vicar said to me as he opened the door.

I looked at him quizzically. 'That's right. How did you know?'

'I've been trying to get my car mended for the last three weeks,' he replied, 'and the mechanic's latest excuse was that he hadn't had time because he was working on your skis.'

We sat down for tea and then he showed me the large leather-bound ledger. There were very few services – perhaps five or six a year for many years – and each was faithfully recorded. At first we couldn't see it. For one mad moment I wondered whether my father's past was a dream. Then, suddenly, in his familiar blue-black ink, I saw my father's spindly signature halfway down a page. *Easter Sunday, 2 April 1961*. It was peculiar and very exciting. It was almost as if he was in the room. It made it all real – far more real than when I was in church trying to imagine him in the pulpit.

My father had been here – my father who always said that if he had his life again he would have been an explorer. And now I was about to set off for the South Pole. The next step of the journey. The one he did not take.

The vicar offered to make a copy of the ledger with his scanner and computer and took me downstairs through his cellar and into his garden overlooking the town. In his garden shed was a modern office with three computers and religious texts in both Spanish and English in bookcases all over the wall.

It took him over an hour to scan the page and, as we waited for the computer to grind, we talked of England. He had never been there and yet he knew where my home in Brick Lane was, about English public schools and a lot about our society.

One of the congregation, Daphne Maclean, invited us to lunch. She lived not far from our hotel in a large solid stone house: yellowing, with slightly tired green windows and paintwork. It was straight out of England in the 1950s: glass in the doors, thin wood panelling, linoleum and 'Strangers in the Night' playing on the gramophone. It was like lots of Cambridge houses and reminded me of family friends. In the downstairs bathroom were cushions made out of towelling and an early twin-tub washing machine like the one we had in Mull.

Daphne rang for lunch with a little silver bell and the maid brought delicious bean soup. It was the best food we had had since leaving home. They told us about Punta Arenas. Daphne's son, Patrick, was at the British School when Father visited. Now he ran a seaweed farm to service the food industry. Otherwise, they told us, most people worked in sheep, salmon and oil.

'When I was a child there were very few Chileans here – just foreigners and lots of factories making tobacco and other things for export,' Daphne told us. 'The population's only grown in the last twenty years. Now unemployment is increasing as the oil reserves are depleted.'

Daphne told us that Shackleton and some of his men stayed with her mother on their way through.

'He gave her one of his skis,' said Patrick, offering to show it to us on our way back.

The good news was that finally we had finished organising our kit. We had moved it all to ANI's warehouse, an old chicken shed filled with dust and green and orange oil drums for ANI's flight operations.

Organising our equipment had been a ten-day game of mud pies and sandpits. We had counted things out of boxes and into bags, discussed them and put them in sledges. Halfway through counting, I usually lost count and had to start again.

We put things to one side for resupply, put them in boxes, labelled them and then took the things out again a few days later to discuss them. Taping up boxes in miles of brown parcel tape and writing M&G ISA in big black felt-tip pen, I felt as if I was back in junior school.

Absolutely everything was weighed and thought about. As we would be carrying it with us for 700 miles, we were obsessed with keeping weight as low as possible. Pen had a pair of electronic scales and we weighed everything and noted down the results in a notebook. Then we weighed the sledges and moved things from one to another to equalise weights. Then we weighed each other. I weighed 11 stone, which is heavier than I have ever been.

We weighed our personal 'luxury' items and complained if we thought the others' were too heavy. Pom had special toothpaste, Ann had a tiny bottle of scent and Zoë had 'nowt' according to her – she took cigarettes which she claimed were a necessity. My nail scissors and clippers came to sixteen grams and Rosie's pencil sharpener was thrown out so she could keep her luxuries (including ear plugs, eye patch and 'Prospice', a poem written by Shackleton) under a hundred grams.

At the same time, all of our possessions – clothes, hats, gloves and so on – were colour coded with ribbon. Ann was green, Pom pink, Rosie yellow, Zoë red and I was purple. Even our sledges had ribbons and everything was put in according to colour.

Again, I found myself feeling grateful for the delay which meant we now felt we knew and understood many of the issues about each piece of kit. It also meant that, when we made decisions to leave things out, such as an extra ice axe, these were group decisions. It gave us each a sense of controlling our own destiny and made me feel more confident.

'If things go wrong now,' I wrote in my diary, 'we are the ones at fault.' That felt scary. 'Yet, we are going to be the only ones to sort out the problems. By going through everything in such detail, I believe we are now as well prepared as we will ever be to solve things when they go wrong and ensure that we do reach the Pole.'

The one thing we could not control was the weather. Pen suggested to ANI that they kept their clients informed by holding a daily briefing. Each day we went and the atmosphere was getting desperate, yet ANI seemed barely to acknowledge it. We had been waiting the longest, but were managing to stay calm. Even so, the days were ticking by. We had to get started soon.

One day, Ginny took us to a smart little solarium and gym she had found. Through all the dramas before we left home, I had done no training at all. I kept thinking that the others must be much fitter than I was, so it was a good feeling to take some proper exercise, and particularly encouraging that I was able to lift the same kind of weights as the others. My arms ached a bit afterwards (I was not used to doing bicep work – except for the last three weeks of humping cardboard boxes) but I was pleased to feel the muscles in my legs again.

I still felt blobby but was not as worried as I had been about my fitness.

From the evening we arrived in Punta Arenas, we consciously kept bringing up the subject of a typical day on the ice. We were keen to talk about this in order to flush out primary responsibility. It helped clear our minds of everything else and focus on what lay ahead. It was a psyching up exercise.

Initially, we talked about taking it easy to start with (perhaps as little as six hours skiing a day) and then building up to ten hours. We didn't talk much about mileage – we knew that, without the pressure ridges we'd had to tackle at the North Pole, we should be able to do ten miles a day in ten hours.

That meant 700 miles in 70 days, which was the length of time we had talked about back home. Seventy days was what we had prepared for – mentally and in terms of our food and equipment.

As the days passed, Pen encouraged us to refine our ideas. He suggested we stopped for a longer rest and a lunch break of thirty minutes halfway through the day. If we took on extra calories then, maybe we would be able to keep going for longer each day.

Pen did not believe – and neither did we – that we would be able to travel faster than one and a half nautical miles per hour. Therefore the only way to cover extra miles was to put in extra hours each day.

This meant strength was even more important than we had originally thought, but I liked the idea. The more we talked about equipment and maximising efficiency through weight, the more I wanted to be efficient in all respects.

'Why take seventy days,' I asked the others, 'when we could do it in much less?'

I also thought it would be great to get to the Pole for the millennium.

'That was our original plan and it would be a good target to aim for,' I told the others. 'It would be fantastic to take people by surprise.'

I also liked Pen's plan because it would be an added satisfaction to get to the Pole before Geoff's team.

'I know we're not as interested as the press in the race between us and the other women,' I said to Pom. 'And every time I've been asked I've said: we don't want to compromise safety.'

'That's true,' Pom said. 'But once I get on to the ice I'm sure I'll want to get off it again as soon as possible. And, yes, of course, I'd like to get there before the others if we can.'

At that moment, Rosie came into the hotel room.

'We're just talking about whether we care about getting to the Pole this year before other people,' I said.

'Oh yes, desperately, hugely, monstrously, with all my heart,' Rosie bent double in her enthusiasm. 'Although of course it doesn't really matter,' she said, suddenly remembering herself.

'No, of course not,' I replied. 'It doesn't *matter* whether I win a tennis match but it doesn't stop me wanting to. What do you think, Zoë?'

'Well obviously we've got to get there first if we can,' she said as she continued to screw bindings into skis on the carpet.

Ann could contain herself no longer. 'Thank God we're having this conversation,' she exclaimed. 'I don't want to do it just to be first, but it would be galling if a commercial team got there before us.'

So it was we restructured our planning and packing. All with the aim of doing at least fifteen nautical miles a day. It meant reorganising our food. Previously we were going to start with about 800g (4000 calories) of food and build up through 927g (4400 calories) to 1077g (5200 calories) after about three weeks.

131

Now that we wanted to hit the ice running, we would have 927g for the Hercules Inlet to Patriot Hills leg. Then, from Patriot Hills, we could increase it to 1348g per person per day. This was 6250 calories per person and included an extra 150g bar of chocolate each and an extra bag of cereal or hot dinner between us.

This meant a lot of sums and recalculation of food weights. Pom and I reorganised all the carefully prepared food bags to make sure we took the right amounts of everything. More unpacking, counting, repacking and labelling with ribbons and the fat marker pen.

We moved hotels to save money. Hotel Condor had a long tradition with pictures of expeditions on the walls, but I much preferred the Hostal Patagonia. It was much less stuffy and there was a good place to sit, chat and watch television.

I began to wonder whether Antarctica existed. I remembered reading that hundreds of years ago people speculated whether there was anything at the bottom of the world and, if so, what it looked like. Terra Incognita they called it. It was not discovered until 1819 and, until then, people agreed its existence only philosophically – there was land in the north therefore there must be sufficient land to the south to balance it.

Our situation was not so different. We only believed Antarctica existed because people said it did.

'Between us, I think we could now write a shopping guide to Punta Arenas,' Ann joked one morning. We knew where to buy sheepskin, ribbon, WD40, video tape, duct tape, parcel tape, pencils, notebooks, cakes, haircuts, screwdrivers, Ibuprofen. We failed only with a Leatherman multi-tool pliers/knife, so Pen kindly offered us his.

Rosie was chief shopper (although sometimes she needed an escort to keep her focussed). Just as in London before we set off, Zoë was director of operations, sending us out with instructions.

Pom found the welders who helped with our skis and Zoë flirted with them to get them to do what we wanted. Pom also found Miriam, a wonderful woman with a sewing shop specialising in parka jackets. She saved our lives.

Miriam's first task was to increase the size of the valance on the tent so we could pile more snow on to hold it down. Also, two days before we left the UK, our thermal underwear and orange skiing outfits had arrived from Rab Carrington. When we opened them up in the hotel, much to the amusement of the others, they were all the same size – much too small for me. The trousers did not reach my ankles and the jacket came nowhere close to covering my bottom.

I had caught a heavy cold and I almost felt like crying. But Pom gathered everything up and said: 'Don't worry Caroline. Miriam will do it.'

She swept me up the road to Miriam's shop. Miriam sat behind a desk with dyed orange hair. She was an ample, matronly figure in lipstick and a floral dress. She spoke no English but, with Pom's pidgin Spanish and me standing there like a badly-dressed clown, she nodded reassuringly at all the amendments Pom suggested. She even had some similar material (albeit in black) to make the extensions with.

'Alicia,' Miriam called out, and a young woman appeared from the back to take instructions. She wore Doc Marten boots under blue-and-orange overalls. We had all sorts of tasks for her (including sewing velcro and sheepskin patches for warmth on to our elbows and knees – a tip from Liv Arneson – sewing on sponsors' badges and putting full-length zips into our wind suits).

Both Miriam and Alicia were unfazed. No sucking of teeth or complaining if any of the changes were not quite right. We made many journeys to and fro.

One day Miriam asked if she could borrow my Mountain Hardwear fleece hat to copy. An old edition of *Cosmopolitan* magazine was on her desk and I wondered whether this was where all the smart women in Punta came to get their clothes made. There were quite a few 'ladies who lunched'. They were stylish in an out-of-date way. Eye shadow and wrap-around sun shades were very popular. Madrid ten years ago, perhaps. Designer clothes without the labels.

A few days later, we hired a car and drove to see the penguins at Seno Otway. As driver, I enjoyed the dirt tracks and skidding on mud. Pom and I had been learning photography: F-stops and shutter speeds, shooting off rolls of film at different settings, learning by trial and error; now Pen wanted to film us training. So, in a screaming wind, we gathered on the beach in our orange jackets. It was freezing cold but they passed their first test.

Pen lay crouched behind a rock with the video camera. 'When I drop my hand I want you to run as fast as you can towards me,' he said.

Despite our training, not one of us thought to suggest we should jog or warm up first. At the given signal, we set off across the thick black sand and rocky beach. White waves crashed in on our left as we ran, arms flailing.

Then we prepared to do it again. We crouched in a line in starting positions and when Pen dropped his hand we powered forward. This time there was a loud scream from behind as Pom's right leg gave way beneath her and a searing pain ran through her calf. I turned to see her struggling up again, her face white with pain as she tried to straighten and put weight on her leg.

I recognised the look on her face from the day she dislocated her shoulder at the North Pole. Her normally animated face was set and pursed.

'It's fine,' she said through a tightened mouth. 'You lot carry on, I just need to sit down.'

But there was no question of carrying on. There was a stunned silence until someone suggested we go into the small café for tea. Zoë made reassuring noises.

'Just take it easy, Pom, there's no rush,' she said. 'Don't put your foot down if it hurts, just lean on me and hop.'

Still no one spoke. I am sure we all held the same thought in our heads. A torn muscle, how long will that take to mend? We've come so far together, surely we are not going to have to set off as a small team of four? No, Pom, you're going to get better, we're not going to have any mishaps now.

On the way home Pom lay on top of the others in the back. Her spirits, at least, began to recover. Even without the narcotic effects of pethidine, she tried to persuade us that a small metal shack was a halibut farm on the seashore. There was a beautiful light from the low sun shining across the water and on the mountains.

We watched *Grumpy Old Men* on television in the hostel sitting room while Pom lay with ice on her leg. Rosie and Ann went to our favourite restaurant and brought back lashings of chicken and chips. We pigged out. It was very cosy and I had to keep reminding myself why we were there. Any day now we would be launched into the most hostile conditions on earth. It didn't seem real.

After the others had gone to bed, I asked Zoë what she thought was going to happen to Pom. I was desperate for information. I couldn't bear the idea that we might have to leave without her.

Zoë was typically discreet, but she did let on that she was pleased by the lack of swelling in Pom's leg.

'What does that mean?' I asked.

'Well, it doesn't mean anything yet,' she said. 'It may just be delayed. We need to wait and see what it's like in the morning.'

'And what if it's still not swollen?'

'Then it may not be a torn muscle after all, it may only be an over-flexed nerve.'

'Is that better or worse than a muscle, Zo? It sounds much more hopeful to me.'

'Oh, does it now Junior Physio? Well you're probably right but we can't do anything until it has settled down.'

I went to bed praying. And in the morning when I was greeted by Zoë's excited face my spirits soared.

'What news, Pom?' I asked.

'The news,' she said importantly, 'is that I am a fraud. I haven't torn a muscle. All I've got is pins and needles.'

It was a typical Pom understatement. She still could not walk and we were all anxious about how long her nerve would take to heal. It seemed terrible to pressurise the natural process. I felt sure all she needed was rest but we didn't know how much time we had, how much longer our flight would be delayed. I clung to the knowledge that if anyone could get her on skis in the next few days, that person was Zoë.

She treated Pom for an hour on the carpet, put foam inserts into the heels of her shoes and taped her calf and foot to keep it pain free. Junior Physio (that was me) watched and listened with great interest. Nerve mobilisation exercises were a whole new game to me.

That afternoon, finally, there was better news. Rachel from ANI called to say that a Hercules filled with penguinos (our nickname for tourists who had come to watch penguins) was on its way.

'The winds are getting up, so it may still turn around,' she said. 'We are all keeping our fingers crossed.'

With my father ...

... and brothers ...

... exploring
began early

Top Trudging across the ice of the Arctic, the way often proved testing

Above Clambering over a pressure ridge

Right At the North Pole

Left Packing up in my flat

Below Sewing on our identifying coloured ribbons in Punta Arenas

Above The team in the bar, working on our navigation

Right Tampons – enough for all?

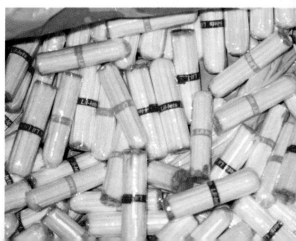

Left Whiteout
Inset And on we trudged through a ground storm of snow

Right Erecting our tent

Above left Pom, sweeping out the inside of the tent

Above right Relaxing at the end of the day and keeping up to date with my diary

Right Phoning home

Top The solar panel, which recharged our electrical batteries, below the white M&G ISA badge

Above Digging out the tent

Left Digging out the 'horses' – the pulks

Above left The entrance to the station at the South Pole

Above right Me and my patch to cover where my skin has been exposed

Left Eating a welcome hot meal at the base. At a table, with a knife and fork!

Left Sleeping the night at the geographic Pole – we had to replace it when Zoë pulled it out!

Below Reaching our goal– the geographic South Pole!

Bottom We went out the next morning to record the event at the ceremonial pole for the world's press

13 Hercules Inlet

B EFORE WE LEFT, WE HAD TO CHANGE hotels again. The last one was run by two women in their thirties and was easily the best: Hostal la Estancia in O'Higgins Street. We virtually took over the place. They let us use their computer and email; lots of faxes and messages to Julian, M&G's PR agents, Holmes PR, and the sponsors to keep them up to date.

It took a lot of energy and time not only to pack the sledges and resupply properly but also to write detailed letters. We explained all our plans to Julian, made comments on the website and contributed PR ideas.

The flights were in chaos. Ginny could wait no longer. The morning she decided to give up on her Antarctic trip and go home, we had breakfast with her in her hotel. It was there we met Bob Elias.

Overhearing us gossiping with Ginny about ANI's overstressed clients, Bob joined in.

'The penguinos are acting kinda weird,' he said with a deadpan face.

A friendship began and over the next few days, Bob told us his story. After making his fortune as an entrepreneur, he had turned to mountaineering as a full-time hobby. He headed a charitable organisation called the Omega Foundation which was interested in funding outdoor scientific research.

After writing a mission statement for Holmes, with Pom and Pen's help, I turned it into a letter to Bob. He and I had coffee in the foyer of his hotel and I explained about the data we planned to collect (we thought 'research' sounded too grand). I showed him our expedition budget and, within ten minutes, he quietly agreed to fund the whole shortfall to the tune of $30,000.

It was extraordinary. After all those months of effort, here we were being given money on a plate. Bob's generosity meant that, even with the extra thousands of pounds we had spent in Punta Arenas, we were now fully funded. Back in the hotel with the others, I tried to be cool, but I could not help grinning as I told them the good news.

The days crawled by.

'We're not going to beat Geoff's team now are we?' I said as we sat in the Corner Bar.

'At this rate we'll be setting off three weeks after them,' said Ann.

'It was pretty daft ever to imagine we would beat them,' said Pom. 'Their expedition has big strong men and two guides. What they're doing is completely different from us.'

'Yes,' said Zoë. 'I think the fun of this is that we're doing it on our own. We've had to make all the decisions about kit and we're going to make all the decisions on the ice as well.'

'And look after ourselves . . . and do the navigation,' Rosie chipped in.

'Anyway I'm glad we're going so much later. Then no one can call it a race,' said Ann.

Two days before we left Punta Arenas, ANI had a meeting where I bumped into Doug. Doug had taken us on to the ice at the North Pole and he was about to fly the same aeroplane, a Twin Otter, in Antarctica for ANI. He was notoriously conservative and nervous about the weather. While we were waiting to be picked up from the North Pole, he was memorably asked by one of the staff at Eureka: 'Hey, Doug, why don't you strap on some balls and go get those goddam girls?'

I greeted him like a long-lost friend.

Three weeks after we had planned to leave Punta Arenas, ANI rang the hotel early one morning and told us we had an hour and a half to get ready. We were off at last. Instantly, all my attention switched to the tasks ahead. Most of our equipment was already at the airport, we just had to gather up last-minute bits and pieces and get dressed in the clothes we would be wearing for the next two months.

The Hercules engines roared and we could hardly hear anyone speak. Ann leaned over her seat in front and shouted in my ear: 'Well, you've done it again Caro, you've pulled it off.'

I felt proud. And very warm. Don't get too excited, I warned myself. It had been such a long wait and we had heard so many stories of aeroplanes turning back because of weather and mechanical problems. I was determined to stay calm and take it slowly.

As a team, we had all been getting on really well but, in the last couple of days, I felt we had taken a backward step. The waiting had finally got to us and Pom had been very tense and worried about her leg. It never became an issue, but we all had to live through it. The strain was beginning to tell. Pom never complained and each day she had made steady progress, but we were acutely aware she was still limping. I just hoped she would be able to ski and if not, I knew she would pretend she was fine until she was.

Sitting in the khaki-green aeroplane, I was also struggling with feelings of disappointment in myself. During our final rope training on the lawn in a street near the hotel, I found myself getting frustrated at the others' attempt to construct a pulley system. As a 'rescuer' I grasped the system quickly but as a 'victim', I had visions of dying down in a crevasse while they faffed on top. My frustration made everyone else tense and ham-fisted.

'We'd like to practise ropes without you, Caro,' Pom said one day.

I agreed it was a good idea but, remembering it now, I was upset that she had had to say it. I definitely felt I should have done better.

I was worrying too about our food. It had sat in the chicken shed for nearly three weeks without refrigeration. Would it have gone off in that time? Would there still be enough calories? Would there be mould on the cheese? Mice had nibbled a hole through at least one of the big blue food bags.

It felt good to allow myself the luxury of worrying. The day before I had withdrawn into myself. Now it was important to refocus and adjust my mind.

When I was little, I remembered hearing about flights to Antarctica and wondering whether I would ever be rich enough to take one. I always knew that I wanted to go there, if only so I could 'do' all seven continents. Yet I never thought I would be sitting here with my polar gear on – complete with harness – about to set off on an expedition.

Curiously, I realised, I felt much more nervous back in the UK than in Punta Arenas. Usually I have a last-minute panic about having left things behind. This time it was Pom.

'I'm having a breakdown,' she said. 'Did we bring any matches?'

'Yes,' I assured her, remembering how, first thing that morning, I had left my card in the cashpoint machine. I was not concentrating and ran back thirty minutes later, sweating in all my kit. (It was gone, of course, but I managed to cancel it before we set off and had just enough money to buy everyone a lucky penguin badge at the airport).

As the worries took shape in my mind and eased away, I began to feel smug about having tied all my possessions on to me. My luxury items – pink scissors, nail clippers and a sheet of aspirin – were on a long string, my pencil was tied to my book, my mittens were on elastic through the sleeves of my jacket and my hat was tied on to my undershirt. This was the way, I felt sure, to keep tidy in the tent and make certain that I did not lose things.

I thought about the task we had set ourselves. The expedition was not just about reaching the Pole, we wanted to come back with meaningful information as well if we could. Flo Howell, for instance, needed to know what the weather conditions were if he was to learn and improve his solar panels and batteries for future expeditions. We were going to take physiological measurements too, such as periods and heart rates. We had some plastic sticks to pee on every day. The sticks would read different colours so we could measure, amongst other things, our pH and ketone levels. This would give some indication of how our bodies responded to the demands. Sitting in the Hercules, I began to feel I was the leader of a *proper* expedition.

The flight from Punta Arenas to Patriot Hills took six hours. The engines were very noisy. Seeing Antarctica for the first time was hugely exciting. At first I could not tell whether what I was seeing was cloud or ice but then, suddenly, I saw black rocks and realised they must be the Ellsworth Mountains. My heart soared. The aeroplane was descending and I could see the coloured tents of the ANI camp at Patriot Hills. The airstrip is several miles of naturally occurring blue ice running parallel to the mountains. (It only exists because the wind is usually so strong it blows the snow off.)

Checking out the runway, the Hercules swooped down alongside the mountains. Then it did a big arc and circled back to land. As we got lower, I could see figures on skidoos waiting at the side of the runway to meet us. The ANI staff were all togged up in layers of clothing and goggles. It looked very cold.

Landing on sheet ice, the Hercules was unable to use its brakes. The landing was fast, big and bumpy. We had arrived. Just as in all the best adventure movies, the big ramp at the back of the aeroplane went down and we took our first steps into Antarctica. The feel of the dry, icy air in my face and lungs was instantly recognisable – it took me right back to the Arctic.

We slithered across the blue ice runway. It was very windy. We piled into a trailer on skis and were taken to the camp about a mile away, where the air was totally still and the sun was shining.

The plan was to fly by Twin Otter to Hercules Inlet, thirty miles away on the coast of Antarctica. We would then ski back to Patriot Hills where Pen would be waiting for us. This meant we could ski with light sledges for a few days. At Patriot Hills we would load up again, make any last minute adjustments and set off on the expedition proper.

From Patriot Hills to the South Pole was about 600 nautical miles. Halfway were the Thiel Mountains and it was there that we planned a resupply of food and fuel. The arrangement was that ANI would fly in to wherever we were on an agreed date just before Christmas. We expected the whole journey to take sixty to seventy days and, when we got to the Pole, ANI would pick us up and take us back to Punta Arenas. Given how late we were starting, we now knew there was no hope of getting to the South Pole for the millennium.

'We've had enough of waiting,' I said to Simon, one of ANI's staff. 'Can we go immediately to Hercules Inlet?'

'I don't see why not,' he said. 'I think we should make use of the window of good weather while it is here.'

'Where do you want to go?' the Chief Pilot of the Twin Otter asked.

'Hercules Inlet.'

'Where's that?' he asked 'My co-pilot and I are both new here.'

Pen ran to the radio operator's tent and came back with a large chart. Most of ANI's other clients gathered round. They had come to wave us off. We unfolded the map on some oil drums and Pen and I did our best to measure off exactly where we wanted to go.

'I reckon here Caro,' Pen said. 'Look, where the contours are not too steep.'

We had a roll-call of everything in our sledges. I shouted out the list:

'Argos. Rope. Cookers . . .'

It took a long time.

Then all aboard the Twin Otter. Our old friend Doug was co-pilot and I had an enormous sense of *déjà vu*.

We flew low over the ice and had a great view of the Ellsworth Mountains stretching out on our left. It didn't look too steep or too hard, especially in the sunny weather.

Beautiful evening. Bright blue sky, no wind. I began to relax and grow more excited. In less than half an hour, the Twin Otter touched down on the sea of white and the engines whirred like a lawnmower as we bumped along to a halt.

'Are you sure this is the edge of the land, Doug?'

I lent forward to catch his attention in the cockpit and Doug lifted one side of his old-fashioned earphones.

'Why sure, Caroline. It's looks to me as if the land is no more than 300 feet away.'

Doug turned off the engines and we got up one by one to squeeze our way out of the aircraft.

'Which 300 feet exactly do you think Doug has in mind, Pom?' I asked as we lowered the sledges gently on to the ice.

Everything looked exactly the same to me. It was incredibly still. Bright white snow with frozen ripples, flat as a sheet of paper. There was no way of telling what was sea and what was land. Then, as I looked closer, I could begin to make out some relief. Doug was right, about 300 feet away, the white began to slope up and away from us.

'That must be land, I've never seen sloping sea before,' I said.

Pom, Zoë and I ripped off the packing tape protecting the runners on the sledges and pulled them away from the aircraft. In the meantime Ann and Rosie checked the readings on our GPS and altimeter with those in the cockpit.

Pen had his camera. We had planned in advance the photographs we needed for press and sponsors. We posed with each sponsor's flag and I felt cold just looking at Pen. His face and hands turned a horrible blotchy blue and red as he crouched and clicked in front of us.

The pilots had agreed to wait an hour but it seemed no time before they were impatient to leave. It was 11.30 p.m. the sun was shining brightly and we were about to be left on our own.

I still did not feel nervous. It was nothing like setting off on our leg to the North Pole. Pen gathered us round to say goodbye and I could not tell whether it was cold or emotion that contorted his face.

'Before you go, I just want to say a few things to you,' he said. 'You are the sisters I never had but I always wanted. Please don't do anything stupid. It can be bloody awful out here and you're going to be frightened sometimes. But I know you're going to make it, I really do. Just keep safe and remember to laugh a lot.'

Only then did I feel tearful. I hoped I didn't show it. I wanted to be brave. Big hugs all round before Pen ran back to the aeroplane and climbed on board. Pom and I stood by with our cameras, expecting it to fly back and dip its wings. But the Twin Otter was up and away and, within moments, it was gone.

It was past midnight. We were alone. I thought I might feel frightened, but what I actually felt was relief. We were away from the ANI mayhem. We were off at last.

'Come on, let's get a few miles under our belts now,' Rosie said excitedly.

Both Ann and Zoë seemed keen to start skiing as well.

'I'm not so sure,' I whispered when Pom was out of earshot. 'I think we should camp. It would be awful if something happened to her while she was tired. It's late and in the morning Pom's leg will be that much better.'

They all agreed and we put the tent up under the clear blue sky and unpacked the sledges for the first time. We unrolled our sleeping mats and jostled for position on the thin foam floor. Half of Pom's ridged sleeping mat overlapped with mine and there was only just room for us all to lie top to toe.

Ann was at one end with her head downhill and Zoë chose the same on her inside. I went between Zoë and Pom the other way up and Rosie was next to Pom with her head in the same direction as mine.

It was quite light inside and I set the alarm on the boys' watch I had bought in Santiago. Eight hours' sleep. I knew I would not hear the alarm inside my sleeping bag, so I fixed the watch to Rosie's Club Class blindfold, which she wore outside her hat. Everyone laughed and I slept like a baby, dreaming about my nieces, nephews and godchildren. I was warm as toast.

14 Ice on Rock

Day 1
6 nautical miles

WHEN THE ALARM WENT OFF I was raring to go. We rolled our sleeping bags up to make room for the cookers, then sat on them in a ring round the tent. Our equipment was shiny and new. We touched it gingerly, fearful of breaking anything.

Breakfast was two mugs of coffee and, in the same mug, toffee and pecan cereal with powdered milk. We had some water from Patriot Hills but had to melt more from the snow outside.

There was still no wind and, when we took the tent down, it did not feel too cold. We clipped our boots into our skis and attached the sledges to karabiners on our harnesses.

Ann and I set our compasses on a direct bearing to Patriot Hills.

'Let's aim for that rock over there,' we agreed, pointing to a shape sticking out of the horizon.

Trudging along in single file was familiar and evocative. The weight of the sledge pulled my thighs and jerked the small of my back. Everything was white, making it difficult to see the gradient and contours. But I could tell we were going uphill because my sledge did not glide and I could feel my calves stretching. As we went up, mountains and lumps of rock appeared, like ships rising out of the sea.

After an hour, the rock had become a large hill at the end of a mountain range. Pulling uphill was hard and I was pleased our sledges were light. I studied Pom's movement anxiously and hoped her leg was not agony. Skiing looked no easier for her than walking.

Parts of my body hurt in turn. First it was the ball of my left foot, next my right heel and Achilles tendon, then a new sensation of the harness chafing my shoulders. The harness was supposed to make me pull from my hips and legs and I checked it was correctly adjusted.

We took it in turns to go at the front. I was relieved nobody seemed to want to go much faster than I did. Pom took my turn at the back, which I thanked her for. She knew from the North Pole how much I hated being the last one trailing along.

We skied for exactly an hour at a time, then sat on our sledges to snack for five minutes. The wind was increasing and it was instantly peaceful to sit facing downhill and turn our backs to it.

Gradually, we could make out the land surrounding the frozen inlet below us as well as the gradient we were climbing. We congratulated ourselves on the progress we were making but, otherwise, were fairly quiet. We concentrated on stuffing our faces with calories from our snack bags.

Nothing tasted quite the same as it had in my flat. The nuts and biscuits were much blander and I decided I did not like almonds. The chopped-up pieces of Mars had stuck together in a lump. I meant to suck and warm it, but I forgot. As I tried to bite, I felt a tooth break in two.

I swallowed the Mars in one, then felt for the tooth anxiously with my tongue. Where a left molar had been, there was now a big piece of tooth missing. I panicked and pushed my tongue into the hole. My jaw froze with pain.

I told Zoë and Ann and did my best not to worry.

Leave it Caroline, I tried to reassure myself, it'll probably settle down.

We set off skiing once more.

After five and half hours we called it a day. We did not want to do too much too soon. We had scheduled a call to

Julian but had to warm the telephone batteries and were late and missed him.

'Leave a message' – I heard Julian's familiar voice on his machine – 'and I'll get back to you as soon as I can.'

I left a message but it felt very odd – getting through to him as if we were at home.

We had covered six miles and climbed 810 feet. It was satisfying to be level with the original rock we had aimed for, but I was disappointed not to make it to the top of the slope (only later would I realise that Antarctic slopes can go on for days).

The wind was blowing hard when we stopped skiing and we had to work quickly not to get cold. No time for chatting and, besides, it was too windy to hear. We camped on a slope. Pom clipped herself to the inner tent as we had practised and, together, we held it flapping to the ground.

At that moment, someone shouted: 'Watch out for that pulk.'

I looked round to see Rosie's sledge hurtling back down the hill. I stood up and sprinted off after it, stumbling in the snow. By the time I reached it, it had come to a halt about 100 yards away.

Rosie arrived panting.

'I did park it sideways, I promise,' she said.

Together, we pulled the sledge back up to the tent.

In the tent, I worried about my broken tooth. It was only Day One – how on earth was I going to eat chocolate in the cold for the next two months? If it got too bad I might have to be airlifted out. I wondered how I would feel when the others went on without me.

Eventually, I let Zoë try filling the tooth with a temporary filling from her medicine cabinet. She made me push it in with my own finger; the slightest pressure made the nerve scream once more.

Day 2
7 nautical miles

Today we learned even more. Bravely, Rosie dressed first and went outside to fetch snow bricks (blocks of hard-packed snow we dug out) for melting. There was a muffled squeal and then her embarrassed face appeared at the door of the tent.

'I'm afraid the wind has claimed its first victim,' she said. 'The big blue snow bag has blown away. Have we got anything else I can use?'

Pom handed her another bag intended to hold the tent, then turned her attention to the cookers. She pumped up the fuel bottles to increase the pressure, opened the valves to prime them and then white gas gushed everywhere.

The colourless liquid evaporated quickly – there was no need to mop it up – but the acrid smell filled the tent. We looked at each other in silence, imagining our house in flames if we tried again. Even Ann, the only experienced camper amongst us, was nervous.

Eventually Ann plucked up the courage to strike a match and brought the cookers back under control.

The wind was still blowing when we set off skiing and, within minutes, we were on a huge piece of sloping blue ice. The wind had blown the snow away leaving shiny, transparent ice like a cube.

It was very steep and the skins on the bottom of my skis would not stick. I found myself teetering sideways, desperately trying to edge my skis like a downhill skier. My sledge had other ideas; it seemed intent on pulling me off the side of the mountain.

The others went the long way round and we met further up the hill. The clouds were low and it was difficult to see. A strong wind blew snow in our faces. The horizon grew more distant and the Ellsworth Mountains appeared one by one to our right. There were rocks up ahead and we kept thinking: that must be Patriot Hills.

'There it is,' one of us would call, 'don't you recognise it?'

Often we spread out in a fan, rather than keeping to single-file. We did not use the compass much, perhaps because I was nervous of being bossy. At the end of the day, though, we paid the price. When the GPS said we were only seven miles closer to Patriot Hills, we all knew what a zigzag we must have travelled.

Lunch was our longest break; we stopped for twenty minutes. Ann and Zoë suggested we put up the bothy bag (a nylon shelter like a giant plastic bag) for our lunch of hot chocolate.

'It's easy,' they shouted across the wind. 'All we do is put two sledges inside to hold it down and then sit on them.'

It was a fiasco. Paranoid about the wind blowing our things away, I ended up lying on the snow outside the bothy bog to hold it down. Zoë kept shouting at me to come in and, when I finally tethered the thing and did huddle with the others inside, we were all too cold to speak.

Worse still, we had to dig our skis and sledges out from the drifting snow and clip them back on with painful frozen fingers. The wind was biting. Rosie set off up another hill at a furious pace as the rest of us struggled to get going and catch up. Heaven knows why she left us behind or in which direction she was heading.

Then I heard Ann's voice behind me.

'Isn't that a crevasse Rosie's just gone over?'

Crevasses are large cracks which appear in Antarctica's glacial ice when the ice is stretched over a slope of rock. They can be over a hundred feet deep, tapering off to a point at the bottom. Part of the reason for going back to Patriot Hills rather than heading straight for the Pole was to avoid crevasses.

I looked down. There was a dip in the snow about six feet wide. It looked as if it had sharp edges of ice underneath.

'What does that look like to you?' I shouted to Pom.

'I don't know,' she said. 'I can't see anything. My goggles are all fugged up.'

'Oh well, never mind.' I tried to laugh. 'If you can't see crevasses, there's no need to be frightened.'

At that moment, there was a loud 'Shit' from Zoë and Ann. Pom and I looked round at once. Zoë's ski pole had gone straight through the snow and she was moving as fast as she could towards us.

'I could see blue through the hole and there was air underneath me,' she cried.

We had been warned about snow bridges – snow which fills a crevasse. They were not a problem unless they decided to give way. Unknowingly we had crossed a field of crevasses – doing exactly what Geoff had told us not to.

'Rosie, stop,' we all shouted together.

She was still up ahead, with the rope in her sledge. She seemed to be carrying on regardless.

Even with nothing to tie us together, it was reassuring to pull the climbing part of our harnesses through our legs and clip them to the karabiner on our waists. It felt secure. At least if we fell, there was something to clip the rescue rope on to.

Slowly, we carried on over several more snow bridges. I did not know whether to go where Rosie had crossed or to try a new route (in case the bridges were weakened). We kept spaced out and watched closely for any movement in the snow.

I was tired and my heart was beating fast. I did not want to believe we were in a crevasse field. I almost hoped that, by ignoring it, it would go away. Four or five bridges later, we were all safe. We pitched our tent once more. Worse was to come.

I lifted the Argos (satellite transmitter) out of Ann's sledge and, somehow, I managed to flip the emergency switch.

'Is this normal?' I asked in a panic. The switch was clearly not pointing at 'normal'. Eleven miles from Patriot Hills, I had effectively asked for an immediate rescue.

'What have you done, Caroline?' Zoë asked. 'It's impossible to turn the emergency switch on by mistake.'

'Well I haven't done it on purpose,' I said rather frightened. 'Quick, call everyone now and tell them what's happened.'

Zoë spoke to Jason the Argosnaut (our name for the radio operator at ANI in Punta Arenas), Patriot Hills, Flo and Julian. To my immense relief, no one seemed to mind too much.

To add injury to insult, that night the temporary filling Zoë gave me came out on a piece of cheese. She put another one in off a dental stick. I was worried and, for the first time, I felt low.

Day 3
11 nautical miles

We were determined to get back to Patriot Hills in three days if we could, but the third day took forever. When we set off, we could see the mountains overlooking the camp, but we never seemed to get any closer.

I kept pinning my hopes on one speck after another. Surely one of them must be a wind sock, tent or some other sign of life. But as we got further and so a bit higher, every speck turned out to be part of the rock. Then the blue sky turned to cloud and it was difficult to see anything at all.

Rosie saw something that looked like a post.

Then Ann stopped and said: 'Isn't that the tail of an aeroplane?'

Ten minutes later, we were all at the site. A crashed DC6 lay buried in the snow. All that was visible was the top of the body and the tail. A huge piece of litter like a white whale or dolphin moving through a white sea. It was eerie and sinister.

Later we learned the aeroplane had missed the runway at Patriot Hills and, with wheels not skis, it was unable to take off again. In just a few years, the snow had all but buried it. Before long, no one would know it was there.

A couple of snack breaks later, we slumped on our sledges, exhausted. Pen was waiting for us at Patriot Hills and I fantasised he was running towards us. I convinced myself I could see his swaying figure, but it turned out to be a radio mast at Patriot Hills.

An hour later, it really was him. He had been looking out for us with binoculars and came out to meet us when we finally came into view. We bubbled with excitement, telling him all that had happened. The elation I felt was almost as if we had reached the South Pole.

We pitched our tent at the end of a row of yellow ANI tents. They were battered old mountaineering tents. I was glad I did not have to spend months cramped inside.

The ANI staff gave us big steaming platefuls of lamb chops and mashed potato.

'I don't want to go to bed on my own,' Rosie said later. 'It doesn't seem right.'

Ann and Zoë went with her and Pom and I stayed up gossiping with Pen. The journey from Hercules Inlet was our first expedition on our own. We had all enjoyed it and it had certainly been a success. I was confident now we could do the whole thing.

Day 4
0 miles

We pigged out on a full English breakfast and made plans with Pen. Ann and I compared blisters. Hers were horrible – bright red and bulging with fluid between her toes – but she managed not to limp as much as I did. My heels hurt a lot when I skied, but it was only when I removed my socks that I realised the extent of the damage. Many layers of skin had rubbed off and what was left underneath was a yellow and dirty green mess.

Doctor Kate, the camp doctor, took a look and advised leaving the blisters untouched to allow the skin to heal. Pom had the mildest form of frostbite on her chin. When I showed Doctor Kate my tooth, she was less reassuring.

'I've got some slightly better temporary filling material I can put in now,' she said. 'It probably won't last more than four weeks and you haven't got much tooth left for it to stick on to. If it gets infected, you can take antibiotics but if they don't work, it will be the end of your trip.'

Either that, or Zoë will want to pull it out with her pliers, I thought to myself, imagining the glint in her eye. I resolved never to eat on the left side of my mouth. I didn't even touch it with my tongue until late in the evening.

I felt sorry for myself and rejoined the others by the tent. They were busy arranging props for our next important task – as many photographs as we could bear for Julian to send to sponsors and release to the press as necessary. We knew from the North Pole how useful it was to have good shots of the team from the start. With Pen there to take them, this was our chance to get pictures of all five of us at once.

It was essential for M&G and our other main sponsors that the photographs were well branded. There was no point giving a newspaper photographs with our M&G ISA badges obscured. Mars and BT Iridium also needed pictures with their products on display. It was harder to be creative about Independent Insurance (how do you advertise an insurance policy?) but we made a list of over 30 setups.

The weather was perfect – bright blue sky and bright white snow with little wind. I knew we would not have time to take such good shots once we were underway. The sponsors had paid for photographs and media coverage – they did not just want us to get to the South Pole. Pom and I were the expedition's principal photographers. With Pen's help, we were keen to get the sponsors' photography out of the way if we could.

Even so we would all have preferred to get skiing rather than to keep posing for the camera. It did not help that we had grossly underestimated how long it would take. The day seemed to go on forever.

After a couple of hours, I made a speech.

'Look, we'll do this much better if we all just relax. Let's reconcile ourselves to the fact we're not going to set off again until tomorrow and concentrate on doing this properly. At the moment, we're all looking grumpy and that defeats the whole object.'

Pen's hands in thin gloves got terribly cold with the metal cameras. He wore an enormous blue parka with a furry hood and we laughed as he peered through the lens like a dirty old man.

Every few hours, we went to warm up in ANI's Cook Tent, which was the only communal area. I wondered what the other clients made of us and our antics. Pom pointed out two aged Americans stumbling along in front of us hand in hand. One of them carried a hot water bottle and they were obviously looking for their tent. I could not help thinking that if I were they, and had spent many thousands of pounds on a holiday, I would want more looking after.

'Poor things,' said Pom, 'they were probably in the party of tourists who had to dig for fuel.'

She was referring to a story we heard about an ANI aeroplane which had to land at an old fuel cache on its way back to Patriot Hills from the edge of Antarctica. Whispers in the Cook Tent were that octogenarian passengers were given shovels and told to dig for fuel drums buried deep in the snow.

'How much fuel do you think ANI have got?' I replied. 'Do you suppose they've got enough to rescue us if we have an emergency?'

'God knows,' said Pom, 'I think it's best not to think about it.'

I agreed. None of us had confidence in ANI but there was no point in worrying. The most important thing was to make sure we kept ourselves safe and never needed help.

By midnight, the sun was still high in the sky and, in theory, we could have carried on. But we were exhausted, so we slumped into our sleeping bags and planned to finished the photographs in the morning.

Day 5
3 nautical miles

The last photographs were the most fun. They included us with our hands on our hips, dressed only in black thermal underwear from Marks & Spencer, black face masks and goggles.

There was also a sequence of shots making use of a transparent bath provided by Ineos Acrylics. This was a replica of my Lucite bath at home; we had brought it with us to considerable mirth. I took all my clothes off and lay alluringly in it, naked except for my boots.

The sun on my stomach was incredibly hot and I hoped I didn't look fat. I didn't like being 11 stone. I took up too much space in the world. After two or three minutes, I shivered and then emergency messages coursed round my body. *Urgent, urgent. All blood must return to headquarters at once. I repeat, all blood to return to the core at once.* Suddenly my hands were incredibly cold.

Finally, all that remained was for us to pack up our sledges. A few last-minute decisions – 'Do I really need a spare thermal vest?' 'How many video tapes do we want?' – and then the moment of truth. Would we be able to pull our sledges?

By our calculations, the sledges weighed between 150 and 160 pounds each, which was heavier than anything we had pulled in the North. We had heard of people trying to set out and their expedition failing when they found they were not strong enough. A few people gathered to wave us off and I did not know how I would face the embarrassment if that happened to us. We had worked so hard to keep weights down, I was not sure there was anything we could leave behind.

It was all right, thank God. The sledges were heavy and uncomfortable but we could move at a reasonable pace. Pen filmed us skiing and then, out of earshot from camp, he wished us luck again.

When we set off on our leg of the relay to the North Pole, Pen wrote me a beautiful letter. I wished from the bottom of my heart I had had time to do the same for him at Patriot Hills. I felt tearful and wished I could find the words to tell him how immensely grateful I was to him. With a choked voice, I shouted my and the team's thanks to him above the wind.

We all gave him an extra big hug. As he turned to go, he stopped in his absurd great parka and we watched him stumble, lonely, back to camp. His head was down and he looked very tired. It was hardly surprising – he had given us his all without resting for over six weeks. I wondered what he was thinking.

The weather was lovely, with blue sky and hot sun, but the wind was getting stronger. I knew it would not stay fine forever. It was comfortable at Patriot Hills – delicious food and friendly people to help us. For a moment, I did not want to leave. I remembered similar feelings when I went back-packing the first few times: I wanted to go but a large part of me did not want to leave the comfort and stability of Mother and Father. We were alone, really alone. For the first time, I wondered what the hell we were doing.

The views from Patriot Hills were spectacular. Surrounded by big slabs of angled and curved rock, it sits in the lea of huge mountains. The camp is a mile from the mountain but we had no concept of scale. (Everything looks much closer than it is because you have nothing to compare it with).

Once we got going, I felt much better. We spent an hour and a half on the relative flat, skiing along the side of the runway. Without any friction, the sledges slipped easily on the shiny blue ice. I was very unstable. As I heaved my hips to move the sledge, I had to concentrate hard. We all fell over – several times – usually because we were knocked in the legs by someone else's sledge.

Littered in the ice were rocks and gravel blown from the mountains. There were little circles of completely clear ice and, a long way down, I could see pebbles trapped inside. Zoë said she saw a circle with a courgette. In places the ice was thick like glass, getting more and more dense until we could see nothing at all.

The runway finished at the end of the mountains where the blowing wind had formed a deep gully. We climbed a steep bank of snow to avoid it. Our sledges felt much heavier now and it was hard work. We took it in turns to lead and, as usual, I found it easier to drive myself forward when I was in front.

We took a bearing and aimed for a distant rock. This time, none of us were going to be fooled into thinking it was close.

'I imagine it will take us several days to get there,' I said. 'And it's probably not a rock at all – more likely a huge great mountain.'

Rosie agreed. 'I think we should abandon any hopes of pitching camp in its lea,' she said.

We had set off late in the day (about 5 p.m. local time) so, as planned, after only three hours, we stopped to pitch camp. The rock had disappeared behind the brow of the hill and I fixed my eyes on the horizon willing it to come back. Without it, it seemed as if we were making no progress.

It was great to be back, just the five of us in our little house.

'I'm so glad we're out of sight of Patriot Hills,' Ann exclaimed. 'I'd hate them to see us making a mess of things.'

Day 6
9 nautical miles

Our morning routine was coming together. It began with the alarm on my watch which I suspended from the roof of the tent three inches from my face. It went off quite gently and I often woke several times in the night, worried we had overslept.

I always slept deeply and it was difficult to haul myself awake. Someone would shout, 'resting heart rate', to remind us to take our pulse for our research and I fumbled around to find mine. I liked that because it gave me a couple more minutes in the warmth of my sleeping bag.

Then came the moment to get up. I slept in my thermal underwear and it was usually damp with sweat when I woke. We had black vapour barrier liners (VBLs) inside the sleeping bags to prevent moisture getting into them and risk them getting wet or frozen. The VBLs were always slimy to get out of – and cold and unwelcoming to get into at night. But they made a big difference to the warmth and, after Norway, we all dreaded being cold at night.

We rolled our sleeping bags in the mats as fast as possible, then sat on them in a circle. The cookers went in the middle and it was a great feeling when Ann and Pom lit them and the tent got warm. We sat in our thermal underwear with our feet in thick socks and the cosies which kept the water bottles warm. Some mornings, with the cookers on and the sun beating on to the tent, it was positively hot – so hot we took our tops off and wrapped them round our boobs to keep cool.

One by one, we clambered over each other to get to the upwind porch which we used as a lavatory. I sat in front of the lavatory door and had to lean right over to let the others pass.

As the cookers were getting going, Rosie dressed in her full polar gear to go outside and collect weather data. I admired her resolve tremendously – she never missed a morning. I was thankful I could wake up slowly by drinking coffee and writing my diary. I also darned gloves, which I found quite soothing, although it turned into a full-time job.

Breakfast was either porridge or toffee and pecan cereal. Zoë and I found the porridge difficult to eat and Zoë sometimes sat with her cheeks filled up like a chipmunk. We ate and drank everything with a spoon and a mug (it was easy to tell which was mine because it was always the muckiest).

We were obsessed with water boiling and how long it took to melt snow each day. Ann and Pom were in charge of the cookers and all three were on full blast. We were pleased the process was improving. When we started at Hercules Inlet it could take up to five hours between waking and setting off skiing in the morning. Similarly in the evening, between stopping skiing and going to bed. It was encouraging when we began to reduce this to four hours.

We needed to make an awful lot of water – two litres each, plus two Thermoses between us to drink during the day, two mugs of coffee each at breakfast and enough water to rehydrate our dinner and drink with our cereal. It had only taken about three hours in the morning in the North and we could not understand what we were doing wrong.

Antarctica has one of the driest climates in the world and as part of our physiological testing, Pom monitored how much we all drank. Ann and Rosie liked up to two litres while skiing. I did not know how they did it; one litre was my maximum and I drank most of it in the first half of the day. After our lunch of hot chocolate, the water was frequently too cold to drink.

Everything took a long time and we were impatient. Having been primarily responsible for our equipment before we set off, Zoë was anxious about it. If she felt the rest of us were not looking after it properly, she was bad-tempered. When I was struggling to put the telephone back in its box, she grabbed it out of my hands with a sigh and put it back herself.

'Don't grab and shout at me,' I said defensively. 'All you have to do is take the time to explain how it fits.'

After about two and half hours in the morning, the water boilers announced it was time for Rosie, Zoë and me to get ready. This meant changing our thermal underwear and putting on whatever we wanted to wear for the day. The others always had a good laugh at my polar bra.

'I don't know why you find it so funny,' I said. 'It may not be sexy but it's very special. There aren't many bras that have been to both the North and South Poles.'

'It's not just unsexy,' Zoë complained. 'It's filthy.'

Eventually I agreed. I abandoned my old friend and it spent the rest of the journey in my sledge.

I was hopeless at getting dressed. I always seemed to forget things and dress in a haphazard order. We put on our orange outer clothing – salopettes (dungarees) and a jacket. Both of these were made from pertex with a thick pile inside.

Next, there were all the little things to be put on – one or two neck gaiters (tubes of fleece we put our heads through), wristlets (homemade fingerless gloves made from fleece), inner gloves, outer gloves, hat (still tied to my underwear or salopettes), face mask and goggles. Then thin inner socks, plastic bags on my feet (to act as a VBL in the same way as the ones in the sleeping bags) and then boiled wool liners with thick socks for the boots.

It was the same, day after day. Rosie liked to go out first. She zipped herself into the downwind porch, or 'space capsule' as she called it, where we kept our boots. When she finished, it was Zoë's turn, then mine.

If the weather was nice, it was great to be able to stand up and stretch when I got outside. Then there were jobs to be done – such as taking the snow off the valances around the tent and digging out the sledges and skis if there had been a blizzard. Moving kept us warm.

The weather continued to be lovely, with very little wind. Some of the ice had a satin egg-box surface which made a satisfying *pee-yong* sound as the skis slid over it. We could not see Patriot Hills any more. We were skiing close to the big black rocks of the mountains and our eyes were filled with wonderful views. The mountains were covered with ice and snow; some had glaciers, like Christmas cake icing, tumbling off the sides.

The wind had made patterns and ridges in the snow, known as sastrugi. Similar to patterns that waves make in the sea – but more disorganised. The surface snow was blown around and formed different surfaces. Some froze and created a hard, smooth surface which was easy to ski over. Elsewhere it remained powdery and sticky; this was hard work to travel through.

Mostly the low irregular ridges were small and we could ski over them without really noticing, in the same way as one walks along cobbled streets. We knew the sastrugi were going to get much bigger and, when we had to pick our way round larger ridges, I wondered how tall they would get.

We skied in single file. It was easier for the person in front to navigate with the sun than to keep stopping to refer to a compass. (We did not use the GPS outside the tent because the batteries would not have lasted in the cold). We therefore made much better progress when the sun was shining than if it was cloudy.

We climbed yet another steep snow-covered slope of ice. But this time, rather than being a false summit, it really felt as if we had reached the top. A great flat plain of white stretched out before us. Antarctica. One rock in the distance to our right but, otherwise, nothing. The sky was pale blue with streaky clouds. Miles and miles of light grey ice.

I felt excited. A sense of awe and wonderment. Now, for the first time, I had a sense of scale. Everything was flat and the horizon was much further away. It was near the end of the day but I had a burst of new energy. Like walking on moors, which I love, there was a sense of open space and being able to see forever. I wanted to carry on going and going.

With no rocks or mountains to aim for, it was difficult to ski in a straight line – especially with our goggles steamed up, as mine were for an hour. I tried to fix my eyes on a slightly brighter lump of ice ahead and kept my shadow at the same angle to my skis.

After seven hours we decided to stop before we got too tired. Even Rosie, who tended to go too fast when she was in front said: 'Let's stop now. Then we can have another good day tomorrow.'

From the tent, we could still see what the people at Patriot Hills called the Three Sails – three pieces of triangular brown rock sticking up out of the ice away to our left. They first appeared on our third day and they really did look like the sails of three yachts leaning into the wind.

'Those rocks are beginning to annoy me,' I said. 'They're like Newark on the A1 at home. Lots of signposts for miles but you never seem to get past them.'

Day 7
12 nautical miles

I only had a certain amount of energy each day. If I used it up on mental effort, it detracted from my physical energy – and vice versa. Skiing along, I had lots of aural mirages. The sledges squeaked along the snow like an unoiled door. The wind sometimes could do funny things. Often I thought I could hear an aeroplane or even barking dogs. Other times, I felt as if someone was tapping me on the shoulder.

We continued to talk about how to improve efficiency. Our water boiling was the principal topic of conversation at snack breaks. We decided to collect better quality snow – hard, dense, squeaky stuff. And Ann and Pom aimed to improve their system.

We were all obsessed with how long everything took. At home, punctuality is not my forte but there, with my new watch, I found myself timing everything. How long it took from waking up to putting the first cooker on. How long from waking to setting off. How long it took to put the tent up, how long to take down.

Everything took so much longer in the cold than it did at home. Our movements were often slow and deliberate and I wondered whether our minds were slower as well. The Americans at the South Pole schedule on the basis that every task takes 2.71 times longer when you're working in the extreme cold than at normal temperatures. The same was true of us.

The tent, sleeping mats and so on were all stiffer too, so we had to be slower and more careful in case we snapped them. Everything behaved differently and was under stress in the cold. It could break much more easily.

We talked about how long we should ski each day and how long our marches should be.

'I think we should try for an hour and a quarter between breaks,' said Rosie. 'That's what we did in the North and it worked fine.'

'That's what we did too,' Zoë cut in. 'But I don't think we should do that straight away. I think we should build up to it gradually.'

We all agreed. If we could get up to eight stretches of an hour and a quarter each, that would be ten hours which would give us a chance of making fifteen nautical miles a day. We were very encouraged that we had managed to do twelve miles in a day already.

We were also aware that the good weather meant the skiing conditions were perfect. It was going to be much harder once the wind got up and we were battling against the elements.

The weather continued to be glorious and I thought a lot about how much I was enjoying myself as we skied along in single file, how lucky I was to have the opportunity to be out here and what a wonderful place it was.

Our pace was very important. If we went too fast at any stage, we could exhaust ourselves and then not be able to keep going for as many hours. My normal walking speed at home is three and a half miles an hour, but there we were travelling at about half that speed.

It seemed incredibly slow at the start but when I got used to the 'polar plod' it was much easier to keep a steady rhythm – left, right, left, right – all day long. On a bad day every step was a huge effort. On a good day it was restful and my mind roamed freely, floating in a daydream for hours and hours. I thought of friends and events I had long forgotten. No purpose, no hauling myself back. It was delicious.

Day 8
11 nautical miles

Cold hands were a perpetual problem. Sometimes I found it difficult to tell whether my fingers were getting colder or warmer. There was an aching feeling and, in extreme cases, it felt as if they were being clamped and squeezed in a vice.

The first time it happened badly, first my index finger and then two other fingers went on my left hand. Then my right hand began to sympathise and I had to stop to unclip my big outer glove from my harness. The others overtook me and Zoë stopped to help.

'No, no don't worry, you go on,' I said stupidly.

I knew I hated being at the back and yet here I was agreeing to go last. Once I had jammed my solid cold hands into my gloves, the others were about fifty yards ahead. I told myself not to be pathetic. What did it matter if I was last? I could just keep on plodding and catch them up at the next break.

But it didn't work like that. Memories of childhood came rushing back: my brothers striding on ahead and me getting left behind at the end of an afternoon's walk when I was tired. I remembered how, as my brothers disappeared around a distant corner, I used to sit down on a rock and give up. I would will them to look round and see me lagging behind them.

Eventually, they would come back for me. Sometimes they were cross, other times they encouraged me. I didn't really care – as long as I got attention. I never told them – or anyone – that I sobbed but I'm sure they knew.

As we skied along with me far behind, I felt like a six-year-old again. The same desire to cry (which I did a little) and the same temptation to give up. Everything was such hard work – my skis didn't slide properly, my sledge felt heavy and my blisters throbbed and throbbed.

I remembered how I felt when my brothers left me – how unhappy I was. And then, the sadness grew and grew. I thought about my father, when he was unconscious in hospital after his stroke. I remembered going to visit him:

the white clinical room, the machines, his steady unnatural breathing. I remembered holding his hand, familiar but limp. The plastic identity bracelet around his wrist.

I thought about the fact that, at the end, my father's hand was the only recognisable thing – his freckles and moles, his beautiful nails. I remembered holding on to it firmly to reassure myself he was still there. I was convinced I could feel a tiny response.

My brother Charles read bits from *The Times* and I tried to talk to my father as if he could hear. I remembered I tried to stop myself crying but emotion kept taking me over. I could not finish my sentences and tears streamed down. I so wanted to be brave and control myself, like my mother and brothers, but I could not.

Now I could not concentrate on skiing. All I could do was feel sad.

It seemed I was at the back forever. Then, finally, Pom peeled off ahead. Despite her goggles and balaclava covering everything, she had I-need-a-poo written all over her face. I didn't even pause to check she was okay. Instead I steamed on past without a word.

Meanwhile poor Pom got her zip stuck halfway and had to spend the next forty minutes catching us up with an icy wind racing up her bottom.

It took a few hours to get out of my downward spiral.

'I've had a perfectly horrid time at the back,' I confided to Pom.

'For God's sake, Caro,' she said. 'Just tell me if that happens again. There's no point suffering. I really don't give a stuff about being at the back.'

I could have hugged her, hard, there and then.

Over the next leg, I began to recover myself. It was midday and the sun was directly behind us. The wind was blowing hard from our right and I kept my head down. My hands were warmer, so I put my big gloves over the tops of my ski poles and marched straight into my shadow.

With my big hood and gloves, I looked like a boxer on the snow. I concentrated on taking long sliding strides as if I was in slow motion. One minute I was a super-cool boxer, the next a lonesome cowboy.

Day 9
14 nautical miles

'The problem with trying to do eight marches of an hour and a quarter,' I said as we sat on the sledges at a break, 'is that there just aren't enough hours in the day. By the time we've had breaks, that's eleven hours. Then we need two lots of four hours, say, for putting up the tent and water boiling. That leaves only five hours for sleeping.'

'I know,' said Pom. 'I've been thinking that too. But why are we worried about a 24-hour day? We've got daylight all the time here, so what's wrong with just making the days as long as we need them to be? Maybe working off a 25-hour day, for instance, and rolling our clocks forward by an hour each day.'

It was ingenious – and obvious. Even so, I did not go for it immediately.

'What about Julian?' I asked. 'We said we'd call him at a regular time. If we move our clocks we won't be able to and I'm not sure that's fair. I don't want to screw him around.'

'Well why don't we ask him and see?' said Pom.

So we did. And he was brilliant. He did not seem to mind at all.

The Three Sails finally left us. No sooner had we got rid of them than another huge mountain gradually appeared on our right. At first it looked like a tanker heaving into view, then it became a vast cathedral way out on the horizon.

Clouds appeared. At first they looked like a giant's smoke signal – great splodges of white in the bright blue sky. Then a larger splash of what looked like paint; then the sun went behind it and cast us in shadow.

There was a band of sunlight on the horizon. The mountain shone in shafts of golden light, it seemed to float above the horizon. For a long time, we stopped and looked. As we did, the mountain seemed to move closer. It was wonderfully beautiful, unlike anything I – or any of the others – had ever seen. I felt lucky to have seen it – as if I'd been chosen to see the holy grail. The Pirrit Hills.

Pom said: 'It's Avalon.'

And we all agreed.

We had two cameras and Pom took pictures of Avalon. The film tore. It felt like part of the experience. We could not capture it.

I flew for most of the day. My sledge seemed light and I felt I could conquer the world. It was exactly as if I had taken drugs. The rhythm of skiing sent me off. I could have been in a club, dancing, dancing to the repetitive beat.

Occasionally, I came sufficiently back into semi-consciousness to be aware that we were marching and to check, half-heartedly, that Ann was still moving in a straight line in front of me. Then, whoosh, I was off again. It was the most fantastic feeling. I did not want to stop skiing and could have kept going all day and night.

I told the others at the next break and they remarked on my wide eyes through my goggles. The next march was our last of the day but, for once, I didn't want to lead.

'I'll probably go round and round in circles,' I said happily.

We slowed down for the last quarter of an hour and finally the rhythm was broken. I came back down to earth. Like a real drugs experience, I felt a mixture of relief and disappointment that the effect was wearing off.

Day 10
11 nautical miles

Today we could see nothing. There was no sign of the horizon and no contrast or shadow on the snow to tell us our direction or whether we were going up or downhill.

Sometimes on a cloudy day, whoever was leading could see just enough to pick out points in the snow to ski towards. We only needed to consult the compass occasionally. If visibility or contrast was poor, we also had the wind and sastrugi to help us. The wind blew into our faces and if we kept it at the same angle, there was a good chance we were skiing straight. Similarly if the sastrugi patterns were even, we tried to keep them at a constant angle to our skis.

The times that were really difficult to navigate were when the cloud had removed all contrast. This is known as a whiteout. Without shadow or contrast, the person at the front could see nothing at all. Everything – the sky, the snow, the air – was white. We could not see any bumps or contours in the snow.

It got worse throughout today. By the penultimate march, which I was leading, we were in a total whiteout. I could see absolutely nothing. I worried about falling in huge holes I could not see. Ann was behind me and we clipped ourselves on to a rope tied around our waists.

'This is how people go mad,' Pom said. 'I imagine we'll see nothing now for fifty days.'

On whiteout days, I wondered how fast I could react if I saw the front of my skis go over the edge of a crevasse. I strained my eyes for any sign of danger but all I could see was the floaty bits on my eyeballs. It was like skiing in a room without windows or furniture – and where the ceiling, the floor and the walls have all been painted white.

Pom called it a Torture Chamber, but I enjoyed wallowing in a fluffy white world. I quite liked being totally disorientated and having not the slightest idea which way we were going. When it was my turn to lead, I stared down at my skis and concentrated on trying to slide them straight with every step. Frequently I believed I was going in circles and the others were watching and laughing.

At other times, I was sure I was going straight when someone would shout out from behind. I was amazed when I stopped to look back. Our orange suits and green sledges stood out clearly and I could see exactly how far off course I had gone. The others might be skiing several yards away or waiting for me to correct myself by standing neatly in a line like lost sheep.

In a whiteout like this it was too difficult to look at a compass and concentrate on going in a straight line at the same time. There were many days when the person in front would be entirely directed by the person going second. Ann and I had a compass each and we took it in turns to shout to someone ahead.

A quiet day was followed by domestic chaos. Ann, the Cooker Queen, had been mending cookers, when the fuel leaked. Flames flared up and all but set fire to the socks and hats drying on the line above. Then a water bottle exploded with too much water. In a moment of vagueness, Pom threw a pan of boiling water all over the tent. The thin black floor was drenched.

We all busied ourselves mopping up the water and making sure our sleeping bags were not too wet. Ann relit the cookers and put the pans back on. Only then did she speak.

'I think I need some help now please,' she said.

Ann was holding the top of her foot, which was red and blistered. Boiling water had gone all over it and no one had noticed.

Zoë dabbed Ann's foot with a damp tissue. Ann winced and looked away. She had already used snow but, with it being so cold, she was frightened it would do more damage.

Zoë covered the burn, which was about two inches in diameter, with a hydrocolloid dressing and gave Ann some painkillers to help her sleep.

In the morning, the burn was stinging and sore. I could see Ann was worried about getting her boot on. She would never say she couldn't ski, but we were all worried for her as well. Zoë made a giant corn plaster out of a piece of camping mat to reduce the pressure and Ann struggled to fit her boot on. She never took the dressing off. She wore the corn plaster for the next three weeks.

'It's going to take more than a boiled foot to stop me getting to the Pole,' she said.

Day 11
14 nautical miles

Zoë's surgery was getting busier. Apart from Ann's foot, Pom's shoulder was the worst injury so far. It had never recovered from being dislocated at the North Pole and the constant ski poling action meant it hurt Pom a lot most days. She was very brave.

There were lots of niggling injuries too. Pom had a sweat rash on her tummy, had lost a crown and had a period that would not stop. Ann and I still had blisters on our feet and chafing on our thighs. I also had my broken tooth, although it was not painful any more. I never brushed it, hoping plaque would help keep the filling in. I was used to eating only on the right side of my mouth.

I was obsessed with the idea we were trudging up a hill. All I could think was we must reach a summit and then everything would be easier. My sledge seemed incredibly heavy and my mind was consumed with putting one foot in front of the other. Over and over. My calves began to burn. There were moments when I even wondered whether the others had put extra weight in my sledge.

At our lunch break, I lay stretched out on my sledge, exhausted.

I shared my obsession with the brow of the hill – which we never reached.

'Tell me that was uphill, please. I think I'm going mad.'

All I wanted was to get to the top where it would be flat and easy.

But the others didn't understand. Why should they? There was no brow, no limited horizon.

I seriously doubted whether I could manage the seven marches planned for the day. The others were tired too, I could see it. Though no one said anything. Nobody complained or moaned.

There was an energy between us, keeping us all going. We were all in pain at times, we all got tired. We were, each of us, pushing ourselves to our limits. But we suffered mostly in silence. Fighting our own battles. Wanting to be a good and useful part of the team.

I led off and went terribly slowly. My calves hurt but I tried very hard to relax. The lunch stop had put things into perspective and I realised far too much of the morning had been wasted on mental energy. I tried really hard then to let my mind wander as it usually did. All this thinking about how heavy my sledge was had sapped my physical strength. I was losing it.

'Is this too slow?' I turned back to face the others.

The wind was blowing in my face and ice was clinging to every part of me. The summit I was hoping we would reach soon – the better place I was holding out for – that was a mirage. I needed to be here. Here. In this moment, in this reality.

'Is this too slow?'

'It's fine Caro, go at your own speed,' I heard Pom's reply.

I knew the things Pom was silently battling with. Her shoulder throbbed, her hands were always frozen and often her goggles were so misted she could see nothing all day.

'Just don't go any slower.'

I heard her voice behind me.

I thought about the others. Further back, I knew, there was Zoë – in and out of moods, the only one to reveal what was going on inside. Taking care of our pains and carrying the burden of responsibility for our health and injuries.

And Ann, she was the first, always, to do any job that needed to be done. She had left her children behind. Rachel, Lucy and Joseph. Without them for Christmas and the New Year. I could hear her voice in my head: 'I love them more than anything else in the world. I wouldn't leave them if they weren't going to be well looked after. But they've got my mum, dad and brothers nearby. I know they'll be okay.'

Ann said they were her inspiration. 'I want to show my children it doesn't matter who you are or what you are, you can still achieve amazing things. I don't just want to tell them they can do anything in their lives, I want to prove it to them. And I want them to be proud of me.'

It never occurred to any of us to sit down and say: I ache, I'm frightened, I give up. We could not. What would we have done, miles from anywhere and anyone?

I thought of Rosie. I worried she sometimes felt left out. She was the one who bravely – foolishly – always stomped off ahead too quickly. I sometimes felt she was lost in her own thoughts rather than being part of a team.

Rosie was on a mission. That was clear. Her grandfather narrowly missed selection for Scott's expedition in 1911 and her husband William's grandfather was on Shackleton's in 1914. Rosie was getting there for both of them. And for herself. Her tough and feisty self.

My father was with me so often. His face, his words, how this would have felt to him. I had always known that a big part of him was coming with me, but I didn't know how much. How very present he would be.

'Go at your own speed,' Pom said, 'but don't go any slower.'

I started to ski faster. I would not give in to my calves. I would not give in to exhaustion. As a child dragging along behind my brothers, so many times I had sat down. Sat down and wept. That child was still inside me. But there was something else now.

We had got to the North Pole against the odds: a meeting with a man at a party and then we got the whole thing off the ground. 'You've done it again Caro,' I could still remember Ann's voice on the aeroplane.

I started to ski faster. Stuff my calves and exhaustion. I would go even faster.

My mind was going. Physical tiredness was affecting my brain; my thinking was sluggish. If there was a crisis would

I be able to deal with it? The hour and a quarter seemed to go on forever.

I looked round and saw a big gap between Pom and myself.

'Only one more march to do,' Ann said joyfully.

'I'm not sure I can manage it,' I said.

We sat on our sledges and rested for ten minutes. I stuffed my face with nuts and chocolate, and loosened the laces on my boots. More importantly, I drank water. It made all the difference. I felt like a human being again. Antarctica contains over 90 per cent of the world's fresh water supply and yet it is a desert. My problem was that I had become dehydrated. I was still tired but my calves hurt slightly less. I had just enough energy to get me through the final march. That night I wrote in my diary:

> Important lessons for me to learn:
> don't do my boots up too tight,
> don't get dehydrated,
> don't go mad.

Day 12
5 nautical miles

We could have been anywhere today: in a cloud at the top of a mountain or cruising the edge of a precipice. We knew we were not in a crevasse area – not a known crevasse area at least – so we carried on skiing in the shrouding whiteness. The others took it in turns to lead and I was second all day, directing operations.

I knew from experience that those at the front could not see anything. It was as if they were blind – simply accepting and acting on instructions. They had to trust me totally.

I did my best to balance with one pole and hold the compass.

'Right a bit,' I called out. 'Left a bit. Too much.'

I felt like Bernie the Bolt on The Golden Shot.

No time for day dreaming.

I enjoyed the challenge of a whiteout, but it was hard work concentrating all day. It could also be difficult to make myself heard with my face mask on. I soon learned Rosie was deaf in her headband and hood.

I preferred steering Rosie to Pom. Pom could not ski in a straight line even when she could see. It irritated me if we travelled in zigzags and I could not stop Pom shooting off in the wrong direction.

Day 13
11 nautical miles

Even when it was sunny, we found it difficult to keep going for eight marches of one and a quarter hours. We got tired, then everything – getting up in the morning, boiling water, taking the tent down – got much slower. We were pleased with ourselves when we managed seven marches of an hour and a quarter. That was eight and three-quarter hours after all.

It was odd to be in a timeless world and yet to be so governed by our watches. Zoë had a stopwatch which she set at the start of our snack breaks. We wanted to keep them to only five minutes (except lunch, which was allowed to be twenty). But we were not very good at it.

Zoë shouted, 'time' thirty seconds before the five minutes were up and sometimes we reacted at once. We stuffed our plastic bags with our snacks back into the pouches on the front of our jackets and got to our feet. At other times, we took no notice and just carried on eating and chatting – if we were tired or it was a lovely day and we were sunning ourselves on our sledges, for instance.

It was easier to keep the breaks short when the weather was bad. Too much time standing or sitting meant we got very cold very quickly.

Today was another day of total whiteout; a day in which we could see nothing. Nothing at all. My mind roamed and I began to wonder if it made any difference. Even when the sun was out there was nothing to see. But zero vision made it much harder to navigate – we could not even focus on shapes of the ice or on shadows.

For a while when I was in front, when all I could see was white stretching out ahead, I was convinced I was walking on a cloud. A fluffy white cloud like the ones you see out of aeroplane windows.

I got used to everyone's different skiing styles. Ann was usually jaunty and upright, waggling her bottom from side to side. Pom made it look easy too, as if she was not pulling anything.

'Pom looks like one of those figures that struts out of a clock and bangs a gong,' Zoë laughed.

Zoë and Rosie both made it look very hard work. Zoë was often hunched and held her poles out at an angle, while Rosie could look quite twisted from behind. I was upright and stiff and took long strides. I tried hard to keep pushing my weight into my knees so I did not lift my feet.

Our faces were totally covered in masks and goggles and it was much easier to recognise people moving at a distance than close up. For a long time I found it impossible to tell who was who. I often got Pom, Zoë and Rosie muddled up.

'Who are you?' I said several times as I skied straight up to them. I often did not know who I was helping or who was helping me.

Gradually, though, I consciously learned their identifying features. Zoë always wore two karabiners on her harness, Rosie had two split gaiters on her boots and so on.

Deep powder snow. Going uphill. And for most of the day it was snowing again. So much snow. It had been snowing for 48 hours. We must have experienced just about all Antarctica's annual precipitation by now, I thought.

It was a quiet tent that evening. Without the sun the temperature inside was still quite warm with the cookers – about 15°C. With the sun it got up to 30°C.

Day 14
9 nautical miles

Julian was a rock. Utterly dependable, he was always there when we called. He made our lives so much easier. Knowing we had him alleviated a lot of our fears. We spoke to him every two or three days during breakfast and our calls were a high spot. Ann usually made the call.

Every conversation began the same way: 'What's your position? Temperature? Wind speed?' And then on to other business. Sometimes there were radio interviews, and always there were messages from family and friends. Julian read them out verbatim with a very straight but slightly humorous voice, and Ann made notes in the Dry Log.

Ann read all the messages to us. It did not matter who had been sent what – we all shared the news. We also loved to hear snippets of what Julian and his family were up to – they kept us going for days.

Nothing amused us more than lavatories. We never tired of comparing each other's bowel movements. We dug a hole in the upwind porch where we all performed and there was no way of hiding anything. It fascinated me that, after a while, all our poo looked exactly the same.

In the morning, after we had wriggled out of the tent and packed the sledges, it was time to take down the tent. Zoë or I filled up the lavatory hole with snow, then we crawled into the porch from the outside together. Inside the fly sheet, the warmth from the tent had condensed and it was all furred up with snow and ice. The ice on the tent poles holding the inner tent up looked like the lime on pipes.

Pom was the last to get out of the inner tent and, as soon as she had packed up the last cooker, Zoë and I would start unclipping the poles. Pom was usually still inside doing up her laces as the tent came down around her. The poles were long thin metal with elastic inside. We could break and fold them in certain places but, almost always, the joints would have frozen. To undo them, we had to rub the joints hard with our hands to warm them.

For the first weeks, we passed the poles out from under the tent and undid them outside. But we found that, even when the sun was shining, the air was so cold the joints froze tight and were much harder to undo. By undoing them under the fly sheet, they kept warmer and so, as Zoë and I worked from one end, Pom and Ann worked from the other.

If the wind was blowing hard, the fly sheet flapped wildly above us. On stiller days, if the fly sheet was frozen hard, it stood up on its own – otherwise I knelt upright supporting it on my head.

Once the poles were packed, Ann folded the inner tent into a large blue stuff sack. From the outside, Rosie would then do the same with the fly sheet. I sat underneath banging shards of ice off it and trying not to feel claustrophobic with the fly sheet pinned down around me with the snow on the valances. The ice went everywhere – into my gloves, into my hood, down the back of my neck – I was always covered in ice when I clambered out.

We were all longing for sunshine and we got a little today. It was great to be able to see again. The drawback was that some of the snow was very sticky.

No gliding, instead as I pushed my ski forward it crunched and sank in the snow. The person at the front and the one immediately behind scraped out a path for the others, who had only to follow their ski tracks. It was a cripplingly slow process and very hard work.

I spent one lovely trudge creating a whodunnit murder mystery around the staff at Patriot Hills. Avalon was still there. We all felt it watching over us. Unlike the Three Sails which were irritating and got in the way of the horizon, Avalon was strangely warm and comforting. Not least because of its outrageous beauty. Because of the undulation of the snow, we might not see Avalon for days. But then it would return, like a special friend.

Finally, just before the end of our last march, we saw another mirage. This time it was a big sea of water to our right and a circular rainbow around the sun (called a panhelion).

At the end of our fifth march, I made a speech.

'I think six marches is enough today,' I said. 'Each march has taken a long time and we've taken longer over breaks too. We tend to be crotchety after seven marches and we're not moving fast enough to make another march worth it.'

Sleep was becoming an issue. Everyone except me was adamant we should have eight hours' sleep every night. I agreed we tended to perform better and were nicer to each other if we slept for eight hours. The problem was we were getting less efficient and our 25-hour day was fast becoming 26 hours.

Before very long, we were going to lose a whole day.

We decided to reduce the length of our marches to see if that made a difference.

Day 15
10 nautical miles

'Do you suppose this is the notorious Marshmallow Valley people forgot to tell us about?' Rosie asked halfway through the day.

It was such hard work. Sticky crunchy snow. The sledges had no glide at all. They were completely dead weights. Our skis crunched and sank in the snow. I felt as if I was on a ghastly machine at the gym – exercising every part of my body: legs, hips, arms, shoulders – with the sledge constantly jarring and pulling in the small of my back.

The difference was, at the gym, the exercise lasted about an hour and then I retired to the pub. Here it went on and on. And our cup of hot chocolate and slab of mullarkey (a recipe invented by Pom and Ann to get more butter and sugar into us) rarely felt equal to a glass of white wine or a beer.

* * *

Mullarkey Recipe
1 pint of water
800 grams porridge oats
1.1 kilos of chocolate
500 grams slightly salted butter
200 grams drinking chocolate
Place water in pan, add porridge and bring to a steady boil.
Cook for four minutes. Add butter. Allow butter to melt
and fold into porridge. Add chocolate (cubed). Melt and
fold into mixture. Add drinking chocolate powder. Cook
for a further ten minutes, stirring continuously. Pour into
a plastic bag and place outside tent to set into sludge.

We had no idea how long the Marshmallow snow was
going to go on for. Would it be like this all the way to the
Pole? We never knew what we would find next.

We tried a new formation. Back to one-hour trudges,
trying to keep up the speed and also keeping snack breaks to
five minutes. It was a long slog. I was very relieved to see the
others were exhausted too. After six marches, Zoë said she
was knackered so we only did one more. We were all very
tired and very cold when we stopped. It was minus 22°C.

'Where do you want the stables, Caro?' was the first
question, as always, when we stopped. I was in charge of
the 'horses' (sledges) and they needed to go near the back
entrance door. Rosie stomped about without her skis
looking for a firm bit of ground (otherwise the tent floor
went squidgy where our feet and knees dented the snow
and this made it difficult to keep the cookers flat).

At the end of each day, Pom clipped herself on to the
inner tent to stop it blowing away. Rosie, Ann, Pom and I
then pegged it into the ground with sawn off ski poles
(made by Billy at The Pride of Spitalfields). Zoë put the
tent poles together, then we clipped the first two black
ones to the tent. My favourite moment of the day was
falling on to my knees and my stomach to clip them on to
the centre point. Such a relief to take the weight off my
legs and back and to lie fully stretched.

The tent was hoisted – Rosie's favourite bit – and we clipped the remaining poles on. Then Pom went in with the insulating carpet (3mm black closed cell foam) and brushed it clean of snow and ice. Meanwhile the rest of us attached the fly sheet – Rosie clipped on this time – and we scrabbled around to clip it on to the loops at the bottom of the poles.

We staggered about drunkenly – skiing every day meant we were gradually forgetting how to walk. Sometimes there was a discussion about where the wind was blowing from and therefore the correct orientation of the tent. But mostly we worked in silence. We were all too tired to speak much.

I tethered the 'horses' to a fixed point – an ice axe or ice screw – and made sure the skis and poles were all tied on to the ropes. Our routine continued. Ann and Pom lit the cookers and started the water boiling. Then I passed all the stuff sacks and so on inside.

'Luggage,' I called out and their hands appeared through the zipped door to receive what I passed in.

Meanwhile Zoë dug the lavatory and Rosie dug the snow to go on the valances. Zoë also built a snow wall to divert the wind. Then she and I finished off the poles in the porches. Rosie, 'the Peat Digger', carved out bricks of snow to put in a big blue sack for water boiling. She also took the weather measurements.

All this took about an hour. Then we went inside. Bottom first, boots off and left in the porch, then clambering over the others and the cookers to sit on my rolled-up sleeping bag and mat. I was usually cold by the time I got into the tent. My breath froze into my face gear and sometimes I had to wait for things to melt before I could take them off. Some days we had competitions to see who could grow the largest icicle off the bottom of their mask – the record was six inches.

I longed to stretch out my legs but mostly we sat up waiting for the water to boil and dinner to be ready. There was always lots of chatting at this time, comparing the day.

Then we tried to guess how many miles we had done before we checked our position with the GPS.

We did our best to change for dinner – take off our wet clothes and put on fresh long johns and vests. Pom was very good about washing. She emerged from the lavatory trying to persuade us how good it felt to rub freezing snow all over herself.

We had soup first with lumps of melted cheese. Then, a while later, it was rehydrated dinner with plenty of extra butter. All to pile on the calories. It was my job to choose the dinner from the sledges. My favourite was beef and potato hot pot.

Then Pom would get out her 'score sheets' – several sheets of scrappy A4 – and note down what we had been doing all day. We told her how much we had drunk and what our mood had been. Then we held up our snack bags to report how much we had eaten.

Ann always won this competition. She ate anything and everything. She even had to count out her squares of chocolate in the morning so she did not eat them all at once. I preferred the decadence of having a big bar of chocolate and shoving the whole thing in my mouth.

'That's pathetic, Caro,' Pom often said to me when I held up my bag. I had rarely snacked enough during the day time, so I tried to finish my chocolate off in the morning. Occasionally I had an excuse.

'Sorry Pom,' I said today. 'Bob gave me some M&Ms and I put them in my snack bag. I was so fascinated by the bright colours all I did was pick them out and look at them. I forgot about my other snacks.'

Day 16
12 nautical miles
Today was my first day without blisters. We started slowly, everyone tired from yesterday's Marshmallow Valley and hoping for a better day. The snow was slightly better – especially for those at the back who could slide along the tracks trudged by the others ahead.

The snow had a crisp outer surface which gave way under our weight. No glide. Just a stomp to lift the skis out again and take the next step. Crunch and sink, crunch and sink, all day. But the sun shone. Beautiful pale blue sky, thin clouds streaked across it. As usual, this lifted our spirits. Nothing seemed as bad and anything seemed possible.

I knew Ann hated leading the last leg so I did it for her. I really attacked it. Bang, bang, bang, keep those legs moving. I thought of my father and wondered how he would have coped with the physical effort.

He taught me to live life to the full and to grasp every opportunity with both hands. I thought: this is for him.

Zoë had her period so Rosie and I carried some of her luggage. I had been very smug about periods. My last tampon was on the Hercules coming to Patriot Hills, which meant nothing was due until close to resupply. But, given Pom's situation, there had been a big run on tampons and I was getting slightly worried there would not be any left for me.

'Don't worry Caro,' Rosie said. 'I've got eight pink Lil-lets squirrelled away somewhere for you.'

Day 17
9 nautical miles

I knew Zoë was tired when she shouted at Ann that the time was up on the first match.

'I was only half a minute over,' Ann laughed.

After the Marshmallow slog of the last few days, the snow was much harder and my sledge glided along again. But, when it was my turn to lead, Zoë told me I was going too fast.

Ann could not get it right, I could not get it right. I called a break early and we all agreed that Zoë should lead the next march – at her own speed.

Her speed was appalling. Her every step looked as if it would be her last. At times, when she got to a piece of 'satin' ice and could slip along, she sped up. Otherwise it was slower than we had ever been. She kept stopping, exhausted. There were times when my skis clattered into the back of her sledge because I didn't realise in time that she had stopped.

I wanted to take some weight out of her sledge. I had done it before at the end of days when she had been tired, but I knew she didn't like it. I decided my best strategy was not to be open to debate. When we finally got to the end of the hour, I went straight to Zoë's sledge.

'What are you doing?' she asked.

'Please don't argue, I'm just going to take some of your weight.'

'Don't,' she said. 'You don't need to.'

'Well, either you're taking the piss by going so slowly – which I'm sure you're not,' I said. 'Or your sledge is too heavy.'

And, with that, I took a large stuff bag and the tent floor out of her sledge and put them into mine.

'Is everything all right?' Ann asked. 'You looked really tired, Zoë.'

Ann meant to be encouraging but, for the rest of the snack break, Zoë sat without talking to any of us. I knew she was cross with me for helping her. I felt sad and frustrated. I wanted to reach out to her, to find a way of making her feel better. I knew Zoë would blame it all on her period but I wondered if she just needed a proper rest.

At the end of the break, when the others shot off, I waited for Zoë. That meant I was at the back which put me in a gloom, but I did not want Zoë trailing along on her own at the back.

Max, a pilot at Patriot Hills, had shown us a hand-drawn map a Japanese expedition had given him several years ago. On it were marked some crevasses and I had copied the map on to another piece of paper before we set off. According to it, we were not far from the Japanese Crevasses (as we called them). We agreed to stick close in one group. We were all worried about Zoë and had little snatched conversations at breaks.

'Perhaps we should take some things out of her sledge at night so she doesn't know,' Ann suggested.

At an afternoon break I said: 'I've had an idea.'

'Go on then, spit it,' said Pom.

'I think we should go on for as long as we want today and then take half a day off tomorrow,' I said. 'We can get up at midnight and set off at 4 a.m. That way we can relax a bit. Ann and Pom never stop working and they must be exhausted. Maybe this will make us all more efficient again. We keep chastising ourselves for being slow in the mornings and evenings but maybe it's just because we're tired.'

'I think that's absolutely right,' said Pom. 'Everyone who does an expedition like this takes a rest day. Otherwise the body can't cope.'

'But what about our schedule?' Rosie asked. 'I do want to get to the top of the Thiel Mountains before resupply.'

'I agree,' I said. 'But if this makes us more efficient perhaps it's the way to do just that.'

There was silence.

'It's only an idea,' I said.

By the end of the next trudge, the idea had taken hold. The more I thought about it, the more I liked it. I hated travelling late in the day – rolling the hour forward meant we were now finishing at 1 or 2 a.m. It was noticeably colder and, with the sun in our faces, we shielded ourselves by skiing with our heads down. When we sat down on our sledges with our backs to the wind, we also had our backs to the sun. Then, at the end of the day, when we were out of the wind behind the tent, we were also out of the sun and it was absolutely freezing. I was convinced it would do us good to have a quiet day.

Zoë apologised to us over dinner and we told her warmly that it didn't matter at all. As we unrolled our sleeping mats, I had another idea.

'Maybe Rosie and I could do the water boiling for a day.'

'Oh no, not that,' said Ann and Pom together, 'that wouldn't be a rest at all.'

It was a landmark day – we had skied a quarter of the total distance – 158 miles. At 3,330 feet, we had also climbed one third of the height.

Day 18
0 miles

Our first day off. Ann volunteered to make the scheduled call to Julian at eight o'clock p.m. GMT. The alarm went off and we all listened. Then we went back to sleep and carried on sleeping. I expected a quiet day chatting and lying around. Instead we slept from 5.30 a.m. one day to 12.30 a.m. the next. It was bliss. We barely stirred.

Day 19
11 nautical miles

So much for the rest day doing us good. I had a horrid day. I thought only of miserable things. The sensation was similar to the helpless-hopeless one I got when I was at the back. I tried to get myself out of it, but I could not.

It was worse when we stopped and I did not even have the effort of pulling my sledge to distract me. The others thought I was in a bad mood. Like Zoë, two days earlier, I sat on my sledge without speaking.

'You're very quiet, Caro,' Pom said.

'I'm concentrating on my snacks,' I said, without looking up.

As well as feeling glum, I felt lethargic. I wanted to be anywhere rather than here. I concentrated on keeping my head down and following the tracks of the person ahead. Their poles made marks in the snow like white ink splats, but even they could not make me smile as they usually did.

The ice looked the same as always – gently undulating and grey. Little sastrugi and bobbles of ice caught the light. Shadows were cast and some ridges looked whiter, like white horses on the sea.

The ice underfoot had different patterns too. Smeared across the surface at different, gentle angles, in places it looked quite smooth. Elsewhere it was crinkly with large wave marks frozen on it.

Then there were places where I had to lift my skis to get from one level to another over frozen ridges two or three inches high. I stopped to poo en route and everyone waited for me. It brought on waves of sickness. I could not eat any of my chocolate at lunchtime and told the others I wasn't feeling well. I didn't want hot chocolate or tea either and hardly ate anything more all day.

By the end of the day I was exhausted. My head was spinning.

'Don't be silly,' Zoë said. 'You've just had a bad day.'

She took my temperature and said it was very slightly up.

'I'm not used to having bad days,' I said. 'Let alone one like this.'

Pom and Ann had laid out my sleeping bag. I lay on top and, as soon as I got inside, I fell asleep.

That night Ann telephoned her children. She spoke to them one by one.

'Am I still your sugar plum fairy?' Lucy asked.

'What are you doing in the Christmas play?'

'How many miles have you done, Mummy? How many more to go?'

When the call was over Ann was beaming. Not suffused with loss and longing as I thought she might be, but filled up with the contact with them. She had a few 'missing children moments' which we learned to recognise – she went quiet for an hour and could sometimes be short. Otherwise Ann talked about her children a lot and always spoke about them after a call, telling us details, filling us in on their lives back home, what they were doing for Christmas, when they were going back to school. I felt they were with us all the time.

'They're doing an interview tomorrow with BBC Bristol,' she said. 'Julian has told them to wear their M&G ISA T-shirts.

'Do you think they're ever not in their M&G T-shirts?' I asked.

'No,' she replied. 'I know my mother – she'll be washing and ironing them every night, I'm sure.'

Ann's high spirits cheered me.

Rosie rang her mother because it was her mother's birthday.

'I just had one of the most coherent conversations I've ever had with my mother,' Rosie exclaimed. 'She was completely unfazed that I was telephoning from Antarctica.'

Day 20
9 nautical miles

'What are we having for breakfast today?' Ann asked as usual. 'Porridge is more filling than cereal and I want to know how much mullarkey I need.'

Ann's appetite remained undaunted. She had taken to eating mullarkey, our nourishing brown sludge in a plastic bag, with a spoon before breakfast. The word *need* in her question always amused me.

I felt very differently – as if I had slept off all the nastiness. I woke with the feeling of a new day.

I led the first march. Before long, a high ridge of ice appeared along the horizon to our left. I wondered if it was the large sastrugi we had heard about. Then I thought of the map I had drawn of the Japanese crevasses.

The thought came and went. Perhaps it was only a trick of the light. The sun played tricks. We had seen mirages of water. The distant contours of ice could look like vertical walls.

The closer we got to the hump of ice, the more threatening it looked. It was unlike anything we had seen so far. Then suddenly it became clear. A giant hole loomed in front of us. We were looking down the mouth of a cavern three storeys deep and fifty feet wide.

The hole was filled with twisted lumps of blue and white ice. It was strangely beautiful and frightening all at the same time. It was hard to look away, I was transfixed.

'It seems to be part of a fault line running east to west.'

'How are we going to get across?'

'Between the cavern and the ridge to our left, there are two parallel dips in the ice where the snow looks softer.'

'We could try going over those snow bridges,' Zoë said.

'Or maybe we should go over there,' Rosie said, 'to the right, where the ice is less disturbed.'

'If we went to the right, maybe we could ski all the way round it. Unless, of course, this fault line runs the whole width of Antarctica.'

'Whatever we do, we should do something soon. We're all getting cold standing here.' Ann was pragmatic, as always.

The advantage of trying to cross here was that we could see what we were dealing with – the sun was shining and we did not know how long that would last. On the other hand, we could not know how many more crevasses might lie beyond this one.

In the end we decided one of us should go over without a sledge to test the ice out and see what it was like further on. Ann and Rosie both volunteered.

'I think Ann should go,' I said. 'Rosie you're not even as heavy as a sledge.'

Zoë got the rope out of Rosie's sledge and, together, she and I organised a fixed point for her to tie herself on to. At the same time, Ann did a spectacular figure of eight knot to secure herself and Rosie unfurled the rope.

In some ways, it was no different from the safety routines we had practised on the grass and pavement in Punta Arenas or the cliffs of Derbyshire. No one had actually fallen in, there was no drama yet. But if we got it wrong there so easily could be. This time it was for real.

Pom was filming and, despite the pressure of the camera, I tied a bowline knot right first time. Zoë sat on the inner tent (in its bag) tied to two ice axes driven into the snow and gradually she let the rope out as Ann inched across.

The rope gave Ann confidence and, rather than thinking about falling through, she focussed instead on testing the snow. I felt helpless standing and watching. What would we do if Ann fell through? We moved every step with Ann. Every shred of our attention was focussed on her.

'It's much firmer over here,' she called.

'Keep going. See if there are any more crevasses.'

When she got to the end of the rope, Ann unclipped herself and carried on. We could see from her familiar waddle that she was growing more confident with every step.

'I think it's better further on,' she called. 'The snow seems much firmer and I can't see many dips.'

The task now was to get everybody over. First Rosie, then Pom, both with their sledges tied on. When they reached the other side and threw the rope back, Zoë and I clipped the remaining three sledges together and the others pulled them over.

Then it was my turn. Very aware there was only Zoë behind me to pull me out, I whizzed over the snow bridge as fast as I could. Without a sledge, I seemed to be flying and I tried to do it on the tips of my toes.

'Well done.'

'Now all we've got to get is Little Zo.'

By now, all our hands were very cold. The others made another fixed point and, this time, Ann sat down on a bag with the rope around her and got ready to belay as Zoë had done for the rest of us. We threw the rope to Zoë and, in a matter of moments, she too was across and standing beside us.

I glowed with pride. My hands were agony and Zoë, Pom and I all waved our arms madly like windmills trying to bring them back to life. It had taken two hours to get us all across the crevasse.

From then on, it was easy to believe that every little dip in the snow was another crevasse. I looked around anxiously for several miles but then began to relax.

'It's not different to so many other miles we have already covered,' I reasoned.

'Who knows how many crevasses and snow bridges we have crossed so far,' agreed Pom. 'The place is probably riddled with them and we just don't know.'

'I thought we crossed some yesterday,' said Ann. 'I even made a note of it in my diary.'

We set ourselves the task, that night, of putting the tent up and boiling water in the shortest possible time. The aim was three and a half hours.

With unprecedented efficiency and much scurrying back and forth to the sledges to unpack, we got organised as fast as we could.

'Snow bricks now,' Ann and Pom called. 'Spare water bottles. Sleeping bags . . .'

Zoë, Rosie and I pandered to their every demand, falling over ourselves in the snow.

Dinner was served before we were fully undressed, hot drinks were rationed and boiling water was sloshed from one pan to another with astonishing speed. Three hours and twenty minutes later we were tucked up in our bags listening to a bedtime story. Rosie wrote regular updates for our website back home and her latest was an enchanting tale of five green sledges and their typical polar day.

Day 21
0 miles

A very windblown Rosie poked her head back into the tent after she had measured the weather. The hairs on her upper lip were frozen into a little moustache.

'*If* we're thinking of travelling today, I think we should get our wind suits out of the pulks.'

So far only Pom had tried her wind suit (the rest of us were intimidated by the palava with zips when she went to the loo).

For Rosie to question whether we might not be travelling was spectacular. Rosie got the most frustrated about waiting for water in the morning, and she was the one most liable to ski too fast when she was leading.

I got dressed and went outside with Rosie. The sledges were deep in drifts and snow was piling high on the tent valances. The wind was whipping along the ground and snow immediately got into anything left open. Not soft, fluffy snow – the wind packed it hard wherever it went.

Snow rushed into the porch, into a sledge we opened and into the side of my suit through a gap in the zip. Heavy cloud cover with the sun just glimmering through. It felt much colder than usual and it was difficult to see and walk against the wind. We stumbled about in deep snow and shouted our thoughts.

'I don't fancy taking the tent down in this.'

'More to the point, what about putting it back up?'

We decided to wait for an hour and see what happened.

The weather got worse. No sun, no contrast and a very big wind. It was only minus 15°C but with a wind of 30 knots that gave us a wind chill of about minus 40°C.

Half dressed and psyched up to leave, I remembered being a child in Mull and longing to go fishing or lobster potting, but being incarcerated because a gale was blowing outside. Then, as now, at the slightest hint the wind was dropping my hopes soared. I used to go outside with my father and look at the trees and the waves in the loch below. As with the sea, we had no choice in Antarctica but to err on the side of caution. If we made a mistake here there was nobody to come and help us.

'I think we'd be all right travelling, but if it got any worse we'd be in big trouble,' I said. 'Also, we don't know for sure we are out of a crevasse area. This weather would make it horribly easy for the person in the front to fall in a big hole.'

It was difficult – none of us knew how bad we could expect the weather to get. Maybe it was going to be like this all the way to the Pole.

'What did Liv say about the weather?' Rosie asked.

'More to the point, what do you think Geoff would do if he was here with his clients?' Zoë asked.

'He'd tell us to stay put, I'm sure,' Pom said.

That was that then. With regret, we settled into the tent for the day. We felt better once we had made the decision. The wind beat against the side of the tent with a clatter.

The snow falling outside could have been rain. I caught up on my diary and darning – little red stars of cotton all over our inner black gloves.

Pen had given us a backgammon board, which Miriam had made out of cloth. Ann played with Zoë, and I had a tightly fought match with Rosie. The score was one all. We chatted about social politics and had beef and noodles for lunch. Pom and Ann wrote letters and Zoë slept a bit.

The wind got stronger as the day went on. We felt pleased with ourselves for making the right decision. We played 'Guess the Speed of the Wind' by blowing into Rosie's anemometer.

We had one cooker on low for most of the day and then got into our sleeping bags. I felt wide awake but fell asleep almost at once.

'We'll wake and get going as soon as the wind drops,' I said.

'Whenever that might be.'

Day 22
10 nautical miles

Once again we slept very deeply. I was woken from my dreaming by Pom.

'What's the time, Caro?'

I reached for my watch, hanging on the side of the tent.

'I'm worried we're late with our call to Julian,' Pom said.

'Oh shit,' I said looking at the watch. 'We're an hour late. Quick, Zoë, get the telephone.'

The wind was dying down. We took vitamin C and a multi-vitamin tablet each morning. We also put sun cream on our faces as protection and used Vaseline as moisturiser for everything – feet, hands and cheeks. Pom peered into her long johns and rubbed Vaseline into her thighs. Ann and I had had chafing there as well but it had gone.

'Isn't it amazing we don't smell,' I said. 'We wear the same clothes every day, sweat like pigs and must be filthy. Look at Pom's and my fingernails, they're always black.'

The others agreed.

'Occasionally I get a slight whiff of myself as I get into my sleeping bag,' said Ann. 'But otherwise we don't smell at all. The cold just seems to freeze it away.'

At the end of each day we pinned our damp clothes on a drying line over the cookers. My view of the tent was almost entirely obscured by goggles, hats, masks, socks and gloves which hung a few inches from our noses. Also there were cameras and the BT Iridium in plastic bags. The plastic bags meant they could warm up without creating condensation.

'I haven't changed my socks since we set off,' Zoë said. ' I can't believe I can sit here so close to them.'

We got very used to each other's bodies. There was no room in the tent to be shy, especially when all we wanted was to get damp clothes off at the end of the day.

'Wow, look at the muscles in your shoulders, Pom,' said Rosie. 'They're amazingly well defined.'

'It must be the effect of lifting so many heavy pans of water every day.'

Proof – if proof was needed – that Pom and Ann worked incredibly hard every day. As soon as they woke up, they had the cookers on – and as soon as we got into the tents at the end of the day they did the same. No rest until they went to sleep.

Rosie looked agonisingly thin and Pom remarked on the veins sticking out on her arms. Pom liked to peer into my belly button on her way to the lavatory.

'You've got an awful lot in there,' she said.

The hairs on our legs fascinated us too. They were so unfamiliar.

'I've never seen them grow so long on anyone,' said Pom.

'Often I catch a glimpse of my ankles and think I have got the wrong legs on,' I said.

'I'm thinking of plaiting mine soon.'

'Mmm, I'm going to miss this when we get back,' said Rosie, pulling yet another hair out of her mouth during dinner.

There was hair and fluff everywhere – in our clothes, the food, the saucepans, the water bottles. It was hair off our heads and from the boiled wool liners to our boots.

Today we skied in a total whiteout. No visibility, no contrast. Strong wind. In my imagination we were in a scene from *The Sound of Music*. I had the sense we were walking along Alpine paths: rolling green fields, purple mountains and flowers.

Pom and Rosie were unable to steer a straight course. They also whizzed off when Ann or I tried to give them a bearing.

'Please try not to get too far ahead,' we said. 'Otherwise it's impossible to see exactly where your skis are pointing and get you straight.'

Day 23
10 nautical miles
The weather was even more hostile today. My serene visions of yesterday were replaced by memories of the selection weekends on Dartmoor. Foul weather, rain and bog underfoot.

It was hard to keep my face warm. The wind lashed in from our left all day, finding its way inside my hood. I often wore a neoprene face mask but today I wore two neck gaiters – one for the draught down my neck and the other for my face. The one round my face got wet with my breath and froze almost instantly. (I also developed a habit of blowing my nose directly into it as I skied along; I got bored with sniffing and it was liberating to blow freely.)

Visibility and contrast were nil. It started to snow. Hoods up, we were battling against the weather. I wasn't wearing enough clothes. The top half of my body felt draughty. This meant my hands kept getting cold and I struggled to put my big mittens on as we skied.

My mittens were too big to hold the poles properly and the coldness in my fingers made me extra clumsy. I tried to keep the openings on the gloves pulled shut to stop the snow going in, but they were wet inside and my fingers numbed. I felt sick with the cold.

I skied with one hand in a mitt held close to my body, wiggling my fingers while I tried to keep my balance with one pole. This was all right when I was going slowly, but harder when the ground was uneven or we were going faster. When one hand warmed, I swapped and warmed the other hand in the same way. The front of my hood was caked in snow made by my frozen breath.

After each break, I rotated the neck gaiter to find a new dry patch to put over my face and nose. This meant the frozen, snotty bits moved round on to my ears or the back of my neck. As the wind hit the frozen areas of the gaiter, it hurt my cheeks.

I led the last trudge. Usually I looked at my watch after thirty minutes, then kept myself going until five or ten minutes before the end. Today, exhausted, I could not stop myself looking at my watch every ten minutes. I started to count. One stride for every second. Usually for the final five minutes, I counted to sixty five times. Sometimes I varied it and counted down from 300.

At the end of each march, whoever was leading lifted their ski poles and crossed them above their head to let the others know. I loved doing that triumphantly at the end of each day.

We did well to keep going for eight one-hour marches. Finally, too, we had made it to the next degree – we seemed to have been in 82°S forever. I was proud of us all.

Day 24
12 nautical miles

Beautiful weather. Huge blue sky. Clouds like feathers suspended over our heads. The wind had blown most of the powder away. Little sastrugi with crisp hard tops – at last something that was fun to ski on again.

The patterns looked like geographical features and I wondered at the assortment: canyons, tidal waves, mountain ranges, desert dunes. As well as crinkly satin sheets.

The ice looked as if the surface had been smeared with a giant palette knife. Now, with the wind, I could see how the sastrugi had been dug out by wind. Any loose powder had been blown away, leaving moulded hard crust beneath. The ice was grey with occasional white patches where sunlight caught an edge. In places it glittered.

'Caro,' I heard my name being called. And then: 'Nose?'

I hastily covered my nose with my neck gaiter.

Since Pom had got mild frostbite on her chin on the way from Hercules Inlet, we made it a rule to point out if anybody had any flesh showing. With everything bound up, it was difficult to know if you were exposed until you turned to face the wind. Similarly, with my hood up, it was easy to believe the wind had dropped. If I put my hood down for a moment, my head was rocked by an icy blast.

The sun came out at last. It was a relief to navigate with our shadows again, rather than constantly looking at a compass. We always skied in single file and we went faster when we could use the sun. It meant we could relax and sink into an easy rhythm.

After so many days of cotton-wool whiteness, it was strange to see the horizon again. I had a clear sense that all the days we were camped and trudging along in a whiteout, the landscape had looked nothing like this. I had seen colours. I felt in my body that we had been going up and down hills. But now I looked around me I saw only flatness. A great expanse of grey flatness. It was not right.

When we had camped on the storm day, I felt the tent was next to a river overhanging with scrub and hazel trees. Then there was the Alpine path along the side of a mountain, then a landscape like Dartmoor.

'Where have all the trees and bogs gone?' I asked Pom at lunch.

'And what about the mountains?'

She knew what I meant.

'I think God must have packed them all up in a shoe box now the sun is out.'

I led today and felt full of energy.

'I love going at the front,' I said.

'We know.'

'Everything seems so much easier. My sledge is lighter, my legs aren't tired and my shoulders don't ache. I feel as if I could go on for hours.'

I could not understand why the others did not seem to object to going at the back.

'Are you really sure you don't mind being there?' I asked Pom, who went last more than most.

'No, I like it, I promise,' Pom replied. 'When I'm at the back there's no one behind me and I'm free to do whatever I want.'

'Strange,' I said. 'That's why I like going at the front – there's no one ahead of me and I feel I can go anywhere and do anything.'

We were one third of the way to the South Pole and I felt elated. Each night I marked the chart with a cross to show where we had got to.

With 209 miles behind us – and 402 to go – I could almost bring myself to open the entire chart and look at the whole distance to the Pole. Up until that moment, I had only looked at the chart in sections. Deep down, I could not get my head around the distance we had to cover. I could only manage it in sections.

We had given up any thoughts, now, of doing fifteen nautical miles in a day. We agreed to aim for twelve nautical miles in eight marches of one hour. That felt respectable. If we could keep it up we should reach the Pole well within our target of 70 days.

Day 25
12 nautical miles

Sun and big wind again. Bigger than yesterday and head on, all day. Rosie's anemometer said 17 knots. It felt stronger, more powerful than sitting on the back of a motorbike.

We experimented with clothing all the time, particularly with different forms of face protection. Today I wore my black goggles with a plastic face mask attached (we called it Darth Vader). It was a triumph. It kept the wind out of my head.

I watched the wind rush along the ground, blowing the snow like a fine silver dust past our skis and in a trail behind us. The dust rushed over ridges, tumbling like water. It gathered in crevasses, filling them for a moment and then blowing on.

When we stopped for lunch, I sat on my sledge. Snow filled my lap, covered my gloves and filled my snack bag and the pouch at the front of my jacket. Less than ten minutes later, my skis were buried in snow.

We spoke to ANI at Patriot Hills. They told us about the storm they had just been through. 90 knot winds.

Niall, the radio operator, called it an arachnostorm because it seemed to have eight eyes. ANI lost nine tents in all, most buried and frozen under six feet of snow.

'The back end of my tent was split open,' he said, 'and in a matter of moments, the wind filled up the space between the inner tent and outer fly sheet with snow. It was packed so hard I could stand on it – it was my very own natural igloo, but I could not get into it. I shudder to think what would have happened if I had been inside.'

'The day we spent in the tent must have been part of the same storm,' said Zoë. 'Thank God we weren't any closer to it.'

Then I spoke to Simon about our resupply, which was due in two days.

'Because the weather is so unpredictable this year, even more unpredictable than usual, we're not going to be able to do it on 20 December,' he said. 'How much food and fuel have you got left?'

'Eighteen days of food rations and about the same of fuel,' I said.

We had a large amount because our plan to go fifteen nautical miles a day had not worked. We had spare dinners and breakfasts as well as chocolate and nuts. The only things we were short of were coffee, sugar and powdered milk (it was rather thin hot chocolate morning and evening from then on).

'In an ideal world, when would you like to be resupplied?' Simon asked.

I thought I might as well go for it.

'At 86 degrees,' I said.

From our chart, it looked as if some of the uphill might be over by then. However, I had no idea whether we could make it that far on the supplies we had left.

There was a silence.

'I don't know whether that will be possible. It's difficult to land up there with the altitude and the snow conditions.'

'What did he mean by that?' Rosie asked later.

'I don't know. Maybe it's harder to fly in the thinner air or something.'

Simon told us to call Patriot Hills again when we had ten days' food and fuel left.

Day 26
11 nautical miles

The worst part of every day was getting dressed and leaving the tent. Rosie and Zoë went first and, while they put their boots on in the porch, I got ready slowly. The tent was so cosy compared to outside; a part of me could have stayed inside all day. I faffed with my clothes and often had a relaxed chat with Pom and Ann as they finished off the water.

Then it was time for me to go outside. If there was wind, I was shocked by the cold every time. I struggled to do up my zips and cover my face with my mask and goggles.

When we went under the fly sheet to take the tent down, our goggles misted up. Sometimes, under there, I talked quietly with Ann or Zoë, discussing the day ahead. My most private moment came when I sat on my sledge to tie my boot laces (I did not do them in the porch because I found it difficult to bend).

Every morning I sat with my back to the wind, my feet sheltered by my sledge. It was amazing how much protection this gave. I felt peaceful.

We could not stay still long. Within a few minutes, we got very cold and it was essential we got our hoods done up and our skis on as quickly as possible. Sometimes ice got into the bindings or the holes in the toes of our boots. This made it impossible to get our skis on; we had to bang them free of ice.

It was easy to feel panic in the cold. There was always the temptation to jam your foot into the binding – even though you knew you risked breaking something. The longer it took, the more likely it was that you or somebody else would get very cold. We all learned to recognise the stages of cold – we now knew when we would be able to warm up quickly and when it was going to hurt.

We put on our harnesses and skis as fast as we could. But feeling my temperature dropping and seeing the others getting colder made it harder to stay calm. We helped each other, especially when someone's hands had 'gone' – or frozen so cold they were useless.

As our journey progressed, so the mornings grew colder. By the end, the linings of our boots had worn thin. Before we got moving, our feet were frozen like ice blocks. It began to take an hour of skiing to warm me completely.

The same big wind against us all day. We kept our heads down and battled. Blurred figures skiing in a blizzard. Hazy sun made us silhouettes.

Day 27
11 nautical miles
News first thing from Julian was that Leeds beat Chelsea and had gone to the top of the Premiership. He gave us the Leeds results every week and the Yorkshire girls, Zoë and Ann, were getting very cocky. There was £5 each riding on this result.

'Tell Caroline she has to pay my debt as I'm not there,' Julian said. 'Tell her to take five pounds out of yours and Zoë's sledges and put it in hers.'

Another telephone interview with a local radio station. It was strange being plugged into the inane chatter before going live.

'Television's not what it was,' said a dreary man from St Albans.

It was a game to see how many times we could mention our sponsors on air. Ann was the best at it – and the first to get a full house. Pom took a direct approach.

'Every day I thank the Lord for M&G,' Pom said on live radio one giggly evening.

We laughed about our media interviews. But they were a brush with the outside world I didn't really enjoy. Like the photographs at Patriot Hills, they were things we had to do for the sponsors.

I froze my bits this morning, trying to change a tampon.

'Oh no, frozen tampon,' Pom said. 'You have to warm them up first.'

'Warm them up?'

'I keep mine next to my heart,' she said, 'along with my batteries.'

I was trying to be as economical with tampons as possible, but now it was Ann's turn to be worried about our supplies. With resupply late, she was terrified of starting again.

'I'm preparing myself already to use wristlets as sanitary towels like we did in the North,' she said.

The poppers on my hood had never worked. I was getting impatient. The more I fiddled, the colder my hands got. I just wanted to move. I didn't care about the consequences of the wind rushing into my face and down my neck.

Zoë was kind and kept me calm. She fashioned a clip with a mini karabiner. The system worked well but I had to be very careful not to let the metal touch my skin. The neck gaiter I used to cover it soon froze stiff.

I liked the theory of sheltering in the bothy bag, but not the practice. At lunchtime today we put it up to get out of the wind.

Bent double, knees round our chins, we chatted and tried to relax. The wind was loud as we huddled under nylon. Our clothes began to thaw and our goggles steamed up. Afterwards, putting on skis and clipping on sledges, we got so cold.

There was a 20-knot wind as we put the tent up at the end of the day. Pom clipped on to the inner tent and Rosie to the outer fly sheet. We all clung on as it flapped madly.

It was very cold. I photographed Zoë's snow wall before I went into the tent. It was a mistake. My left hand was agony, so cold I could not get it back into my mitten. That night Ann and Zoë had to untie my boot laces for me.

Day 28
13 nautical miles

Rosie's alarm went off early. I looked at my watch.

'Aren't we supposed to have another hour?' I said.

There was consternation before we agreed and fell blissfully back to sleep.

'I can't believe you suggested we sleep on,' Ann said later.

I knew she looked at her watch in the morning and that she did not always trust me to tell the truth about how much sleep we got. We had planned our 25-hour day around eight hours sleep but most nights we only slept for seven and a half hours. I did not tell the others – sleep was a sensitive subject – it seemed simpler to keep moving the clock forward by one hour and keep quiet.

The wind had dropped and the weather was beautiful and sunny again. We skied into the sun and the ice was grey. Smooth slippery ice. We whizzed along. Familiar crunch and squeak of skis and poles. The scrape and rumble of the sledges behind.

The snow reminded me of a battlefield. The jumble of surfaces and twisted sastrugi could have been the dead and wounded lying in several feet of mud. I skied behind Ann and watched her pick a course between them.

For the first time our sledges felt noticeably lighter.

But, after a few hours, the sun went in.

'Is there no such thing as the perfect travelling day?' Ann complained uncharacteristically.

Ann and I took it in turns to lead. We were better at steering a straight course than the others. With the going good, it was no harder work at the front and I much preferred it to shouting instructions from behind.

Through the cloud, Zoë spotted a rock on the horizon. We could not find it on our chart so we named it: Hudson (after Zoë Hudson) Ridge.

By the end of the day the light was spooky – soft white, so white it was almost dark. It was about midnight local time and I imagined I was walking alone down an unlit country lane. If the others had not been behind me, I would have been afraid.

Now that our sledges felt lighter, we planned to increase our skiing times.

'Let's add five minutes on to the morning marches,' Zoë said in the tent that evening. 'That means doing five marches of one hour and five minutes before lunch. Then three one-hour marches in the afternoon.'

'We'll never notice the extra five minutes, ' I agreed. 'But an extra twenty-five minutes in our day could mean we cover an extra mile.'

Day 29
14 nautical miles

We continued to work off a 25-hour day. This meant we woke an hour later each day. We were now starting to ski in the evening and finishing after midnight local time. We were getting used to the cold and, for now, it did not matter travelling into the sun because it was cloudy every day.

No wind. Then suddenly the sun came out. The snow glittered with light. It reminded me of a tacky Christmas card – even the air had water droplets that twinkled like fairy lights. The snow was a jumble of textures. Another circular rainbow around the sun.

Labouring behind Zoë, I felt exhausted. Zoë's skiing looked such hard work. When I was tired, going behind her made me feel worse.

'Now I've eaten *all* my chocolate, I feel a bit better,' I laughed at our second snack break. 'The trouble is, I'm just not interested. My sledge is too heavy and I can't be bothered.'

We laughed. We all felt the same so, for the rest of the day we pottered. I didn't concentrate. Instead, my mind whizzed. For the first time, I thought about work. I also tried to work out a plot for a novel.

We took longer over our snack breaks, chatting and gossiping. When Zoë called time, we took no notice. I had no concept of the speed we were travelling.

Towards the end, the light disappeared again. We were skiing into white cloud. The snow was the same but it no longer looked crisp and hard. Instead it seemed to be fluffy white powder and we could see dim blue shapes at either side.

'They're just big sastrugi,' I kept telling myself.

But I went very slowly.

No one mentioned the word crevasse, but when Zoë said: 'Don't you think we should put the leg loops on our harnesses?' we all did it without saying a word.

With no visibility, we shuffled about, trying to find a site to camp.

'I never thought we'd make it back to the tent,' Pom said later.

'Let's just hope we're not parked in the middle of a giant crevasse field,' I replied.

It was wonderful to discover we had covered fourteen nautical miles. Our plan of skiing eight hours and twenty-five minutes a day had worked.

Day 30
Christmas Eve
14 nautical miles

No wind again. And thankfully no crevasses. The snow was crisp. The sun was out again and the sastrugi were such magnificent shapes I spent the first two breaks photographing them. This meant I only had time to stuff a few squares of chocolate into my mouth before setting off again. The time after breakfast was the longest we went without food and I was always hungriest at the first break.

The lack of food had a dramatic effect. On the third march I felt weak. I could not keep up. My sledge felt suddenly monstrously heavy and I had no strength in my legs.

In front were Ann, Pom and Zoë. I could see from their strides that they were not moving unusually fast. The gap between Zoë and myself was widening, yet I could not rouse myself to go any faster.

My spirits plummeted and I went even slower. Thank God Rosie is behind me, I thought. I'm not left behind, I'm not at the back. I tried to will myself on.

'What's wrong?' the others asked when it was finally time to sit on our sledges and snack again.

'I don't know,' I said. 'I think it's because we've travelled for more than three hours and I've had almost nothing to eat or drink.'

'Are you mad, Caro?' Pom said. 'That's like trying to run a car without fuel.'

I felt foolish. They waited patiently while I demolished most of my snack bag.

Gradually my strength returned. And so too did my spirits. A band of golden light appeared to the east and I imagined a bay of white sea between us. Still no sign of the Thiel Mountains, even though they were only thirty miles away.

Incredible to think we were nearly at the Thiel Mountains. Suddenly every mile we did made a real difference. We all felt we were making progress.

* * *

'Have you thought what you are going to say to him yet?' Zoë asked.

'To who?' I said bemused.

'To Prince Charles, of course.'

I was so wrapped up in myself I had completely forgotten. Prince Charles had asked us to call him on the morning of Christmas Eve – we had been told he would wait for our call before leaving for his family Christmas in Sandringham.

Given our longitude, breakfast time at Highgrove was towards the end of our day. Zoë was in charge of the BT Iridium telephone and she took it carefully out of its box. Everyone, except Pom, who was filming, squeezed on to my sledge.

It was extraordinary. Sitting in the middle of Antarctica and telephoning our future king for a chat. Ann called out the number and I dialled it as if I called royalty every day.

I could hear the telephone ringing. A man's voice answered.

'Hello.'

We had been told Bernie the Butler would answer.

'Hello. Is that Bernie?' I asked.

'It is.'

'This is Caroline Hamilton,' I said. 'I am calling from Antarctica.'

'Ooh spooky, you sound as if you're just next door. Hang on a minute. I'll put you through to the Prince. He is expecting your call.'

Then: 'Hello. How marvellous to hear you. Are you all well? '

It was the Prince of Wales' unmistakable voice.

'I hope you're safe and warm in your tent.'

'No actually, we're sitting outside on our sledges. The sun's just come out again and we're having a wonderful time,' I enthused.

'Is it terribly cold?'

The Prince was easy to talk to. I felt very privileged to be chatting with him as I would a friend. As usual he was anxious to ask all sorts of questions. How many miles had we done? How many more to go? Did our sledges feel very heavy? He was particularly interested in what the ice looked like and Pom interrupted to say it was flat like Norfolk.

'What's your food like?' he asked.

'Your special fudge and Duchy Original biscuits are a high spot,' I said and thanked him profusely. 'But I have a confession to make. I'm afraid we couldn't wait until Christmas Day and we've been scoffing them all the way.'

'Well it was a very small contribution, I'm afraid,' he said.

We passed the BT Iridium between us and the Prince spoke to each of us in turn.

'Who am I speaking to now?' he'd ask. 'I can't tell who is who.'

'I know, we've been together for so long now, we all sound the same,' I replied.

The call lasted twenty minutes. We described the landscape and how we were getting on. It felt surreal. I imagined him sitting at the breakfast table with William and Harry and a large plate of kippers.

'I think you're all absolutely amazing, I really do. You will be in my thoughts and prayers,' he said. 'I wish you the very best of luck for the rest of the expedition. Goodbye.'

'Happy Christmas,' we all yelled down the telephone.

Suddenly it was quiet again. There was no wind any more and no prince to talk to. We all felt cold. We put on our skis and tried to return to our own reality. It was beautifully clear and we trudged along the side of a very gentle slope.

The ice stretched away for miles to our left. My eyes ranged across it. Something unusual caught my attention. Way out on the skyline, there was a shape – and then, to the left, three or four more. As I looked closer, they darkened.

'Look, I think those are crevasses over there,' I pointed and shouted to the others.

Pom skied up alongside me and spoke quietly.

'You could be right,' she said. 'They're just like the ridge next to our big crevasse. Aren't they sinister? Like a monster lurking under the sea.'

In my mind the shapes were the dark triangles of shark fins moving silently past us.

We were getting slower at everything. I thought we could benefit from another half day off. But there was no wind and it would have been a shame to waste the good weather.

'Besides,' said Rosie, 'we all really want to get to the top of the Thiel Mountains before resupply.'

Day 31
13 nautical miles

At last the Thiels appeared. Rosie went outside the tent twice without seeing them, and then she shouted: 'There's a huge great mountain in our way.'

I was in the porch putting on my boots. I shoved my head outside at once. On the southwest horizon there was a long jagged ridge sticking out of the ice.

'Oh wow, Rosie. Those must be the Thiel Mountains at last. Why didn't you mention them before?'

'You must think I'm stupid,' she said. 'But I didn't look that way when I came out to do the weather. And the mountain is in the direction of the wind so I had my poo with my back to it just now.'

Looking at the Thiel Mountains I felt excited. I remembered the day I first heard about them, sitting in Geoff's kitchen eating his homemade grapefruit and lemon marmalade. It was our first conversation about the South Pole and he had pointed to the Thiels on a map. Now, over a year later, we were nearly there. We had trudged almost 300 nautical miles in this great wilderness and managed to find them.

I felt a rush of pride in our compass – and in Ann's and my navigation. The Thiel Mountains meant so much to us all. We did not know what they looked like, but they were the only landmark we had had. There was something oddly familiar about them. They had acquired a powerful and magical significance.

I had yearned to see the Thiel Mountains. They were the halfway point on our journey. They were also the place we planned for our resupply.

We had made it this far. That was a triumph.

Christmas Day in England. A day for treats. Pom gave herself clean socks and new VBLs (vapour barrier liners – cheap plastic bags) for her feet. Ann washed with soap, gave herself a squirt of scent and put on clean socks. Rosie also had new VBLs and allowed herself a nutmeg and spices tea bag.

'I'll recycle this,' she said, wrapping the damp teabag in another plastic bag. 'Something to look forward to on millennium day.'

Zoë had nothing special except a Christmas cigarette.

'What about you, Caroline?' Ann asked. 'How are you going to celebrate Christmas?'

'With beef and potato stew, of course.'

It was my favourite dehydrated dinner and it did taste delicious.

Zoë and Ann called Niall at Patriot Hills to wish ANI a Happy Christmas. Then we set off.

The ice undulated gently as we skied towards the ridge. There was no way of knowing how far away it was. At times it loomed large to our right, at other times it disappeared beneath the horizon. Rocks began to appear and I wondered how large the mountains would be.

The sun shone brightly, bathing the Thiels pink. They glowed. Clouds striped the sky. *The Thiel Mountains*. I could hardly believe it. For two years they had seemed mythical. Impossible to imagine we would ever see them – but here they were.

I was elated, awestruck.

'I feel as if the mountains have just been sitting here,' I said, 'waiting for us, all this time.'

Zoë was quiet and insisted on skiing at the back. I looked round a few times and her movement looked painful and laboured.

'Is your back okay, Zoë?' I asked at a break.

She refused to speak and glared at me through her goggles.

Later, as we skied, I hung back at the end of the line.

'Come on, Zo, you've got to tell me. You're so good at helping other people when they're in pain, you're just stupid if you don't say what's wrong so we can help.'

After considerable cajoling, she eventually told me.

'The whole of my back hurts and my shoulder. I've got shooting pains down my arm like sciatica.'

It was clearly agony and I could see she was worried. We stopped a few times and I tried to adjust her harness. But nothing seemed to help. Later I took one of her poles and she skied slowly along with her bad arm tucked into her harness as a sling. I saw her lifting her arm behind her head, stretching her back to ease the pain.

It was frustrating not being able to help, but I could not help thinking how cross Zoë would be if her patients were as uncommunicative as she was. She sat on her sledge away from us all and continued not to talk.

'Ask her what she would do if it was me who was injured,' suggested Pom.

'I'd give you an anti-inflammatory,' Zoë responded quietly.

Well that was the answer, then. I took the medical bag from Zoë's sledge, tipped the contents out on to the ice and rummaged around for some tablets. To my relief, she took them willingly and her spirits revived a little.

As the day went on, though, her arm and shoulder got worse. A deep ache kept spreading from her back down her right arm. She tried to give herself energy by imagining she was a fearsome warrior. She had waves of sickening pain – she felt so nauseous she could hardly eat.

The black rocks sprinkled with snow loomed closer. It was difficult to tell but we hoped, when we pitched our tent, we were level with a ridge on Pom's map called Hamilton Cliff. Zoë was very tired. So too were Pom and Ann, who had spent far too much energy today trying to keep warm.

I was cold too. Wearing the wrong clothing again. We had a limited choice of layering to put on. Each morning, it was a tricky decision – one we had to live with all day. Should it be the thin thermal underwear, the thicker Rab Carrington ones or nothing at all? Did we need our all-in-one wind suit over the top? Through trial and error, we each developed the systems which suited us best. Even so, I always looked anxiously at what the others had chosen.

For most of the journey, I found the Pertex/pile jacket and salopettes supplied by Rab Carrington kept the wind out superbly. I started the journey without any long johns but then, as it got colder and windier, I wore the Rab long johns every day. Similarly, on top, I wore a thin thermal vest for the first few weeks before graduating to the Rab Pertex/pile one.

Ann and Pom decided to see what would happen if they did not wear vests. It was a disastrous decision. The jackets did not fit closely enough and the icy wind blew straight up from their waists and down into their legs. No matter how fast they skied, the blood ran cold in their veins. They could not warm up.

At lunchtime, they stripped off to put on more clothes. They shivered uncontrollably. Ann's flesh felt so cold I could have believed it was frozen.

As we pitched camp at the Thiel Mountains, we watched the cloud lift in a straight line across the sky. It was as if someone was lifting a blind.

Despite the traumas, everyone was cheerful when we settled into the tent. It was early afternoon on Christmas

Day back home and Ann was bursting to speak to her children. They were at home in Yeovil with her parents, her brothers and their children as well.

'Hello, darling,' she said to each in turn. There was chaos the other end as the five-year-olds frantically grabbed the telephone from each other. Their high-pitched voices filled the tent.

'What did Santa bring you?' Ann asked each of them – as if she didn't know what she had wrapped herself.

Everything she said was followed by more high-pitched squeals and unintelligible noises.

'I know what Santa gave them and I still didn't understand what they said,' she told us.

Next it was Rosie's turn. Her parents were with elderly relations and their Christmas was much more sedate. A call from Antarctica was treated quite normally.

'Happy Christmas, Uncle John. It's Rosie here . . . Oh, I'm sorry, Aunt Pay, I thought you were Uncle John.'

Embarrassed but unbowed, Rosie then asked for her mother.

'Hello, Mummy. Happy Christmas. We're nearly halfway there.'

Her mother was unmoved by the news.

'Still a long way to go then, dear,' she said.

My mother was staying with my brother Charles and his family and I called them slightly nervously. I thought it might make my being away worse if Mother heard my voice. But I could not have been more wrong. She was overwhelmed by the call and spoke almost as fast as the triplets had done.

'I'm sorry,' she said, 'I'm so excited I can hardly think let alone speak straight.'

What was clear was how extraordinarily well-informed my whole family was. They hung on to Julian's daily progress reports and I realised what a fantastic job he must be doing to keep them calm.

Mother wanted to know our exact coordinates so she could mark our position on the map she had bought.

'So you're nearly halfway,' she gushed. 'You're doing incredibly well. I can't believe the miles you're doing each day.'

Charles asked about battery power and how the solar recharging panel was working. They all asked detailed questions about our clothing systems and how we coped with the cold. As a family we do not normally communicate much, but there was so much love and support I got a real buzz. When I put the telephone down, I could not stop grinning.

Meanwhile, the Telephone Show continued. It made a welcome change from staying in every evening and watching the cookers.

Pom called Kent and was admonished by his mother.

'Why haven't you overtaken that husband and wife team yet?'

She appeared not to listen when Pom explained we had set off three weeks after them.

Last to go was Zoë. She had spent the last few days complaining her family was away and she did not know how to contact them. Finally, encouraged by our successes, she decided to call her grandmother.

She too was hugely excited.

'I never thought I'd hear from you, Zoë. The others have called me but I never thought I'd hear from you.'

Zoë asked if her grandmother had a number for her mother and sisters.

'Yes, dear, I do. Hold on a minute.'

And with that the telephone went dead. Zoë called back and it was engaged. She tried again and soon got frustrated. The minutes wore on and we got ready for bed.

Finally, Zoë got hold of her grandmother again.

'Sorry, dear. I thought I'd speak to your mother first and tell her you'd be calling.'

Poor Zoë. The fun of surprise was lost. I went to sleep to the sound of her chatter and thought about the days of the very first telephone. I wondered whether the thrill of our calls from so far away was comparable to the excitement generated then.

Day 32
Boxing Day
14 nautical miles

When we woke, I had a flash of inspiration. According to our local time, it was late in the evening on Christmas Day. By the time we got going it would be Boxing Day. It was Boxing Day in the UK as well. Because of our 25-hour days, it made sense to lose a calendar day at some time, so why not do it now?

It was a wonderful feeling of power.

'At last I've done it. I've finally done it. I've cancelled Christmas,' I wrote in my diary. No being cooped up indoors on top of my family, eating too much and arguing about what to watch on television. In 1999, for me at least, Christmas Day is erased.

Both 24 and 26 December appear in my diary but Christmas Day is missing.

Ann did not like what I had done. She insisted on calling it Christmas Day all day.

'This has been my best Christmas ever,' she enthused. 'Yesterday was my day for the kids and I did miss them, it's true. But today was our Christmas and I can't think of a better way to spend it.'

I also had an excellent day. The sky was blue, there was not much wind and we had a wonderful view of the mountains. They were big, black and strong – vast, immovable beings guarding the ice for millions of years. Steep cliff faces with roughly hewn features, each different and distinctive.

Zoë's arm was better with tablets but she still skied with one pole. Unable now to use her right arm and her pole to lean into the weight of her sledge, Zoë was exhausting herself. And that was quite apart from the pain which was draining her energy.

Rosie, too, was having a bad day.

'A porridge day,' she called it. We all had them. Days when everything seemed gloomy, your sledge was heavy and nothing – absolutely nothing – was right. It amazed me how we could all swing from good days to bad. There seemed to be no transition. One day you felt fantastic. The next, you were in the depths, thinking all the things you did not want to think. The vast white space opening up in front of you like a canvas with only your thoughts to fill it.

It seemed only Ann and I could keep a reasonably straight line. We were also the ones with the compasses and understood navigation best. One by one, the others were banned or banned themselves from skiing at the front. Today, the decision was made that Ann and I would take it in turns to lead.

As a present to Ann and Pom, Rosie and I took over their water and cooking duties for the evening. Like parents with small children, they sprawled in the tent watching us anxiously and laughing as we attempted to copy them.

Rosie was in charge of digging snow bricks. At the end of each day, she looked for snow that 'squeaked like polystyrene'. The quality was vital. The important thing was the density. Much of the snow was powdery, like granulated sugar; it had too much air in it.

As Ann and Pom did every morning and evening, we emptied all spare water bottles back into the pans for reheating. (We needed water to start the melting off – without it the snow burned the bottom of the pan and we were left with nothing.) It was a laborious process. One six-litre lump of snow melted down to only one inch of water.

There were three cookers and three pans each with coloured electrical tape on the handles: one black dinner pan, one silver six-litre pan, and one tall pan with a spout called Billy. Despite their different names, we used all of them to melt snow. It took forever.

Rosie and I sloshed water from pan to pan. All water was sluiced into Billy before being poured into bottles, mugs and the two vacuum flasks.

During the day, we carried hot water on our sledges. The bottles were stored in red cosies (ideal tent slippers when not being used) but the water was often too cold to drink by the end of the day – sometimes frozen. Even in the tent overnight, the bottles cooled considerably if we did not keep them in their cosies in our sleeping bags.

Water dripped from a glove on the drying line. The flame on a cooker sputtered but carried on.

'Oh, this is a good little cooker,' I said, mimicking Pom.

'Mugs,' cried Rosie, doing the same. 'Over here, now, otherwise you won't get any dinner.'

Each night, Ann wrote up the Dry Log.

'311 miles done, 299 miles to go,' she said, consulting the GPS.

Ahead lay 300 nautical miles. We were halfway. That evening it felt easy.

I wrote in my diary: '299 miles now seems like nothing at all.'

Day 33
15 nautical miles

The Thiel Mountains, they were my first thought – and my first words upon waking.

'The Thiel Mountains. I can't believe we're here.'

After yesterday's excitement, today it was business as usual. My lower back hurt and, at breaks, I lay on my sledge to ease the pressure.

I turned to Rosie, who had led the last march.

'Good effort, Rosie,' I said. 'But I'm afraid you've failed.'

'Failed?'

'We've been trudging along for four hours and twenty minutes,' I said, 'and the mountains aren't a millimetre closer.'

Eyes fixed upon the mountains, we gave each shape a name, spotted pictures in the snowy peaks.

'Look, a pussy cat's face.'

'That one looks like a Toblerone.'

'A sleeping donkey and a guinea pig.'

Pom had a bad day. Her left shoulder and arm ached again. She spent much more time than the rest of us with her goggles entirely iced up.

'You look tired,' I ventured.

'No, no, not at all. I'm fine. It's just that I can't see out of my frozen goggles,' she said.

I knew she was being brave. Pom and Zoë were now both skiing with one pole.

At last, the mountains got closer. Rising from the horizon. Snowy slopes. Huge hunks of rock, rising two or three thousand feet out of the ice.

'I wonder how high the mountains really are?' I said. 'How much rock is buried in the ice?'

We knew the ice beneath us was several thousand feet deep but Rosie's altimeter watch had gone mad. It kept insisting we were going downhill.

In order to avoid some known crevasses, Charles Swithinbank had given us a piece of advice: 'It's very simple,' he said. 'Aim for the Thiel Mountains and leave the left-hand nunatak [mountain] one mile to your right.'

So we did. From Patriot Hills, we skied every day on a slight diagonal, gradually making our way west, as well as south, towards the Thiels. As soon as we could see the mountains clearly, we aimed straight for the most easterly point of the Toblerone. Pom had drawn a simple version of one of Charles Swithinbank's maps and, according to it, the left-hand point was called the Nolan Pillar.

So far so good. The next problem was: how were we to judge a distance of one mile? Everything was so huge, we knew things looked much closer than they actually were.

In the tent, I looked at our chart of Antarctica. I studied the crosses that marked our progress.

'If we calculate how many miles west we've been going in the last few days and then keep the same course, we should be able to estimate when we're going to reach the line of longitude which is one mile away from the Nolan

Pillar,' I said. 'By my measurements, we need to be on 86 degrees, 45 minutes West.'

'We're on 85 degrees, 16 minutes South and 86 degrees, fifteen minutes West now. We've been travelling about 50 minutes West each day,' said Ann, consulting the Dry Log.

'That means in about another half day, we should be there,' I said.

'Oh wow. At lunchtime tomorrow, we can turn left and head south for the very first time.'

Ann and I looked at each other excitedly.

Day 34
13 nautical miles

We tried various tricks to dry and clean our clothes. Rosie and Zoë dried their jackets by hanging them up in the tent, but there was not enough room for us all to do that. The tent was always cluttered with food and cookers, stuff sacks with clothes in, diaries, toothbrushes, the medical bag and repair kit as well as all the wet things we hung on the drying line.

Pom and Ann often put their jackets in the porch with our boots overnight. The moisture froze and, in the morning, they could bang a lot of the ice out. Another night, Pom and I tried sleeping with our jackets between our sleeping bags and the ridged camping mats. It was a dismal failure.

'They look like toasted sandwiches,' laughed Rosie.

We tried cleaning our thermal underwear too. The best technique was to stamp on it outside in the snow and then 'dry' and air it in the sun. We tied things on to our sledges – again the snow would freeze and we could shake them dry.

Last night, Zoë went a stage further. Our salopettes and jackets wicked away our sweat as we skied but, by the end of the day, they were damp (the dampness never affected their warmth). Zoë poured water on to her salopettes, put them outside and, in the morning, they were a frozen lump. It took several hours of hard skiing before they dried out.

* * *

As we got closer to the Thiel Mountains, they lost their animal features and became primeval. Black rocks sticking out of the ice. For millions of years, I thought, they have been here, waiting and watching, for something to happen. They had seen no life – nothing growing, no birds, no trees, no insects. Just a handful of people, like us, on expeditions.

'No sign of the wingless midge then,' I joked. I had talked about the wingless midge before. 'The only permanent inhabitant of Antarctica. It's hard to imagine how it gets around.'

'I expect the mountains will be talking about us for years,' Zoë laughed.

Today we turned south.

Now, for the first time, we were heading directly for the South Pole. We began a steep climb. Down below, we could see blue ice strewn with boulders and rocks. Four weeks since we left the Ellsworth Mountains, four weeks of nothing, it was strange now to see such detail. For a moment, I thought the boulders were birds flocking on the ground. The wind had scooped out the snow around the southern end of the Nolan Pillar in just the same way it did around our tent.

Today the enormity of Antarctica hit me. I was struck, suddenly, by the total improbability of what we were doing – finding our way through a great, white nothing.

The GPS was there to reassure us – and to encourage us with our mileage – but, otherwise, we had navigated the entire distance with a watch, the sun and a £30 compass Pom's friend Errol had bought in Sydney.

The dog leg was over and every mile we did now was directly towards our goal. There were still 280 nautical miles to go – but one day soon the South Pole would appear in front of us. Until now, my sights had been set on the Thiels. Now, for the first time, I let myself wonder what it would be like when we saw the South Pole.

There was a sharp, icy wind. I kept my face down. All I wanted to do was to gaze to the south and dream of what lay ahead.

We were all very pleased with ourselves. After over 300 miles of 'left a bit, right a bit', we had arrived at the point Charles Swithinbank had told us to head for. The navigational challenge now was to keep going in a straight line south all the way to the Pole.

Day 35
12 nautical miles

Zoë's back was causing her terrible pain. I tried to mobilise it, but it didn't help. The waves of pain continued. As we set off, I saw that Zoë couldn't use her pole. I watched her trying to find a comfortable position. At snack breaks, she lay on her back on her sledge, staring at the sky.

With no differentiation, it was difficult to know we were going uphill. The only clear signs were that the horizon was shorter and our pulks felt much heavier. We were leaving the Thiels behind us. The best part of the day was sitting on our sledges looking at the view.

Up, up and further up. It was a slow, hard trudge. Each time we got to what I thought was the top, another steep climb appeared on the horizon.

'Do you think we're ever going to reach the top of this hill?' I asked.

'No, it's like Scotland,' Zoë said. 'One false summit after another. I hate it there.'

A triangular rock appeared to our right. It looked like a Cornish pasty. It was so unimpressive after the Thiels, yet it was the top of a mountain taller than most mountains in Europe. Just the very top peeking up out of the ice. The Lewis Nunatuk. Charles had told us about it and suggested we look at it. But no one wanted us to go out of our way. There was no need to discuss it.

We stopped after seven marches, and were amazed when Ann read our mileage off the GPS.

'Yesterday we were at 85 degrees, 29 minutes South and

today we're at 85 degrees, 41 minutes. That's 12 miles,' she said, triumphantly.

'Just shows the power of the polar plod,' Rosie said.

We had ten days of supplies left. I spoke to Julian. 'We need to start organising the resupply. It would be great to keep going with lighter sledges,' I said, 'but we only have enough food and fuel for ten more days.'

Later that night ANI told us our resupply would arrive the next day. I was off darning duty. Everyone's gloves had huge holes, but I was not about to mend them – not with new ones on the way.

Day 36
14 nautical miles

With resupply due, I wrote a letter to my mother and brothers. Ann telephoned Niall to finalise arrangements.

'No resupply today,' he told her.

'What do you mean?'

'You're not down to your last Mars bar yet, are you?'

'No.'

'Well then you're not high priority.'

'Everybody lies about how much food they've got,' Pom said. 'We're being penalised for being honest.'

We had no choice but to set off again. More uphill.

We were rather relieved not to have had the resupply that morning. Our sledges were light and the sky was like blue glass. Today the sastrugi looked like speedboats and shark heads. They tended to be a similar size throughout an area. We might have a hundred miles of small sastrugi, then larger ones for the next hundred miles. I wondered how long the sastrugi lasted – whether the same area had big sastrugi all year round.

As the sastrugi got larger, they were more uncomfortable to ski over. If the side of the ridge was soft, our skis could slide through. But if they were harder, we had to lift our ski tips up and over. (Our ski tips were broken and splintered by the end of the journey from bashing into sastrugi – and other people's sledges in a whiteout).

The end of the ridge pointing into the wind was V-shaped. The wind rushed past and granules of snow were blown along the ridge on either side. If there was lots of snow blowing along the ground and past the sastrugi, it was like standing in a shallow fast-running stream and watching the water rush past you. We could see the sastrugi changing in front of our eyes.

Pom's hands suffered most from the cold. I sewed patches on the thumbs and fingers of her gloves.

'Bit chunky,' I said when I handed them to her. 'I may not qualify yet for the Honorary Company of Glove Makers. But they are certainly classier than Rosie's French seams on her frayed blue gloves.'

'They are keeping my hands much warmer Caro,' Pom said triumphantly. 'And a red-letter day: the first when my goggles didn't entirely freeze up.'

'Hoorah,' said Zoë. 'It worked then, not covering your nose and mouth under the face mask.'

It was a mystery why some days our goggles misted up and on others they did not. It seemed to help if you could prevent your breath getting in from under your mask.

Pom and I both cut large square holes in the mouths of our balaclavas to make more room for our breath. Pom looked very sinister in hers. I chuckled when we posted our snacks.

Day 37
Millennium Eve
14 nautical miles

I spent most of the afternoon in a trance, thinking about the millennium. I had been looking forward to the year 2000 all my life. As a child, I remembered imagining what I would be doing. I could never have envisaged I would be skiing to the South Pole.

Now I was here, the date seemed meaningless. The five of us scarcely mentioned the millennium. I thought about that a lot. I did not miss being at home at all. Instead I had a sense that where we were was more important than the rest of the world.

Antarctica is timeless. For millions of years it has remained the same. While the rest of the world gets up to its trivial business, Antarctica is a white, unchanging giant. Bigger and more powerful than anything else.

With not many days before resupply, our sledges were light. I was weightless in my trance and, as I skied, I wondered what the millennium had in store. I hoped for a fresh start for the world. I had a sense of wanting to wipe the slate clean – and where better to do it than on an enormous icy white slate? For myself, I had no plans beyond reaching the South Pole.

Skiing in front of Pom, I heard a noise like a jet fighter.

'What was that?' Pom started like a frightened horse.

The snow seemed to move and sink beneath us. We were surrounded by a reverberating thunder.

'What was that?'

'I don't know.'

'It could be anything.'

'It could be a crevasse.'

The noise was everywhere.

It only lasted a couple of seconds, but there was no way of knowing where it came from.

We skied on.

And it happened again. And again.

The ice was trembling. I felt very afraid, acutely aware of how small and insignificant we were – pitted against the forces of nature. Tingles ran down my spine.

'I feel as if at any moment, we could be crushed to nothing,' Pom said.

At the end of the penultimate march, it was past midnight GMT. We gave each other a big hug and a kiss.

'Happy new year.'

That night, sitting in the tent, I reminded myself this was the new millennium that, as a child, I had so looked forward to.

'I had all sorts of imaginings for my future self,' I told the others. 'But I never thought I'd be sitting in a tent in Antarctica, patching gloves for Ann and Pom.'

Day 38
1 January 2000
8 nautical miles

Strange that we should call a day in which we trudged for five hours through snow at minus 20°C 'an easy day'.

'What's your position?' Niall at ANI asked again.

'The same as it was last night. 86 degrees, 8 minutes, 57.2 seconds South, 86 degrees, 29 minutes, 12.2 seconds West.'

'Sastrugi?'

'Completely flat.'

'What's the wind speed?'

'Two knots.'

'What about contrast and visibility?'

'The contrast is excellent and visibility unlimited to the horizon.'

'Well you won't have a resupply today,' Niall said. 'Our Twin Otter's only just got back to Patriot Hills and the pilots need a rest.'

'Why do they keep asking for all these details if they're not going to come?' Zoë complained.

Our resupply had been due eleven days before. Thanks to the extra rations we started with, we had been able to carry on for a further 147 miles (our fuel consumption was less than we had expected as well). ANI had said they were coming two days ago. Now we only had seven days' food and fuel left. The snow conditions and weather were perfect, but we didn't know how long it would last. Each perfect weather day without resupply felt like an opportunity wasted.

We talked a lot about ANI and the nightmare job the staff had at Patriot Hills. We tried to work out why they had changed their minds about resupplying us. Why had they chosen to resupply Geoff's clients before us? We did not believe that Geoff would have been down to his last day of food, as they told us. Also, it did not fit in with an earlier report from ANI that two of his party wanted to give up and be flown the last miles to the Pole.

As we had light sledges, we decided to make the most of it and get as far uphill as possible before resupply. This meant not having another rest day until the resupply came. But we were getting more and more tired – and frustrated. Our heads were telling us to keep going but our hearts and bodies were telling us to rest. We grew irritable.

'An all-time record this morning,' I said as I prepared to follow Rosie and Zoë out of the tent. 'Four and a half hours since waking up.'

'There are reasons for that.' Ann was defensive. 'We're still waiting for resupply, you had to wake up in the middle of the night to do an interview with Radio 5, we're tired, Pom and Rosie both had massages in Zoë's shoulder clinic . . .'

'It's not a criticism,' I rushed to reassure her. 'I know there are reasons. I know we need a rest day. It's just I'm worried that we've been rolling the clock forward more than an hour and a half each day; we're travelling later and later.'

'We're banking on a whole day of sleep when the resupply comes,' Ann said, 'but I'm worried that, by the time we finally get to our rest day, we'll find it's in the middle of our night and we won't get any extra rest at all.'

'That's why I was tense about the length of our breaks yesterday too,' I explained. 'Every extra minute is eating into our rest day.'

'I agree,' said Pom. 'I think we should try to get our clocks the same as at Patriot Hills so it's easy to call at a useful time for them. Maybe we should only do five hours' skiing today. That would be good for Zoë's shoulder too,' she said.

I went outside and told the others our plan.

Later, in the tent that evening, Rosie said tentatively: 'I'd just like to make a point. I don't want to make an issue of it. But I do think –'

'Go on, spit it out,' Ann laughed.

'You should have involved Zoë and me in this morning's discussion. It's not that I don't agree with you, but we should have been part of the decision-making process. It's our decision too.'

'You're right,' I said instantly. 'I am very sorry.'

'That's an end to it,' said Rosie. 'I just needed to get that off my chest.'

Day 39
0 nautical miles

We called ANI with our position and weather reports. They said they would try and send the resupply early the next morning. They told us to call again in a few hours' time and we decided to undress and get back into our sleeping bags again instead of skiing.

Day 40
11 nautical miles

'It's not coming today, is it?' said Ann who had woken early to call ANI with our position and weather reports again. There was a slightly desperate tone in her voice. 'It is? Oh fantastic. Thank you.'

After two weeks of waiting and anticipation, the re-supply aeroplane was finally on its way. It was tremendously exciting. We had discussed resupply so many times. Once it was completed, we knew our sights could be set on the Pole. Nothing else, we believed, would stand in our way.

But first we had to get the resupply right – and we only had one chance. We went through the list of equipment again over breakfast. Pom had been awake a long time and seemed very tense. The others said I was too. I was aware only of wanting to concentrate.

We knew the pilots would not wait long on the ice so it was essential for us to be efficient. When our resupply boxes arrived on the aeroplane, we needed to be certain what we were taking and what we were sending back.

Some important issues still needed to be resolved.

'Have we made a decision about the rope?' I asked, going through the list.

We only needed the rope for crevasses and we all remembered someone had told us we were unlikely to find crevasses this far South. The problem was none of us could remember who it was.

'Who told us we wouldn't need it?' Pom asked. 'I think it was Pen. I don't know how he knows since he hasn't been here.'

Ann and I thought it was Geoff.

Or was it Liv when we visited her in Norway?

'The problem is,' Ann said, 'we won't know until it's too late.'

In the end, Rosie said she would be very nervous if we left the rope behind so, on the strength of that, we agreed to take it.

'How about the harnesses?' I asked.

If the risk of crevasses was reduced, we had discussed taking the safety leg loops off the harnesses to reduce weight. Other decisions had to be made. The tent poles, for instance. They had stood up to the cold brilliantly so far. They were still quite flexible and, provided we undid them under the fly sheet, the joints came apart well (we undid every other joint). There was one small crack we had mended with duct tape. There was a spare set of poles in one of the boxes.

'I think we should take the spare set, just in case,' Pom said.

'You mean have two sets of poles?' I asked. 'I thought we'd agreed to swap them over so we've got a new set to see us through to the end. Otherwise, it's an awful lot of excess weight.'

'Yes, Caro, but it's going to get much colder and I don't think any of us fancy pitching the tent with broken poles,' Pom said.

I was perplexed. But there was no time to argue. We needed to eat and sort out our things as well as get outside to mark an airstrip. As we had told ANI, the ice could not have been flatter, with very few bumps or sastrugi. It was nothing like trying to land amongst the broken sea ice of the Arctic.

We knew from our experiences there how important it was that the pilots had confidence in us. On the North Pole expedition, the pilots said they did not trust Matty's weather reports or her ability to find suitable smooth bits of ice. There were occasions when aeroplanes had to turn back.

We did not want the pilots to think we did not know what we were doing, especially if we needed them in an emergency. While Ann and Pom continued water boiling, Zoë and I assembled our rubbish and the few other things we were sending back and Rosie set about pacing an airstrip.

This needed to be parallel with the wind and at least 1,200 feet long and 50 feet wide. Any bumps more than six inches high might damage the aeroplane and we had been told to mark them with a sledge or dustbin bag. We marked the four corners in a similar way and put another sledge halfway down the left-hand side.

I was still towing my sledge when we heard the Twin Otter arrive. A whirring, mechanical noise somewhere in the sky behind us.

'Quick, it's coming,' Zoë shouted.

I stood transfixed. The aeroplane came closer and circled above us. For an awful moment, I thought the pilots had decided they could not land. But no. Predictably, perhaps, they had seen somewhere better and, within no time, the aeroplane was taxiing towards us. It stopped thirty yards from our tent, huge and incongruous.

There were colours on the aeroplane we had not seen for weeks – including yellow and brown – and the hard lines of the fuselage were all wrong. We ran towards it as Ann and Pom came out of the tent, struggling to put on their hats and gloves.

'You're half an hour early,' we cried and gave the pilots big hugs.

One of them was John, who had flown us in the North.

'Why, it's good to see y'all again,' he said. 'It looks as if all's going well here. Can I take your photograph?'

It was lovely to see him. Somehow it felt less of an intrusion than if they had both been strangers.

We unloaded the boxes, rummaging around for what we needed. We wanted to catch up on gossip with the pilots. But at the same time, we needed to concentrate on finding what we needed and counting out the correct number of days' food and fuel.

After an hour, we were done. The pilots wished us good luck and climbed back into the aeroplane. The engines were deafening. Hard pellets of snow flew up from the ground and covered us as we stood waving goodbye.

Suddenly, there was nothing but silence.

'What a relief to be on our own again,' said Rosie, as we hurried back to the tent to warm up.

'Hoorah. We've done it.' Zoë flung her arms around Ann and me.

I too felt a sense of relief. But I was also feeling upset and unnerved.

'What's wrong with Pom?' I asked Zoë. 'She's been horrid to me all morning. Not just in the tent but also when we were going through the boxes.'

'Oh, don't worry about it,' she said. 'I think we've all been tense.'

Zoë lit a whole cigarette from one of the resupply bags. She took her first long, contented drag since Day 23, when she started cutting each cigarette in half to conserve them.

I could not get Pom's coldness to me out of my head. When we discussed whether we needed all the food and other equipment we had taken (including the tent poles), she seemed to think I was stupid. Everything I said earned a put-down. Everything I did seemed to irritate her.

I convinced myself Pom hated me. I got myself into a terrible spin. I knew I was getting things out of proportion and that I should talk to Pom, but I did not trust myself not to say something dreadful. I feared I would break down in tears.

I stayed silent for most of the day, wanting to keep out of the way. I tried to think about other things. But for large parts of the day, I was overwhelmed with self-pity. I felt completely worthless. I found myself sobbing into my goggles unable to stop.

Everyone asked me what was wrong.

'Oh, nothing,' I said to each of them, still crying.

I knew they wanted to help but I did not know how to ask. I felt pathetic – as if I was letting them down by not being an emotional rock.

Day 41
11 nautical miles

The journey was beginning to take its toll on our bodies.

In addition to all her other tasks, for several weeks now Pom had been making bespoke snack bags for us all. Responding to our childish whims about food, she took almonds out of my bag and replaced them with extra chocolate and she gave Rosie extra nuts. Rosie rarely ate all her rations and I was not sure she believed the rest of us when we told her she was losing weight.

'No chance of me starving,' said Ann, patting her stomach.

Ann and I had put on the most weight before we went out – 28 pounds and 18 pounds respectively. We reckoned it would just about see us through.

'In fact, I'll be bloody annoyed if I don't lose it all by the time we get back,' said Ann.

Today was no better emotionally for me than yesterday. Beautiful weather – a huge blue sky and hot sun. The others were relaxed and enjoying themselves. When we pitched camp, I sat alone on the ice some way away from the tent. I adored the simplicity of the ice, the cloudless blue sky and the simple line of the horizon. I found it calming to be with it on my own for a change.

For the first time, I listened to Antarctica. Without any wind or the sound of our cookers or sledges, the silence was deafening. More powerful than any silence I knew. My slightest movement seemed to echo in the blue dome of the sky. I scarcely wanted to breathe.

'Shall we have our Christmas tonight?' Ann asked.

It was quiet in the tent and Ann looked at me. 'Or are we all too glum?'

'I'm not glum,' chirped Pom.

'Yeah, let's do it,' I said, very flat.

When we had planned our resupply in Punta Arenas, it was scheduled for 20 December and we had put our Christmas gifts to each other in the resupply boxes. Now Ann cracked open the whisky mac (whisky and ginger wine) Julian had sent us for New Year's Eve. It tasted like nectar. I wished I was in better spirits.

The challenge had been to find something excessively small and light. In the spirit of Christmas, I also chose to make my gifts useless.

'Condoms?' Ann guessed when I told her my plan.

'No, we've got those from Julian's secretary Chris,' I said, holding up what she had sent us.

I gave everyone false stick-on fingernails. Ann gave us each a miniature bottle of alchohol and a St Christopher medal. I put Pom's present on the same chain – a silver Spanish pendant. Zoë gave everyone a miniature book. Mine was *A Little Chicken Soup for the Soul – Inspiring Stories for Self-Affirmation*. It could not have been more appropriate. I was very touched by the gifts the others had brought. They made me realise how much we relied on each other and how lucky I was to have their love and support.

We had letters too and we read out snippets or passed them round. There was a letter from my mother.

Darling Caro,
All's well here, though of course I miss you. Every time the wind blows more than its usual norm I think of you. I wonder if it's being a tougher expedition than you had anticipated. Julian writes very informative emails every

other day, so with the Internet as well I feel very much in the know, and it's very exciting which removes any fear that I might have felt.

There was a letter, too, from my brother Charles.

My dear Caro, he wrote, it is very strange that you will be receiving this in the middle of absolutely nowhere and I hope that it finds you all in good heart.

Mum has been in pretty high spirits once you got going and is obviously very proud of you, as of course are we. We will be on Mull for the New Year which is not quite as romantic as the Antarctic but it is the best we can do! The whole country is going to grind to a complete halt for about a fortnight and I am very envious that it is not of the slightest concern to you.

Keep walking and keep warm and the very best of luck. We are thinking of you.

Day 42
12 nautical miles

Started the day doing a live interview with Jenny Murray on *Woman's Hour*. I wasn't in the mood, but she asked good questions.

'Do you mind my asking – how do you go to the toilet?'

'It's very easy. We've got a zip which runs between our legs and all we have to do is unzip it and squat down.'

I made it sound easy. I did not mention that I planned each loo stop in advance. Didn't tell her that I psyched myself up for the nightmare of the cold – and the wind blowing up my bottom and spraying pee over my harness and compass as they dangled down. I loved using ice wedges instead of loo paper but gosh, they were cold.

I also omitted to tell Radio 4's listeners about the zips. The problem with my wind suit (a layer of Pertex worn like a petrol pump attendant) was the palava of undoing the zip. There was also the difficulty of negotiating Miriam's Velcro (which could have moored the *Titanic*) and undoing the zip on my salopettes. For this, I needed to take my big gloves off, leaving me with only thin inner gloves. By the time I squatted and checked the gap in my thermal underwear was in the right place, I was usually too numb to feel anything. We helped each other constantly.

'This has to be the biggest reason not to do the expedition solo,' I said to Ann as she fumbled between my legs for the umpteenth time.

'Very easy,' I told Radio 4. 'No problem at all.'

'How do you feel about the news that the other group, led by Geoff Somers, has reached the Pole?' Jenny Murray asked.

'I'm absolutely thrilled,' I said.

The truth was I felt nothing. I was more concerned with us.

At the end of the call, Jenny Murray said Julian needed us to call him urgently. Julian said he had an email from Anne Kershaw at ANI saying we had not paid for a dedicated pick up from the Pole and that we were scheduled to fly out that day or the next.

'What on earth do you mean?'

He told me Anne had been 'following the expedition closely' and she estimated it would take us another twenty days to reach the Pole. The implication was we would have to pay more money if we wanted to keep going.

'Now,' said Julian, 'I have to ask you a very important question. Did anyone from ANI ever inform you of the consequences of setting off three weeks late? That is, did they ever tell you that if you didn't get to the Pole by 5 January, you'd have to come off the ice?'

'No,' I said. 'Absolutely not.'

'Good,' said Julian. The relief in his voice was palpable.

'And when Pom asked Anne in a fax before you left England what would happen if you didn't get there by a certain date, did you get a response?'

I repeated the question to Pom.

'She said not to worry about any of the dates,' said Pom. 'She said the dates were only there to make sense of the contract. She said we shouldn't worry when we arrived, ANI would just have to accommodate us.'

'I've been speaking to Bob Elias,' Julian said, 'and we're very worried about the potential psychological impact of this on you girls. I don't want you all worrying about it. Your job is to get to the Pole. Leave me to deal with this. And keep a look out for the others too, Caroline. You must keep focussed. We don't want anyone thinking this is a good excuse to get home to a nice warm bed . . .'

When I got off the telephone, I repeated our conversation to the others. It was the final straw for us with ANI. Why had they not said anything before? Why did they bother to resupply us? What did Anne mean when she said she had been watching the expedition closely? Surely it must have been obvious from the day we set off we were not going to get to the Pole before the end of January.

We were outraged. The ANI issue focussed our minds again on how to improve efficiency. Fired up, we went at a furious pace. At breaks, we talked hurriedly about possibly reducing our food and equipment so we could go faster.

'I don't think we should throw away food. Two hundred miles is still a very long way,' I said. 'Anything could happen. Potentially we may have five days' too much food, but I don't think that's a very big contingency. If our mileage drops because of bad weather or someone sprains their ankle, we may need to use it.'

Zoë, too, was measured. 'I don't think we should panic on the basis of one telephone call,' she said.

We agreed to stick to our plan, keep plodding and we would get there.

'If we go mad and go too fast, we're bound to compromise safety,' we agreed.

Day 43
12 nautical miles

Another long call to Julian meant a record slow start of six hours this morning.

Julian said: 'I've spoken to Anne Kershaw. She needs to keep the camp at Patriot Hills open longer than she anticipated, and she's asked us to pay another $175,000 so they won't have to come and pick you up off the ice before you get to the Pole.'

Julian had obviously spent a frantic forty-eight hours, speaking to Pen, Flo and Bob, as well as a lawyer. We did not have any more money, and we'd already paid handsomely for ANI's services before we left the UK. We drafted a letter with Julian to send them.

Big sastrugi. Much bigger than anything we had seen so far. They were eight or ten feet high and looked like frozen sand dunes. Very beautiful. The surface of the snow was mostly grey, not white, but the sastrugi caught the light and were dazzlingly white.

We had to zigzag our way through to avoid having to climb or step up and down. The sun cast the sastrugi in long shadows. Our sledges felt slightly less heavy again. We went back to our five marches of an hour and five minutes with three one-hour marches after lunch.

The lunch break was an important psychological boost. It was possible to have a bad morning and a good afternoon, especially as the one-hour marches seemed much shorter. Ann was motherly at lunch. She poured hot chocolate for Zoë and me and tea for Rosie and Pom and passed it to us on our sledges.

Sitting there, feeling proud, I said: 'Who would ever have imagined we could ski 500 miles?'

'I know it's amazing,' Ann said, 'but we've still got another 200 to go.'

It didn't seem possible. I still couldn't visualise 200 miles – or 500 miles. It was an unimaginable distance. We had been prepared and focussed about everything – except the distance and what that meant. When we had talked or written about it, they were just words. They didn't mean anything. We were beginning to face the fact that 604 nautical miles (695 statute miles) was an awfully long way to ski.

Normally I felt slight pain in my leg at the end of each day – a pulling at the front of my left shin. Today it came on badly on the third march. I used my right pole as a crutch and leant on it at an angle as I skied for several hours. During breaks, I checked my laces were not to blame and there were no knots in my VBL. Then Zoë gave me some anti-inflammatory drugs.

'Are you sure you're all right to carry on?' the others asked at the end of the penultimate march.

'Provided nobody minds going very slowly,' I said.

They shook their heads and I shuffled off at a snail's pace. My shin hurt slightly less and I realised we were going downhill for the first time since we started. The sastrugi were up to ten feet high. They looked old and gnarled, stretching as far as we could see.

I looked round to check the others were OK. There was Ann tripping along as usual, and Zoë labouring with one pole. Pom was taking photographs and Rosie was dreaming with her face tilted to the sky, enjoying the sun. I did not like skiing directly into the sun. I was alarmed to see Rosie was skiing without any protection for her eyes.

'It really worries me when you don't wear goggles,' I said to her later in the tent. 'The sun is incredibly bright and it would be such a stupid thing to do to go and get snow blindness. It's incredibly painful and, apart from being a hospital job for you, Rosie, it might be the end of the expedition for all of us. ANI could claim that we didn't know what we were doing and evacuate us.'

'Don't worry, I won't do anything stupid,' Rosie replied. 'It's just that I love the sun on my face and seeing the colours as they really are without a tint from my goggles. This way, I feel part of Antarctica, as if I'm really here.'

In the meantime, Zoë was prodding my leg.

'Feel that crunching,' she said with glee, inviting Ann to press the offending shin as well.

I wiggled my foot up and down. It hurt.

'You have crepitus in one of your tendons,' she advised.

'Are you sure? That sounds rather too old and unglamorous for me,' I replied.

Zoë put me on more tablets and told me to take three a day until we reached the South Pole.

'Charles Swithinbank told me what the booming ice was,' Julian reported back that evening. 'Firnstofs.'

'What are they?'

'Layers of hoarfrost – which can be very big – being dislodged slightly and then settling three or four feet down.'

Only 190 nautical miles left. We were down in the hundreds. I began to get a sense of the huge distance we were travelling – and the unrelenting nature of our journey. As I put down my mat and got into my sleeping bag, I thought this is the forty-third time I've done this. Every day began and ended the same way. I began to feel impressed with myself.

I always knew we wouldn't give up. Yet, I had never really focussed on what sixty days of concentrating on only one thing – going south – and doing the same thing over and over would be like.

'Please can we do something different tomorrow,' I joked to the others.

We laughed. We were all feeling the same.

Day 44
10 nautical miles

The ANI situation was slowing us down. We had agreed to call Julian every day so we could keep up to date and discuss it. Today he told us Anne Kershaw had received his letter and was refusing to deal with him as our representative. She wanted to speak to me direct.

It was Friday afternoon in the UK. I left a message at her office to say I would call on Monday.

* * *

As soon as I stood in my boots outside the tent, my tendon hurt. Over the first marches it got worse and then worse. We skied for eight hours and twenty-five minutes – that was 30,300 seconds, which was 30,300 strides. 15,150 strides with my left leg and, with every single one, my left shin throbbed.

All day we clambered up and over icy snow dunes, trying to steer a course between them. I wasn't in the mood. Head down, trying to keep sliding my left foot forward and ignoring the pain.

The ANI saga continued to dominate as we trudged. I was aware we were beginning to concentrate on external forces now, rather than thinking about ourselves as a team. I worried about the effect ANI's threats were having on our morale.

It was getting much colder. The hazelnuts in our snack bags froze like pellets. Minus 25°C and an eight-knot wind blowing continuously into us from the southeast. Snow like big crystals of sugar. Cold wind made it difficult to talk at breaks. I wanted only to relax my leg.

At the last break, I was relieved everybody was exhausted. Together we limped the last march.

'What were you thinking when we were skiing along then?' Ann asked.

'Thank God we haven't got to ski back like Scott,' I confessed.

We all laughed.

'Did you really think that?' Ann asked. 'I thought I was the only one feeling crap. As I skied all I could think was: I hope it's not going to be like this all the way to the Pole.'

Tonight everything was frozen. The tent was so cold my goggles did not steam up when I came in – even though the cookers had been on for thirty minutes. As usual, we put things on to the pan lids to warm – Vaseline, butter, sun cream – but it did not work. Even the seals on the freezer bags stayed frozen. Instead of our usual starter of hot soup, we went straight to dinner and one hot drink before bed. It knocked an hour off the whole process.

Day 45
11 nautical miles

The sastrugi slopes reminded me of scrapyards of twisted ice. Some looked very old; lumps of bright white ice. Silent and unchanging. The wind making patterns around them. Wind patterns like waves. Shapes of white horses, ripples and tidal swell – frozen in one moment of motion. Our skis and sledges clattered over them. The sledges jerked and pulled as they fell in troughs.

We developed different mental techniques for keeping going: Ann and I counted our steps, while Zoë found it helpful to try to imagine we had taken everything out of her sledge.

We were hopeful the ANI saga was drawing to a close. We relaxed a little and invented stories about ANI to keep us amused.

'What will you do if they come to pick you up?' Julian asked on our call.

'We won't get on the aeroplane,' I said simply.

'I advise a starburst,' he said. 'If you all ski off in different directions they won't be able to catch you.'

'I have fantasies of burly men trying to bundle us into an aeroplane while you film the whole thing and I'm on the telephone to ITN,' I told Pom.

'I have visions of pilots trying to trap us with giant shrimping nets,' she replied.

Day 46
11 nautical miles

The sun was hot. Seeringly, unbelievably hot. Even with my goggles on, if I looked at the sun it hurt my face. It pierced my eyes – like something sharp. Yet the ice did not melt at all.

It was minus 25°C and falling, but we could sit on our sledges without down jackets and not get cold. A few days earlier I had developed a brown stripe on my left cheek – the effect of the cold wind creeping under my mask and lashing my face. Slightly sore and itchy, the skin went dark and then hardened before peeling off, like sunburn.

I applied cream and always kept it covered – even when the sun was hot and I longed for fresh air. Just as it was beginning to heal, along came the wind and split the skin again.

Zoë fashioned a piece of white lint and stuck it across my face with zinc oxide tape. I looked as if I had been in a pub brawl. Today Pom, who had also developed a brown mark on her face, copied my cheek patch. With a white lint patch on her left cheek and a preventative one on her right, she called herself Apache Indian. We agreed Zoë's invention was a brilliant device for keeping out all weathers.

The last three hours we had the sun directly in our eyes again. Zoë skied up to me while I was leading and I could see she was agitated. I could not hear exactly what she was saying through her mask – something about Rosie ignoring medical advice.

I turned round to look and then gestured to Zoë to keep calm.

'Please don't ski without your goggles on,' I said to Rosie quietly as we flopped down on to our sledges for a break.

Rosie roared back. 'I don't need you or Zoë or anyone else to tell me what to do. I can tell whether the sun is too bright for my eyes or not, thank you. I'm certainly not going to jeopardise the expedition, if that's what you're worried about.'

There was a stunned silence.

It was the first time any of us had lost our temper and I was completely taken aback.

'I'm terribly sorry Rosie, I really didn't mean to make an aggressive statement,' I said.

Zoë was very quiet that evening in the tent. The tensions between her and Rosie had not gone away. Zoë felt Rosie lacked concentration. Rosie felt Zoë was impatient with her. The rest of us babbled that evening about nothing much. I wondered whether to mention the goggles again. Rosie liked to emphasise how important it was that we all looked after each other. How unfair it seemed now that she did not want to be reminded.

Day 47
10 nautical miles

A quiet day. Zoë did not talk to anyone and Ann was edgy and tense. The needles on both our compasses were moving increasingly slowly and they had developed air bubbles which interfered with their movement. We shook them to get them to perform but, quite often, the needles went mad.

Ann eventually gave up on her compass and, when leading, just used the sun. Occasionally, according to my compass, she went slightly off course. Today, when I suggested a small change of direction, she was very annoyed.

'Why don't you use my compass?' I asked.

From then on we both used my compass. We wore it on our harness on a piece of pink string, swapping at breaks.

I was quiet. I felt Rosie had over-reacted about her goggles and wondered if anything had gone wrong between us. Having so little time or space away from each other was difficult. Private conversations were impossible.

I worried about Rosie. I worried she was getting too thin and she seemed to be losing her memory. There were occasions where she appeared to forget conversations that had taken place that day.

Rosie was not the only one. We were all more tired than we liked to admit. We had skied 460 nautical miles and still had another 145 to go. It was getting much colder. The uphill slope must end soon, I told myself. Why do people refer to a Polar Plateau, if it doesn't flatten out at the top?

I thought about the others. We all wanted to get to the Pole now. We laughed about the situation with ANI but I knew it was adding to our stress. None of us could help thinking about what might happen. It was a constant topic of conversation at our breaks. Someone would start the conversation and then, an hour later at the next break, someone else would carry it on. I was one of the worst offenders, I knew that, but the more we thought about ANI, the less we thought about each other.

Day 48
0 miles

I spoke to Anne Kershaw.

'When do you think you'll reach the Pole?' she asked. 'I'm wondering whether I can jolly you along a bit.'

'We're doing 11 or 12 miles a day,' I said. 'You can rest assured we're not hanging around.'

'So that would mean another ten or eleven days, would it?'

I was very unwilling to make a commitment. I did not want to give a date and then not be able to make it.

'I'm not really sure why you're asking me this,' I said. 'We're certainly within the 60 to 70 day schedule we always talked about. If you're asking us to go faster and compromise safety . . .'

'I'm just asking you to do the best you can. We've worked so well together in the past, Caroline, I'm hoping you'll help me out.'

I didn't know where the conversation was going and it made me nervous.

'If you're asking us now to pay more money . . .'

I was on the telephone for half an hour. At the end, Anne agreed to confirm that ANI would pick us up from the Pole when we got there and take us back to Punta Arenas. She also said we did not owe them anything more for their support.

I was shaking when I turned the telephone off. It was such a relief.

'Well done, Caro,' said Ann. 'I could never have stood up to her like that.'

'Phew. I never thought that, for us, dealing with ANI would be the hardest part of getting to the South Pole,' said Rosie.

The anxiety now over, I made a little speech to the others.

'I think we're all focussing too much on how many days we have to go,' I said. 'Rosie makes no secret of the fact she wants to be home for her birthday on 25 January. And Pom, in particular, often mentions the distance still to go. We should be concentrating on enjoying ourselves again. We need to put our energies into being nice to each other. I think we've become too insular. There's no point in sulking, even if we think we're justified. Perhaps we should think about re-allocating tasks,' I added.

'There's no point in that,' Ann said.

Zoë agreed. 'Especially as the water boilers have got so efficient.'

Time for a rest. We set the Argos satellite transmitter to one of its prearranged codes. Most days it was 00, which meant 'all OK'. Today we put it on 04, which meant 'strong winds'. That way Julian would know why we were not travelling.

We wanted to move the clock so we didn't ski into the sun. We also wanted to be refreshed for the last 135 nautical miles.

Ann telephoned her children – which put a huge smile on her face – then we all went back to bed.

Outside, a gale was blowing. It was blissful to spend the next six hours dozing in our sleeping bags.

Day 49
8 nautical miles
Woke at 9 a.m. local time, much refreshed. It was such a relief the ANI saga was over. We chatted and laughed about what we had been through.

'Thank God for Julian. What would we have done without him?' we all said.

We were now at 7,500 feet. The effects of altitude are worse near the Poles. Today my sledge felt as if it was filled with lead weights. My legs felt as if they had no muscles; I couldn't get any oxygen down to make them work. I had to keep stopping to lean on my ski poles. Breathless and heaving, I was loud inside my mask.

Since resupply – as my contribution to helping Zoë's back to get better – I had carried a large stuff sack for her. At the first break, Zoë took the stuff sack back.

I knew it didn't matter – I knew each team member played their own part. I also knew that some days it all seemed easy and other days the weight was impossible. But I was unwilling to give weight up. I knew the others would not judge me. It was me, judging myself.

Closer now to success than failure, there was an optimism between us. We were beginning to feel proud.

The homeward stretch.

I thought about the outside world. It had rarely been very far away – always the telephone, Julian and going live on radio. The experience was surreal – and in that way, quite magical.

So different from the experiences of the early explorers – and yet, in many ways, no less powerful. Conquering your fear and pain barriers, the limits of what you can do easily – it makes you grow inside. Gives you something unshakeable – a confidence.

With these thoughts, always, inevitably, my father. And my brothers too. Growing up, wanting to compete. They were boys and they were bigger, older. I had felt successful before. But this was something else entirely. I knew it would change me. I had no idea in what way.

Rosie, Pom, Zoë and Ann – closer to me than anyone had ever been. We were sharing an extraordinary adventure. Their lives were as important to me – every bit as important – as my own. I felt their aches with them – I had them too. I knew the euphoria and the empty hopelessness. We rarely expressed our fullest feelings – we hinted at them and stepped around them. Just enough for each other to know. Keeping a lot to ourselves.

I wrote in my diary. Page after page. I wanted to record the whole thing. One day I will look back and there will be proof that I did it: I skied to the South Pole. I made it happen. It's easier than you think.

* * *

We were all breathless. Whenever we stopped we could feel our hearts thumping. Ann had a headache and her nose bled. We went very slowly, heads down in our hoods. Faces covered against the wind. Impossible to chat at breaks because of the wind. Goggles so misted we could hardly see.

Sometimes the sun kept the mist watery. It was like looking through a bottle of vodka. When it was my turn to lead, my goggles turned to thick ice. I fell over.

'No bumps for miles and Caroline chooses the only one to clamber over,' Zoë laughed. 'You looked like Pom when she crashed into my snow wall.'

Zoë took over at the front.

'Just follow my sledge,' she said.

But I couldn't even see that. Or a shadow.

Every few minutes, Zoë turned and called out. I could just hear her voice through the wind and set off towards it. Later I discovered Ann and Pom were in the same state. We made a sorry gaggle staggering along in different directions.

At the end of the hour, we stopped as usual, lifted our goggles an inch and looked at each other. The weather was closing in, visibility was worse and the wind was much stronger. We were loathe to stop but worried about putting up the tent in a storm.

We had skied for just over six hours. Eight miles, we told ourselves, was much better than nothing.

Day 50
11 nautical miles

The scenery changed again. Now we were skiing through an eccentric jumble of surfaces. Lots of ridging and small sastrugi. Very tiring to ski over, difficult to get a rhythm. Our skis and sledges kept getting stuck.

Big news: without a word to anyone, Zoë started using two poles again. Since Christmas Day she had been using only one. 186 miles in 18 days – no wonder she was tired and losing weight.

'At last we've made it to 88 degrees.'
'We were in 87 for seven days – that's far too long.'
'We're on our way again.'
We all felt that.

We really were getting closer to the end of the earth. The lines of longitude on our chart were getting closer and closer. We had followed a pinstripe between 85° West and 86° West all the way from the Thiel Mountains. Never deviating. Now, at 88° South, there was no space to print the pinstripes and we were into a blank bit of white. Another navigational triumph. We had steered an exact course since we turned left at the Thiels. Over 150 miles in a dead straight line.

Day 51
11 nautical miles

Sticky snow all day. Beautiful sunshine. No wind. It was good to be able to relax a little. And chat during breaks.

'Just imagine,' Rosie said, 'if we could open a door and walk right into a nice warm tent.'

'Cookers on,' Pom extended the fantasy. 'Luggage in, a chalet girl, perhaps, to prepare everything.'

All I could think about was a warm bath. I wanted that more than anything.

'Poo-yee, Zoë,' I said as Zoë climbed back over me in the tent from the lavatory.

Rosie poked her head out to look.

'That's amazing, Zoë. I'd have asked for an epidural if I'd done one that big,' she said.

'You should try my technique,' said Ann proudly. 'Yesterday, when I was outside, I made a hole with my pee and then managed to poo straight into it.'

We were all impressed.

Our conversation most days revolved around lavatories. We were paranoid about getting our periods. There was a panic every time somebody's pee was pink – although usually this was a reflection of our orange trousers or red wind suit. We developed a group superstition: if we did not talk about periods (more than once a day that is) we wouldn't get them.

Whoever had a period – at this point it was me – was seen as having the power to jinx the whole group.

'That's it, we'll all be on now,' Ann said.

'If you bring me on, Caro,' Pom said, 'I'll never talk to you again.'

Today we completed 500 nautical miles.

Day 52
9 nautical miles

Antarctica wasn't going to let us within one hundred nautical miles of the Pole without a struggle. One of our hardest days so far. Minus 24°C and gusting 15-knot winds.

I fought with my hood all day. It was too small and the poppers were frozen. For the first two marches I had to ski with my hand holding the hood together.

I had to keep stopping. The others did their best to help, providing safety pins and karabiners – all the time battling against cold hands – but nothing stopped the wind freezing my face.

We needed to keep moving. Snack breaks seemed impossibly short. No sooner had I got my hood undone and plunged my mitten into my pouch for food, than Zoë would shout 'time' and the others got up to set off.

The hood exhausted me. Zoë took my hat off and lent me her balaclava to wear underneath. Then she fixed up a contraption to try to keep the hood shut, but this only added to my helplessness. I could not see how the arrangement was fixed so I could not undo it. I could not eat because I was frightened of burning my mouth on the metal. I felt my heart thumping with every step. I told myself it was just the altitude.

We were just over 100 miles from the Pole – and from the 220 people who were based there. Yet today I suddenly felt very remote. For the first time, I began to feel a long way from anywhere. I did not feel frightened. I took strength from the fact we were winning – we were on the homeward stretch.

The sun was out all day and, in the late afternoon, I was able to use the sun to melt the ice in my goggles and then chip it out. The wind swirled the snow towards us over bumps and troughs. The ice looked like an ocean frozen in a storm.

Despite the difficulties, I enjoyed battling the elements. It was exhilarating. When we got home – home being the tent which I looked forward to more and more – I felt a great sense of achievement. As the first black poles went in, I felt elated.

At the end of the day, 95.5 nautical miles to go. We had travelled a very long way. After dinner we cracked open Pom's miniature Jack Daniels. It was a landmark, we felt celebratory.

'I still can't grasp what 100 miles means,' I told the others. 'Let alone what it means to ski it.'

Day 53
12 nautical miles

Every day when we got up, the snow looked different. The wind was constantly changing the size and shapes of the sastrugi. In the morning, the sun would have moved 180 degrees from the night before. It would play on the ice in a different way, always changing.

The wind dropped and we set off at quite a pace.

I loved having time to daydream. Extraordinary memories drifted in and out of my head. All sorts of people – friends and acquaintances, many of whom I had not seen for years. Each person triggered memories of events and other people. Thoughts stretched. An hour or more, weaving idly.

We saw our first double rain circle around the sun. A faint double rainbow, very soft and beautiful, throwing a bright white light on to the horizon.

'Perhaps this will be our last Sunday on the ice,' Pom said.

'Don't say that,' we all tried to shut her up quickly.

We were unwilling to count the days, terrified to make a commitment, even to ourselves. We were frightened to tempt fate.

The tent was freezing. At this altitude, the cookers were difficult to handle. When first lit, flames two or three feet high leapt up. Ann and Pom had to coax them down with pan lids.

The cookers had also started to play up – a combination of altitude and the long hours we had put them through. Now we often only had two working at a time. We reduced our intake of drinks.

Ann kept a record of how much fuel we had: 'We've got lots,' she said. 'Even though the cookers use more because of the cold and the altitude, our consumption is about the same.' (1 can – 3.78 litres – every 3½ to 4 days.)

One less cooker made a big difference to the temperature. It was minus 5°C in the tent and minus 21°C in the lavatory this evening. We shivered and were so cold we could hardly speak. We longed to get into our sleeping bags.

Day 54
11 nautical miles

This morning I got very excited about reaching the Pole.

Then, as a penalty, the world went mad. Cloud came down, the wind rose wildly and then, for the first time ever, swung round to the north. This was very disorientating. I was leading but I could see nothing. I kept stopping, convinced I had turned 180°. I consoled myself with the thought the others would call out if I was veering off madly. But then I remembered their goggles were probably as iced up and opaque as mine.

Ann was having a bad day; she had no energy. Zoë too was struggling with her back and with gout in her right foot. I took some of her luggage. It made my sledge feel much heavier – a heaviness disproportionate to its new weight.

Rosie went in front and I attempted to navigate, but it was difficult to shout loud enough through my mask and balaclava.

Then, just as it seemed we were getting nowhere, the sun came back. Suddenly the cloud opened up and there was an enormous dome of bright blue sky. Shadows came back in the grey sastrugi.

My goggles froze completely.

Our equipment was showing signs of wear and tear. The soles of Ann and Zoë's boots had split near the toe. The snow and wind found their way in and their feet were very cold.

The plastic baskets on the ends of most of our ski poles were also close to breaking off. We only noticed when one of mine broke completely, leaving a sharp tip which kept sinking into the snow. Mostly the ice was so hard it made no impression but then, suddenly, without warning the pole would sink in up to twelve inches. It affected my rhythm; falling sideways was tiring.

I mended the poles with thin paracord, winding and knotting it in a way I hoped I could remember from watching people making fishing nets as a child. It made me think about the equipment used by explorers in the past. Their clothing must have been so awful. How they coped in leathers and tweeds I could not imagine. Everything – their boots, jackets, sleeping bags – must have got so heavy and wet. Everything must have been frozen solid. I wondered if they ever felt warm.

Our clothing was amazing. We were out in temperatures close to minus 40°C and were still only wearing two layers plus a wind suit.

Day 55
12.5 nautical miles

Every night we slept in the same formation, squidged like black sausages into the tent. Pom's face was in the pots and pans, mine was six inches from the lavatory. On some nights, the wind came racing through and we made barricades with stuff sacks and clothes to keep warm.

Today we woke full of expectation. We were nearly at the last degree.

'Morning Wod,' said Zoë, unusually cheerful for the morning. Wod was Pom's name, visible upside down on the stuff sack she used as a pillow.

We spoke to Pen, who sounded a bit miffed we hadn't called before. I explained we tried to call him on Christmas Day (always engaged) and left him a message on Boxing Day. Pom had written him five pages at resupply, which he should get today or tomorrow. I tried not to feel guilty.

We spoke to Geoff, back home in the Lake District, to congratulate him on having made it.

'Did you ever think we'd make it after Norway?' Zoë asked him.

He did not answer.

'You are my heroines,' he said. That made us all very proud.

My skis and sledge flew. The hours passed more quickly than on almost any day so far. I didn't think of anything except we were nearly there. I kept imagining seeing the South Pole on the horizon.

'What's that?' one of us would say – and we would all stop and look. It was nothing.

We agreed we should make a big effort today to get to the last degree. For an hour, I had a rush of excitement and skied faster and faster. I wasn't thinking about the fact it was a major achievement – all I could feel was excitement, like a child at Christmas. *I simply could not wait*.

At the end of our customary eight and a half hours, Ann got the GPS out.

'Welcome to Garmin . . .' it read as usual. We waited for it to warm up and find its satellites.

'88 degrees, 59 minutes and 41 seconds,' announced Ann. 'Just a third of a mile to go.'

I set off at the front for another twenty minutes, skiing, skiing, one foot in front of the other and then – at last – we were there.

'Hoorah,' I shouted.

When we first looked at the map, 89° South seemed such a long way. Now we were there. Just one more degree – 60 nautical miles – to go. We were still on 86° West. The same longitude as we had when we left the Thiels – this gave Ann and me immense pleasure.

Back in the tent, I realised I was the only one who had had an easy day. Everyone else was exhausted.

'Can we get there by 5.00 p.m. GMT on Sunday?' Ann wondered. 'On the telephone, Julian said that would be good for the media.'

We thought about it for a while.

'If we do nine hours' skiing,' I said, 'maybe we could do 14 miles for the next four days. That would leave us with just a few miles to do on Sunday.

'I think we should try to stick to GMT now,' Ann said. 'Otherwise the hours will slip forward and it won't be Sunday at all.'

We were all agreed. It was very cold again, but we had hit the last degree and that gave us all a gentle smug pleasure.

Day 56
12.5 nautical miles

Our first day in 89°S. We had always contemplated that, when we got to this stage, we might throw food away. We each ate about 1.1 kilos of food a day – so an extra day's food was heavy.

'Even if we're not going to use it, I think we should carry it rather than throw it away,' Rosie said. 'It doesn't seem right environmentally.'

'I think you're getting things out of proportion,' I countered. 'To me, the concept that a bag of peanuts is going to interfere with the world's climate is ludicrous. I want to enjoy the last degree,' I said, 'not get there on my knees because I've been pulling extra weight.'

Antarctica is enormous – so enormous it is hard to get your head around its size – even when you are there. It is larger than America and Mexico combined, its ice is up to 14,000 feet deep.

'What's much more damaging is aircraft,' Pom said. 'There are eight Hercules flights to the Pole a day.'

'Yes,' agreed Zoë. 'And it's still the cleanest air on earth.'

'If we don't throw it away,' I continued, 'what happens to our bag of peanuts? An aeroplane comes to pick us up and burns extra fuel carrying the extra weight – much more damaging than a bag of peanuts. And what do we do with the extra food when we get it home? It doesn't mysteriously evaporate – it has to be disposed of in England and damage the atmosphere there.'

'Over these two months, we've caused far less damage to the planet than we ever would at home,' Zoë continued. 'We haven't driven a car, used a fridge or gone shopping and come home with loads of plastic bags. People have this romantic notion that, when they're at home, they don't cause any damage – but it's just not true.'

'The same goes for human waste,' Ann added. 'You read about people on expeditions claiming they take all their waste home with them, but I don't believe it. Apart from anything else, how do you physically collect your pee? And imagine how heavy it would be.'

We remembered the DC6 we had seen abandoned in the snow just outside Patriot Hills.

'It will be buried in a few years and no one will ever know it was there,' I said. 'The same goes for a bag of peanuts – or a human poo.'

We left ourselves with five days' food, plus two spare days' dinners and breakfasts in case of storms or anything else that might keep us stranded. The sledges were lighter again but I was slightly scared. This was it. If we didn't make it on these rations we would fail.

We all thought the scenery was boring today, although it was not actually much different from so many other days. We were excited inside, so the outside became something to get through.

So much for adrenalin coasting us home. My sledge felt like a Mini Metro. I had no energy, my back hurt and I had crepitus in both legs. I thought again about our plan to ski for nine hours.

'I think it's self-defeating,' I said. 'We've agreed to try and get to the Pole by 5.00 p.m. on Sunday if we can. In order to do that, we can't afford to roll the clock forward at all. The trouble is, if we ski for too long I don't think we'll be able to function without rolling it forward. If that happens, we may find that by the time we arrive, it's a day later anyway.'

Pom stuck her thumbs up in agreement.

'We know we can do 14 miles in eight and a half hours,' I said. 'I think that's what we should aim for.'

Rosie nodded. 'I like going faster anyway,' she said.

At the end of the day we only had 48 nautical miles to go. I began to feel excited. I knew what 48 miles meant. 48 miles was the distance from London to Cambridge. If I had to, I could imagine myself walking along the M11. It began to feel very real.

Day 57
12 nautical miles

We decided we would do just 12 nautical miles a day – and enjoy it. We renewed our efforts to be quick in the morning. Zoë won a race with Rosie and me to get ready and was out of the tent first.

My coldest day. It wasn't just my hands that were cold – my whole arm felt draughty. I didn't understand why and kept checking everything was done up. When we stopped because Zoë and Pom were having a poo disaster, I jumped up and down and waved my limbs about, but the arm was numb. It felt lifeless, frozen, hanging by my side. It didn't feel like me – as if it didn't belong to me. It was cold to touch, dead.

I waved my arm around to get the blood going, but it didn't seem to make any difference. I could move my arm, but it still didn't really feel like a part of my body. If I had stuck a pin in I would not have felt it. I was scared, worried the coldness would stretch through my whole body. I couldn't believe anything was wrong, yet it felt unnatural.

It took a couple of hours skiing to warm up. I didn't mention it to the others. Everyone had something they were battling with.

'I don't think we'll be seeing the Emerald City today,' I said to Zoë.

The Emerald City was Zoë's vision of the South Pole. Before we came, she had not wanted to look at any pictures of where we were going (she even went so far as to run out of the room at Liv's house when she showed us her photographs). Her South Pole was a vision out of the *Wizard of Oz*.

I knew there was a scientific base at the South Pole. I knew there would be people and frenetic activity. I expected them to overlook us when we arrived. We had been told to expect them to be unfriendly. It could be an anticlimax, the moment of arrival at the South Pole. I hoped Zoë wouldn't be disappointed.

Someone had told us we would be able to see the polar base from miles away. The trouble was no one could remember how far they had said.

'Didn't Liv say 50 miles?' said Rosie.

'Surely not,' Ann replied, 'I think it was more like 30.'

A dark blue line appeared on the horizon. We could have been on the moon. At times I wondered about my next venture. A summer by the Sea of Tranquillity, perhaps.

Day 58
12 nautical miles

Today I thought about the enormous distance we had travelled. I thought of all the different stages of the journey – Hercules Inlet, the Ellsworth Mountains, Marshmallow Valley, our big crevasse, the Thiels, resupply, big sastrugi, ANI, the last degree.

I had no sense we had skied in a straight line. In my head there were bends and turns and gentle, undulating slopes. It did not seem possible we had gone uphill all the way, or that we had been at it for sixty days. Sixty days, what did that mean? It now felt like no time at all.

As lunch breaks were longer stops, we sometimes put on down jackets. Today we sat still for too long. When I took my jacket off to start skiing again, I realised it was much colder than I thought. An icy coldness spread from my waist up, right inside my body. It made me breathless. I was far too cold to think about anything but moving desperately fast to get warm.

I was at the front but I couldn't concentrate on going in a straight line or looking at the compass. I didn't care. All I wanted to do was move, move, move.

I put my hands in my armpits and then between my legs. Nothing made any difference. I needed my hands close to me, needed to hold them. There was a moaning noise we all made when our hands hurt like this. I moaned and moaned.

Zoë was behind me. She took hold of one of my hands and tried to rub it, but it had no effect. I felt cold from my core. The only thing to do was move again.

My body took an hour to start to warm up – the moment it did, I became aware of my hands, which were in agony. When my body was freezing I didn't notice my hands – the body, it seemed, had a physical hierarchy of attention.

A reflective day. We were all thinking about the journey, remembering. For the first time we allowed ourselves to think – and talk – about what we most looked forward to.

'I've been trying to imagine my first pint of beer back home,' Zoë said at once. 'Spending all day in the pub with the Sunday papers, endless beer and cigarettes.'

'I'm looking forward to real beer too,' I said. 'But, first of all, I really really want to go to our Corner Bar in Punta Arenas.'

'Yes,' said Pom. 'One of those ridiculous tall vodkas with no more than a splash of tonic. I imagine I'll fall over in a moment.'

Then I thought about it further. For two months I had not been able to stand up in the tent or sit comfortably. 'Actually, what I want most is a chair . . .'

Rosie looked dreamy. 'A lovely deep armchair. With big soft cushions,' she mused.

'No, it doesn't even have to be comfortable for me. All I want is to sit upright with my back against something. In fact, I think a simple wooden chair would be best.'

'I'm looking forward to Lucy and Rachel rubbing cream into my back on a Saturday morning,' said Ann.

'What about Joseph?' I asked.

'Oh, he doesn't do it. He prefers watching telly,' she said.

I thought of other things I missed: warmth, spontaneity – deciding to go out without having to put on layers of clothing – variety, speed. Everything we did was so slow.

'How about spending a whole day in a beauty parlour in Punta Arenas?' said Pom, reviving a dream she had had from early on. 'If I don't get my legs waxed soon the hairs are going to touch the floor.'

'Do you think they'll be able to dye my eyelashes?' Rosie asked. 'I'm so glad I haven't been able to see these ghastly blonde ones.'

We all enjoyed not having a mirror. We had had sixty bad hair days but missed every one of them.

'What about eating with a knife and fork? That's going to be quite a thrill as well,' I said.

'Mmmm, I could just murder a huge great plate of liver, bacon and spinach,' said Rosie. (Despite the iron in our rations, Rosie had longed for that all the way.)

The rest of us had very few food fantasies. Pom talked occasionally about roast lamb and I dreamed of mashed potato. Zoë had buttered tea-cakes and Yorkshire Pudding on her mind for a week.

That night, Julian told us he would prefer us to arrive on Monday morning. This took the pressure off. We really could take our time and enjoy the last few Antarctic miles.

Day 59
12 nautical miles

Still no sign of the South Pole.

'I think the Pole is part of a giant Stealth Experiment by the Americans,' Pom said.

'I think they've buried it so it's now undetectable and we're going to walk straight past it.'

For a moment I worried we might be going in the wrong direction. Perhaps the GPS and Argos had been hit by the millennium bug – and we were nowhere near where we thought we were. 'Oh yes,' I could hear myself saying to the media, 'the great thing about this expedition is that we've done all the navigation and everything all by ourselves. We've planned our food and fuel and now we haven't got enough to make it the last 150 miles to the Pole . . .'

In the middle of the day, I got terribly excited for several hours. Any minute now, we're going to see it, I thought. (Ann thought she did see it several times, but it was an illusion.)

We spoke about all that the weather had thrown at us in the last few days.

'Whiteout was the first thing,' I said.

'A double rain circle around the sun,' Ann said.

'Hot sunshine.'

'Big winds.'

'Ground storm.'

'Amazing blue skies, piebald clouds.'

'Mackerel sky,' Pom said.

'And streaks of white like aircraft streams.'

'It's amazing what the mind does. It's still so vivid to me – the mountains, the lakes and hills my mind told me we travelled through. I'm still certain about it,' I said. 'Absolutely certain.'

By the end of the day I was playing it cool. I didn't like talk that this was our last evening. It was tempting fate. I was trying not to think about it.

We skied just over 12 nautical miles. 11.4 to go.

As I lay in my sleeping bag, I thought of my father. He would have liked the simplicity, the single-mindedness, the remoteness. The South Pole was as close to us now as Patriot Hills had been on our third day. The mountains looked so clear then. This time we still did not know where our destination was.

Day 60
11.4 nautical miles

'What's that?' I shouted and stopped in my tracks. Was it another false alarm? We strained our eyes to the yellow haze on the horizon once more. Sure enough, there to the left was a strange rectangular shape.

'Oh, wow, that's it,' cried Ann. 'Look, there's buildings everywhere.'

Dark, square boxes and a long, low building like an aircraft hangar slowly emerged from the mist. It was an extraordinary moment. This place we had longed for for so long was suddenly upon us. The miles we had travelled all fled from my head. Now nothing mattered but the last one or two.

The Pole could not be more than a few hours away and, as we skied on, all I could think of was trying to find it.

I called out to Ann at the front and caught her up when she stopped.

'Where do you think we should aim for?' I asked. 'We don't want to end up at one end only to find it's miles away.'

'That's true,' she agreed. 'Shall I get the GPS out to get the bearing exactly?'

Ann was already reaching for the batteries in her undershirt pocket where she kept them warm.

Time for a snack. Potentially our last snack on our sledges.

'This can't be right,' Ann was confused. 'It says we're at 89 degrees 59 minutes South but the Pole is on a bearing of 43 degrees, from here.'

'How bizarre,' I replied. '43 degrees is over there, at right angles to us, isn't it?' I checked my compass. 'Perhaps Pom was right about the Americans hiding the base after all.'

'Which way are we going?' Rosie asked, rather irritated.

'What's the longitude say, Ann? Or has that gone mad as well?' I asked. 'Let's reset our watches exactly and just use the sun.'

So that is what we did. In a new time zone 5 hours, 56 minutes behind GMT, we picked out a square box on the horizon and set off towards it. I felt no tiredness and my sledge whizzed along. The wind slashed my cheeks like a knife but my eyes were fixed straight ahead and I ignored it.

For sixty days I had taken really good care of my face and made sure it wasn't exposed. I had been frightened about the cold and getting frostbite. Now I didn't care. All I wanted was to get there.

Gradually, we could make out more and more of the base. The buildings were square and simple – no sign yet of the dome we had seen in pictures. There were flags everywhere. Surely some of those must be at the Pole. We knew it was surrounded by flags – but we could not make out one from another.

Then, suddenly, to our right, there was a fresh flurry of snow and a Hercules landed a few hundred yards away. The wind must have taken its roar away and it had arrived completely unnoticed, about to taxi in front of us.

'Oh shit, it's the runway,' Ann said. 'Oh well, let's just go across.'

'Time to get the Union Jack out, Caro,' called Pom.

I tied the precious flag we had flown at the North Pole to my ski pole. It was bitingly cold and, as I struggled with the thin thread, my hands hurt in an instant. The flag flapped wildly as we skied five abreast.

'It looks as if we're invading,' I shouted to Pom.

Then, before we had even reached the runway, two figures emerged from the base. Half-running, half-walking, they were clearly coming towards us.

'Stop,' Pom and I shouted to the others. 'We may not be allowed here.'

We all stopped together and waited. I expected to be told we were not allowed near the base. The figures drew nearer and we could hear their voices. They sounded female but they were wrapped in heavy canvas clothes and red anoraks so we could not tell.

They wore black face masks and goggles, which they removed with a flourish.

'Hoorah and welcome. You made it. Congratulations.'

They were women and they rushed up to embrace us.

'The natives do appear to be friendly,' I whispered to Pom and we laughed at our previous nervousness.

'Do you want us to show you the way?' the women asked.

We nodded at once.

We crossed the runway, then made our stately progress towards the base. It looked completely chaotic, messy and dirty. Lots of ugly prefabricated buildings. Machinery, planks of haphazardly stacked timber and oil drums half-covered in snow. Snow was heaped up like mud on a building site.

Overwhelmed by different sights and sounds, it was hard to remember I was at the South Pole. Nothing on earth would induce me to be here during the winter, I thought – through temperatures of minus 90°C and total blackness.

The base was fast upon us and the silhouettes we had seen from a distance began to make sense.

'There it is,' the women called out. 'Up that bulldozer track to the right.'

By now it was obvious. We clambered up on to the track – my sledge knocking Rosie flat on her back. Then we regrouped to travel the last fifty yards. Lots of people appeared and began clapping and cheering us on.

It was an excited crowd. They had identical red parka jackets, their names on their breasts. I spent a lot of time focussing on the cheap sticky labels – all those names.

It was very noisy. Strange suddenly to hear people's voices other than our own. We were crowded in – we could no longer ski five abreast. It was terribly cold and very windy. It was difficult to organise ourselves. We weren't used to people.

They ran backwards beside and in front of us, taking our photographs. Then as they let us through, there was the Pole. A little ceremonial red and white striped pole with a silver globe on top. A few yards away, a signpost marked the Amundsen-Scott Polar Base and the South Geographic Pole.

'Plant your flag,' our audience cried.

I stepped forward to plant it right in front of the cameras. More clapping and cheering and people wanting to shake our hands. We fell over each other and the crowd as we struggled to undo our skis and sledges. Clumsily we hugged and congratulated each other through our frozen balaclavas and masks.

The temperature with windchill was minus 55°C.

'What's this?' Zoë asked, yanking a hollow piece of scaffolding stuck in the snow. 'It's in the way of the photos.'

It was the Pole, apparently.

'Do you think we dare sing the national anthem in front of these people?' I asked the others through a photo smile.

'Oh yes, we must,' Pom said, 'they'll love it.'

Our voices filled the air.

Afterword

T HE CROWD LISTENED RESPECTFULLY while we sang our national anthem. When we finished, there was more cheering then a woman came forward and said very gently: 'We understand if you would rather be on your own, but we would be delighted if you would come into the base to celebrate.'

We did not need to be asked more than once. We tidied up our sledges and followed a man across the snow. The silver dome of the American scientific base was in front of us at last. We slithered down a snowy ramp into our first real warmth for sixty days.

I blinked in the artificial light. After shuffling on skis for so long, it was difficult to walk. When we came to the stairs, my legs failed to respond and I fell straight over Pom, who was face-down and giggling with the same problem.

We were given champagne and the Americans allowed us to pitch our tent right by the South Pole. For the next four days, we could almost reach out our hands and touch it.

The Americans overwhelmed us with their hospitality – they looked after us like royalty. They fed us constantly, showed us round the base and even gave us a party. We were all so hungry. For my first breakfast I ate seventeen sausages. We had arrived at our goal, yet there was no sense of anticlimax. Being at the base was a new adventure.

* * *

Flying back to Patriot Hills, I looked out of the aeroplane window. Our route took us over almost exactly the same ground we had covered on skis. We stared at the ice. Miles and miles of grey and white ice. I felt as if I knew every inch.

There were an unimaginable number of crevasses, one crevasse field after another. From the air, they were large patches of ice which looked as if they had been scratched by a giant's fingernails. We looked at one another.

'God,' said Ann. 'What would we have done if we'd found ourselves in crevasses like that?'

'Perhaps we were there,' I said, 'and we just didn't know it.'

'I can't believe what we have just done,' Ann said.

'Nor can I.'

It was at that moment it hit me – the enormous distance we had travelled and the conditions we had endured.

'Look,' said Ann.

And there they were – the Thiel Mountains.

The flight to Patriot Hills took four and a half hours. From the sky we saw the Cornish Pasty, Hudson Ridge, Avalon and, finally, the Ellsworth Mountains.

'Our friends,' I said.

When we arrived back in civilisation in Punta Arenas, we were horrified by the sudden darkness of night. After sixty days of 24-hour daylight, none of us wanted to give up the energy the perpetual sun provided.

'Don't you hate the night?' Pom said. 'It's such a waste of time.'

Back at the Hostal la Estancia, we sat up drinking champagne and talking.

'Look,' Zoë suddenly exclaimed. 'A fly.'

It was the first life other than human we had seen for over two months. We watched in silence as the fly crawled across the table. It suddenly seemed a wondrous thing.

* * *

For months after my return from the South Pole, I had only one speed. I did everything very slowly. I had got out of the habit of switching my mind quickly from one thing to another. As on the expedition, I could do only one thing at a time.

In London people seemed to move so fast. Ambling along, I bumped into them in the street. People in shops had to help with my change. Back at the office, I felt no rush to do anything. My interest in my work was undiminished, but deadlines did not mean anything to me any more.

It is very difficult now to put into context what we did. Going to the North and South Poles was never a dream, but it seems dreamlike now. I think of skiing almost 700 miles through the wind and hostile conditions of the Antarctic and can't imagine myself doing it. I look at pictures of myself and I can't believe it's me.

I know with all my heart I could never have done it without Zoë, Rosie, Pom and Ann. Their strength, support and unfailing good humour made it possible for me to do something that seems impossible now. Even so, when we sit around talking about our adventure, it seems too incredible to be real.

I feel lucky I found something in life to inspire me. It means nothing to me that I achieved notoriety. What is important is that I achieved something for myself. I reached my goal.

I don't know what comes next, only that I want to do it again. I want to set myself another target and, no matter what obstacles stand in my way, I want to experience the thrill of success once more. That is what kept me going. That is what it's all about for me.

I am very proud of our achievement yet I don't believe that I – or any of the women who travelled with me – have special qualities. Everyone has their own mountain to climb. For some people, getting to the end of the road, competing in the Special Olympics or recovering from a major illness may seem a massive hurdle.

Yet success in these is no different to our success in reaching the South Pole. If that has taught me anything, it is: if we think without limits, have the courage to try and the determination to see our goal through, all things are possible.

Appendix 1

Acknowledgments

Hundreds of people made my polar adventures possible. Without their support and enthusiasm, the North and South Pole expeditions would never have succeeded, let alone been such tremendous fun. The following are just a few of those who contributed. I cannot thank them all enough.

Selection Weekends

Marian Benjamin, Kirstin Bruce, Ruth Charles, Heather Clanfield, Nina Coon, Emma Coop, Heidi Corbridge, Louise-Ann Corlett, Jennai Cox, Margaret Croad, Monica Cummins, Pauline Cuthbertson, Rosy Fabian, Susie Fairfax, Kathy Farquhar, Susannah Farr, Linda Glogg, Lissah Hall, Ali Hay, Liza Helps, Louise Hutchinson, Anne Mattison, Katherine McKay, Moira O'Toole, Susan Ovenden, Fiona Owens, Paula Phillips, Alison Prain, Gillian Price, Rebecca Reid, Pauline Renz, Ginny Rhodes, Bernie Rochford, Sue Self, Jacqui Smithson, Lianne Spencer, Anita Templar, Karen Troy Davies, Jane Webb, Linda Yarr

McVitie's Penguin Polar Relay

Alpha: Ann Daniels, Claire Fletcher, Sue Fullilove, Jan McCormac
Bravo: Rose Agnew, Karen Bradburn, Catherine Clubb, Emma Scott
Charlie: Lynne Clarke, Paula Power, Sue Riches, Victoria Riches

Delta: Andre Chadwick, Sarah Jones, Juliette May, Rosie Stancer

Echo: Caroline Hamilton, Zoë Hudson, Pom Oliver, Lucy Roberts

Guides: Denise Martin, Matty McNair

Serena Chance, Mike Ewart-Smith, Dawn French, Gary and Diane Guy, Pen Hadow, Mary Nicholson, Peter Noble-Jones, Sue Self, Jacqui Smithson, Geoff Somers

M&G ISA Challenge

Ann Daniels, Caroline Hamilton, Zoë Hudson, Pom Oliver, Rosie Stancer

HRH The Prince of Wales, Pen Hadow, Lawrence Howell, Julian Mills, Geoff Somers

Christine Adams, Suzanne Alwes, Hugh Anderson, Paul Anderson, Amundsen-Scott South Pole Base, Jerry Arcari, Jill Arch, Liv Arneson, Alan Axon, Scott Bailey, Jeannie Baker, David Baldwin, John Barwick, Philippa Baker, Barclays Bank, Mr Ballinger, Dr Ian Beasley, Hafdis Bennet, Jen Benton, Peter Bierdo, Peter Blackman, Ed Blain, Chris Bloor, Susie Bohn, Nicholas Bonham, Martin Booth, Dave Boreham, Hugh Bourne, Helen Boyd-Carpenter, Brian Brown, Kate Brown, Adrian and Natasha Bridge, David Broucher, Nick Bryce-Smith, Elisabeth Buchanan, Gary Buck, Helen Bunch, Karen Bunton, Russell Burgess, Jean Burrows, Humphrey Butler, Steve Chadwick, Carol Cheesman, Anton, Alison and Diana Coaker, Chris Court, Fiona Coutts, Gary Cross, Mark Cross, Dave Cummings, Simon Curry, Cus, Penny Daly, Joseph, Lucy and Rachel Daniels, Kevin Davies, Nick Davies, Tim Delaney, Colette Denihan, Rob Dixon, Roger Daynes, Christian Duff, Andy Dunn, Lars Ebbeson, Dr Edwards, Bob Elias, Vernon Ellis, Ercol Furniture, Lucian Ercolani, Charles Evans, Dawne Everett, Richard Everiss, Richard Field, Sir Ranulph Fiennes, First Aid Nursing Yeomanry, First Air pilots, Alex Fontaine, Tina Fotherby,

Sue Fullilove, Rick Gaulton, Robin Gibson, Sue Glasgow, Angela Gordon, Professor Frank Gould, Peter and Elizabeth Grace, John Green, Anne Hadow, Jane Hamilton, John and Kathleen Hardaker, Christine Harris, Robert Harris, Jemima Harrison, Neil Harrison, John Harvey, Robin Hawes, Andy Hawkes, George Hayles, Julia Hayward, Sandy Henney, Harriet Hewitson, Commander and Mrs D Hewitt, T Hitchings, Helge Hoflandsdal, Michael Holmes, Mark Horgan, Hostal la Estancia, Hotel Kennedy, Janie Howell, Mark Hubbard, Billy Hughes, Sue Hunter, Peter Hutchinson, Imagination, Chris Ingram, Allen Jewhurst, Tim Jeynes, Matthew Judd, A Kay, Paul Kelly, Diana King, Caroline Kinsey, Petra Kocandrlova, Paul and Nicola Krusin, Judy Lampson, Paul Landry, Randy Landsberg, Tim Langton, Sharon Lathey, Ian Lauder, Steve Laycock, Dan Leaman, Belinda Lehrell, The Hon Niall Leveson Gower, Lord Lichfield, Dee Livingstone, Susie Llewellyn-Jones, Andrew Logan, Karl Longley, Flora and Sebastian Lyon, Sara Madgwick, Jennifer Maguire, Tony Manik, Dominic March, Valerie Mars, Peter Martin, Steve Martin, Sir Arthur Marshall, Jerry Marty, Judy Maude, Caroline Mayhew, Jan McCormac, Eddie McGrath, Jeremy Merckel, Ginny Michaux, Sir Peter Middleton, Tony Minx, Miriam, Amias Moores, Sjur Mørdre, Mr P Morse, John Mortimer, Chris Moseley, Tessa Murray, Jo Musgrove, Rick Myles, Narwhal Hotel, Annarita Negrini, Esther Nicholson, Gillian Noble-Jones, K O'Byrne, Michael and Sally Oliver, Tim Oliver, Jonathan Page, Boyce Partridge, Ginny Paton, Karen Peterson, Tim Pettifer, Bianca Piper, Pitcher & Piano, Ian Pitchford, Angus Porter, Humphrey Price, Chris Proctor, John Rand, Resolute Bay Nursing Staff and School, Arthur Reynolds, Roman Reznicek, Jeremy Riches, Mrs C Roberts, Dave Roberts, Martin Robson, Clinton Rogers, Lynda Rose, James and Sarah Ross, Amanda Routledge, Jenny Ruler, Jack Russell, Sue Sadler, Susan Sawtell, Niall Saunders, Louise Selby, Rick Selleck, Lindsay Sexton, Sarah Sharples, Gary Shaughnessy, Sir Neil Shaw, Oliver Shepard, Rachel Shephard,

Singer & Friedlander, Barbara Sinclair, Terry Sinclair, Geoffrey Smith, Ian Smith, Amanda Smithson, Jennifer Sparks, Graham Staley, William Stancer, Alex Stappard, Lord Stone, Gordon Storey, Charles Swithinbank, Rod Taylor, Donna Teasdale, Chris Terrill, P Treadwell, Mike Tomes, Clive Tovey, Sean Turner, University of East London, Dave Urquhart, Eric van Dal, Caroline van der Straaten, Kent Walwin, Paul Ward, Sophie Ward, Stephen Warren, Phil Way, Richard and Jose Weber, Greg White, Araminta Whitley, Julia Wilson, Andy Woodward, Chris Woolterton, Marina Wyatt, Rob Wylie.

And finally, a huge thank you to Rosalyn Chissick for her tireless work and creative input.

Appendix 2

South Pole Sponsors
M&G Group
BT
Independent Insurance
Ineos Acrylics
Marks & Spencer
Mars
Omega Foundation

South Pole Official Suppliers

Amway	vitamins
Ajungilak	sleeping bags
Åsnes	expedition skis
Atomic	training skis
Breitling	watch
Bridgedale	socks
Carrington Performance Fabrics	sledge covers
Cébé	goggles
DMM	ice axe, ice screws
First Choice Expedition Foods	
Helly Hansen	pile clothing
Lancaster	sun protection
Simpson Lawrence	general camping equipment
Mountain Hardwear	tent, hats, gloves
Perseverance	Pertex for clothing
Rab Carrington	expedition clothing system
Rottefella	ski bindings

Appendix 3

M&G ISA Challenge
Kit List
Official Log Book – includes
Argos Codes & Procedure
Charts & Maps
VIP Tel Nos (Patron, Technical Advisors, Patriot Hills,
   Sponsors, PR Agent, Journalists)
BT Iridium Codes & Procedure
Airstrip Preparation
Time Zones (Punta, Patriot & Zulu)
Kit Manuals (EPIRB, GPS, Stoves, Iridium Pin Codes &
   Relevant Tel Nos, Video Filter, Cameras)
Insurance Details
Kit List & Weights
Flip-out Prompt Sheet

320g

	Unit Weight in grams	Total Weight in grams	Manufacturer	Model
Navigation				
GPS A (exc battery)	162	324	Garmin	12XL
GPS B (exc battery)	156	156	Garmin	12
GPS Cells ×4	92	92	Energisers	Lithium AA 1.5V
Chronometers ×5	30	150	Timex/Casio	Expdn/Barometer
Magnetic Compass (main)	38	38	Suunto	M-5
Magnetic Compass (spares) ×2	28	56	Silva	–
Chart (see Dry Log)	–	–	NOAA	JNC 120/121
Communications				
Argos Platform (inc battery & aerial)	1,195	1,195	NACLS	TAT-3 Platform
Argos Case	90	90	NACLS	As for above
Argos Spare Battery	330	330	Will	Lithium 10.8V
Argos Codes (see Dry Log)	–	–	–	–
Satellite Phone (exc battery)	400	400	Motorola	9500 Portable Tel.
Satellite Phone Batteries ×6	100	200	Motorola	3.6V 1990mAh Lith
Anti Condensation Bag	92	92	Ortleib	47×32cm
Sim Card	–	–	Iridium	–
Satellite Phone Protective Case	582	582	Peli-Products	1120 inc aerial case
Emergency Beacon	104	104	Breitling	'Emergency'
Aircraft Mirror Signaller	16	16	BCB International	–
Power Supply				
Primary Battery A (40 hrs)	1,805	1,805	Woolsery	Lithium 16 cell 14V
Primary Battery B (20 hrs)	1,425	1,425	Woolsery	Lithium 12 cell 14V

Rechargeable battery	1,440	1,440	Flo Howell	Ni-Cad 12V
Solar Panel (inc cabling)	694	694	Flo Howell	See Flo
Solar Panel Protective Backing	106	106	Flo Howell	See Flo
Video Voltage Adapted Cabling	272	272	Flo Howell	See Flo
Iridium Voltage Adapted Cabling	220	220	Flo Howell	See Flo
GPS Voltage Adapted Cabling	64	64	Flo Howell	See Flo
Crevasse Safety				
Safety Rope	3,100	3,100	Lanex	50 m × 9.2 mm
Ice axe (hammer)	680	680	DMM	The Fly 45cm
Karabiner (Screwgate)	290	58	HB Wales	9KN-9-28
Leg Loops (detachable)	1,000	200	Wear & Tear	Custom-made
Prusik Loops (leg & waist)	300	60	Homemade	Acces. cord 6mm
Ice Screw				
Tent Inner (inc hanging line & pines)	3,178	3,178	Mtn Hardwear	Weather Station
Tent Outer	4,078	4,078	Mtn Hardwear	Weather Station
Tent Poles	2,950	2,950	Mtn Hardwear	Weather Station
Tent Poles (spare)	48	48	Mtn Hardwear	Weather Station
Tent (extra floor)	994	994	Homemade	3mm closed cell
Tent Stowage Bags × 2	144	72	Homemade	Pertex/drawstring
Snow Stakes × 8	976	122	Homemade	30cm, special cut
Bothie Bag	990	990		Standard 8 person
Snow Shovel	718	718	Voile	Extreme
Pee Bottle (900ml)	144	144	Nalgene	1 litre
Special Pee Bottle	196	196	Suba-Care	Plastic, domestic
Snow Brush	82	82	—	
Multi-Tool	226	226	Leatherman	Wave

	Unit Weight in grams	Total Weight in grams	Manufacturer	Model
Kitchen				
Stoves (×3)	330	990	MSR	Dragonfly
Fuel Pumps (×4)	54	162	MSR	Dragonfly
Wind & Base Reflectors (×3)	68	204	MSR	Dragonfly
Base Boards (inc bungee wraps ×3)	323	969	Homemade	–
MSR Maintenance Kit (see Repair Kit)	–	–	MSR	Dragonfly
Stowage Bags	28	84	MSR	Dragonfly
Fuel Bottles ×4	140	840	MSR	0.975 litres
Reserve Non-Pressurised Fuel Bottle	228	228	Sigg	1.5 litres
Cooker Fuel				Naphtha
Funnel	26	26	Stewart	Plastic 9.5cm diam.
Snow Melting Pan (inc lid)	840	840	The Metal Corp	Open Country 6L
Cooking Pan (inc lid, handle & bag)	564	564	MSR	Guide, 4 litre
Drinks Billy (inc lid)	392	392		4 litre
Chef's Spoon/Ladle	52	52	Lexan	Lexan
Vacuum Flasks (no mug-lids) ×3	684	2,052	Vango	Stnlss Steel 1 litre
Meteorological				
Temperature & Rel. Humidity Gauge	114	114	Vaisala	HM34C (exc batt)
Temp & Rel. Humidity Battery	44	44	Varta	IEC6F22 9V
Anemometer	26	26		W 10
Wrist Barometer	30	30	Suunto	Vector
Met. Log	80	80	–	–

Video

Camera	568	568	Sony	DV DCR PC3E
Battery (high capacity) ×2	114	228	Sony	NP-FS31 Lithium
Micro-phone (lapel)	80	80	IQ Video	TMM1000
Tapestock ×17	20	340	Maxell	MiniDV Cassette
Memory Card	20	20		3×16MB & 2×4MB
Protective Case	48	48	Homemade	Closed cell foam
Anti Condensation Bag	72	72	Ortleib	29×29cm
Outdoor Camera				
Camera Body	604	604	Nikon	FM 2
Lens	260	260	Nikon	35–70mm
UV Filter	20	20	Hoya	(non-snow)
Filmstock (inc cases) ×40	28	1,120	FujiColour	Superia Reala 100
Spare Lithium Batteries ×4	–	–		
Protective Case	52	52	Homemade	Closed cell foam
Anti Condensation Bag	72	72	Ortleib	29×29cm
Indoor Camera				
Camera Body (inc lens)	500	500	Voightlander	Bessa-1 25mm lens
Filmstock (inc cases) ×17	28	476	Fujicolor	Superia Reala 100
Spare Lithium Batteries ×2	–	–		–
Protective Case	48	48	Homemade	Closed cell foam
Anti Condensation Bag	80	80	Ortleib	29×29cm
Digital Camera				
Camera Body	368	368	Kodak	DC280
Memory Cards	–	–	Kodak	1×16 & 1×20MB

Clothing	Unit Weight in grams	Total Weight in grams	Manufacturer	Model
Spare Clothes Sack	116	580	Homemade	—
Socks				
Vapour Barrier Liner Socks	—	—	—	—
Calf Sock (thin) ×2	66	330	Bridgedale	Cool Max Liner
Alfa Liner Bootee Spare	186	930	Alfa	—
Calf Sock (thick) ×2	148	740	Bridgedale	—
Hands				
Wristlets ×2	20	200	Homemade	Fleece
Liner Gloves (v thin) ×2	16	80		Silk
Liner Gloves (thick)	42	210	Mtn Hardwear	Polartec
Main Mitts	422	2,110	Mtn Hardwear	
Trousers				
Thermal Bottoms	162	810	Helly Hansen	TR48603
Under-Trousers Rab			Rab Carrington	Pile/Pertex
Salopettes			Rab Carrington	Pile/Pertex
Tops				
Thermal Top	74	370	Helly Hansen	OX48506
Under-Top Rab			Rab Carrington	
Smock (with fur ruffed hood)	1,150	5,750	Rab Carrington	Pile/Pertex

Extreme Outer				
Wind suit	—		Rab Carrington	Pertex
Down Jacket (inc sack)	1,300	6,500	Rab Carrington	Expedition
Head				
Balaclava (inner)	24	120	Helly Hansen	Silk, HH OX57800
Headband	24	120	Helly Hansen	57707
Neck Gaiter	26	260	Homemade	Windproof Fleece
Nose Beak	4	20	Homemade	Fleece/Pertex
Wrap-Around Face Mask	58	290	Stomatc	Proline Support
Face Mask	132	660	Scott	Safari Vee
Goggles	106	530	Cébé	Tinted lenses
Hat	62	310	Mountain Hardwear	Gore Windstopper
Sunglasses	44	220	Cébé	4000 Cecchinel
Sledging				
Sledge	6,710	33,550	Snowsled	Glass fibre, 1.6m
Trace	146	730	—	Kerm. 6m × 6mm
Shock Absorber	106	530	Wear & Tear	Custom-made, 1m
Harness	1,055	5,275	Wear & Tear	Custom-made
Karabiners (Regular) × 2	44	440	HB Wales	KN 24-9
Skis (inc skins & screws)	1,662	8,310	Åsnes	190cm
Skins & Screws	—	—	Pomoca	Mohair/Synthetic
Bindings (Toe)	935	4,675	Rottefella (hybrid)	SuperTelemark
Bindings (Cable – see wgts above)	—	—	Rottefella	Chili cable
Ski Poles	798	3,990	Åsnes	Military (NATO)

	Unit Weight in grams	Total Weight in grams	Manufacturer	Model
Sleeping				
Ground Mats ×2	322	3,220	Cascade	RidgeRest
Vapour Barrier Bag (inner)	340	1,700	Peter Hutchinson	Custom-made
Main Synthetic Bag	3,440	17,220	Ajungilak	Denali
Outer Down Bag	910	4,550	Peter Hutchinson	Custom-made
Foldaway Straps	74	370	BCB	1 metre
(Personal) Camping				
Insulated Mug (inc lid)	140	700	Aladdin	0.5 litres
Spoon	12	60	Lexan	–
Nalgene Flasks (no jacket)	144	1,440	Nalgene	0.9 litres
Flask Parka Jackets	114	1,140	Outdoor Research	1 litre
'Spare Clothes' Sack			Homemade	–
'Day Bag' Sack			Homemade	–
Private Log	312	936		
Pencil(s)				
Whistle	20	100	Storm	–
Christmas Presents	–	250	–	–
Toothbrush	16	80	–	–
Toothpaste	68	272	Colgate	Total
Vitamins	116	580	Amway	Multi & C
Moisturising Suncream	122	1,220	Lancaster	SPF25
Lip Protection	28	280	Lancaster	SPF25
Tampons ×10 boxes	110	1,100	Lil-let	
Vaseline	92	920		

Repair & Maintenance

Stowage Sack
Thread
Needles
Duct Tape
Spinnaker Tape
Tent Pole Ends
Binding Screws, Philips Driver & Micro Spanner
Binding Toe Straps
Spare Harness Buckle
Argos Tools
Thick Wire
Paracord
Tent Pole Repair Sleeve
Superglue
MSR Stove & Pump Maintenance Kit

Total 558g

Medical

Analgesics
Pethidine Tablets 50mg × 50
Temgesic Tablets (sub-lingual) 0.2mg × 100
Meptid 200mg × 50
Aspirin Tablets 0.5g × 50

Anti-infection
Chloramphenicol eye ointment × 1 tube
Flucloxacillin 250mg × 120
Canesten Cream

Anti-inflammatory
Sodium Diclofenac Tablets 50mg × 100
Ibruprofen Tablets 200mg × 24

Other Medicines
Loperamide 2mg × 30
Zovirax
Glycerine Suppositories 3.5g × 20
Throat Strepsils × 5 pckts
Cymalon × 2 courses

Dental
Cavit – Emergency Filling Stick

First Aid
Water Resistant Tape with Gauze Strip 10cm × 30cm
Strappel Zinc Oxide Tape 2.5cm × 1 roll
Petroleum Jelly Dressings 10 × 10cm (× 2)
Sterile Absorbable Dressings 5 × 5cm (× 5)
Steri-Strips (× 6)
Compeed assorted sizes (× 30 pads)
Bactigras Antiseptic Wipes 5 × 5cm (× 10)
Antiseptic Cream
Hypothermia Thermometer
Mersilk Suture Kit (black silk with curved needle)
Sterile Disposable Scalpel
Tweezers
Sterile Drainage Syringe
Sterile Latex Gloves
Melolin Gauze Dressings/Swabs 10 × 10cm (× 5)
Flexible Cohesive Bandage 7.5cm × 3 metre
Directions for Use Drugs Notes
Accident 'Vital Signs' Monitoring Form
Stowage Bag

Total 922g

Private Bags

Caroline	40
Pom	106
Zoë	0
Ann	32
Rosie	99
	Total 277g

Standard Rations per Day	Individual grams per day	Team grams per day	Calories	Manufacturer	Comment
Matches	1	5		Swan Vesta	Wood, Non-Safety
Milk Powder	29	145		Taj Stores	Full Fat
Tea Bags	8	40		M&S	
Coffee (Caffeinated)	6	30		M&S	Italian Blend
Sugar	29	145		M&S	Granulated
Hot Chocolate Drink	54	270		Mars	
Porridge/Toffee-Pecan Crunch	104	520		M&S	
Nuts/Shortbread/Chocolate }	340	1,700		M&S	Brazil, almond, hazelnut, walnut, pecan & cashews
Mars Bar			Mars	Mars	
Chicken & Vegetable Soup	145				
29					
Supper Dish	128	640		First Expedition	Various
Cheese	100	500		M&S	Cheddar
Butter	100	500		M&S	
Totals	1,077	5,385	5,200		

Appendix 4

Navigation

I still find it difficult to grasp how enormous Antarctica is. Just how big is an area of over five million square miles? The answer is it is nearly half the size of Africa and one and half times bigger than the whole of the United States. 98 per cent of the continent is permanently buried in glacial ice – ice which is so heavy that most of the rock underneath has been pushed below sea level. The average depth of the ice is around 6,000 feet and it represents between 70 and 95 per cent of the world's fresh water (depending on whether one includes moisture in soil as well as rivers and lakes).

We started our journey at sea level at Hercules Inlet on the edge of the Antarctic continent. Over the next 604 nautical miles (or 695 statute miles), we climbed to 9,300 feet at the South Pole. Whilst the South Pole itself never moves, the glacier on top of it moves about ten yards a year towards the coast. Contrast this to the North Pole which lies in the middle of the Arctic Ocean. The sea there is frozen for most of the year and the ice can float many miles each day with the ocean currents. However, like the South Pole, the geographic point which is the North Pole does not change.

The North and South Poles are at opposite ends of the axis around which the earth spins. They are sometimes known as the North and South Geographic Poles to distinguish them from the magnetic ones. The North and South Magnetic Poles are the ends of the giant bar magnet inside the earth which an ordinary compass points to. Therefore, if we had simply followed a bearing of 180 degrees, we would have found our way to the South Magnetic Pole, not the South Geographic Pole where we wanted to go.

Our compass bearing to the South Geographic Pole was the angle in relation to us between it and the North Magnetic Pole. The bearing changed as our own position changed. At the start of our journey, the bearing to follow to the South Geographic Pole was 169 degrees and it reduced steadily to 114 degrees towards the end.

We checked the bearing with a GPS, or Global Positioning System, every evening in the tent. The same size and shape as a mobile telephone, the GPS used satellites in the sky to tell us exactly where we were on the planet. (It is the same system as most aeroplanes and boats use.) At the same time, the GPS calculated how many miles we had left to the South Pole and the bearing to follow the following day.

The GPS gave us our position in longitude and latitude. Both longitude and latitude are measured in degrees, minutes and seconds (60 minutes equals one degree, and 60 seconds equals one minute). The longitude told us how far east or west of the Greenwich Meridian we were and the latitude how far south of the Equator. The Greenwich Meridian and the Equator are at 0° West and 0° South respectively. We started at a position at Hercules Inlet of 79°56′ South 80°11′ West and every time we crossed a degree of latitude, I unfolded the map we carried and marked our progress with little pencil crosses.

The map reminded me of a chart of the sea – an almost blank sheet of paper with only lines of longitude and latitude marked on. There were no contours or definite landmarks, just a few splodges where mountains (known as nunataks) might appear above the ice and one or two clusters of blue sausage shapes to mark known crevasses. When we started, none of us liked to look at the whole map unfolded. It was such a desperately long way – over two feet of chart and we only moved half an inch a day. But towards the end, I held it up ceremonially and retraced the crosses with my finger for all to see. We were never shy of congratulating and encouraging ourselves.

Lines of longitude and latitude circle the earth at right angles to each other. The lines, or degrees, of latitude run parallel to the Equator. There are 90 degrees of latitude North and South and they are all an equal distance apart. Each minute (one 60th of a degree) is equivalent to a nautical mile. Therefore by knowing our position each day, we were able to calculate the nautical miles we travelled, excluding of course any zigzags or diagonal lines which we might have skied in. A nautical mile is the unit for measuring distance along the earth's surface rather than in a straight line like a statute mile. A nautical mile is roughly equal to 1.15 statute miles and most references to mileages in this book are given in nautical miles.

Since the earth is round, the circumference of each line of latitude gets smaller as one goes north or south from the Equator. The lines of longitude, by contrast, are all the same length. Like the lines between the segments of an orange, they get closer together as one reaches the ends of the earth and all lines of longitude run through the North and South Poles, where the 'circles' of latitude have been reduced to mathematical points.

All the lines, or degrees, of longitude converge at the North and South Poles and therefore they are the only points in the world where there are no east or west coordinates. When I stood on the North Pole, it made no difference whether I was at 0° West or 180° West, my position was 90° North full stop. Every direction was south and nothing was east or west from me.

I never quite got used to travelling south and not north. I instinctively thought of the east to my right and the west to my left and I often had to think twice when I was navigating. But once I was at the South Pole, there was not a problem. I could not look east and I could not look west because at 90° South everywhere else was north.

We used our longitudinal position to calculate the exact local time each day. There are 360 degrees of longitude and the earth completes one revolution every 24 hours (which is 1,440 minutes). This means that the earth takes four minutes to turn through one degree of longitude and we are accustomed to grouping these degrees into time zones. For much of our journey, we skied in a straight line south along the line of longitude which was 86° West. It takes the earth 344 minutes to turn through 86° and therefore the local time was 5 hours 44 minutes after Greenwich Mean Time.

We kept our watches to the exact local time so we could navigate using the sun. (Mine also showed GMT for reference.) We used our own shadows as sundials and, provided that we knew what the local time was, we knew where our shadow should be. At local midday, the sun was due north and all we had to do to go south was to ski straight into our shadows on the snow. As the day went on, our shadows rotated 15 degrees every hour. Therefore, if we were still going at midnight, we were skiing directly into the sun. (In the northern hemisphere, the sun is due south at midday and so to get to the North Pole we did exactly the opposite.)

Appendix 5

Table of Temperatures and Positions

Day	Position	Nautical miles South	Statute miles South	Temperature °C	Wind speed knots	Windchill °C
	79°56′S 80°11′W			−16	8	−21
1	80°02′S 80°24′W	6	7	−17	18	−30
2	80°10′S 80°32′W	8	9	−16	10	−23
3	80°18′S 81°20′W	8	9	−12	1	−12
4	80°18′S 81°20′W	0	—	−15	8	−20
5	80°21′S 81°12′W	3	4	−16	10	−23
6	80°30′S 81°18′W	9	10	−16	6	−19
7	80°42′S 81°17′W	12	14	−14	3	−15
8	80°53′S 81°20′W	11	13	−14	12	−22
9	81°07′S 81°27′W	14	16	−12	5	−14
10	81°18′S 81°35′W	11	13	−14	3	−15
11	81°32′S 81°43′W	14	16	−15	4	−17
12	81°37′S 81°49′W	5	6	−18	5	−20
13	81°48′S 82°04′W	11	13	−15	6	−18
14	81°57′S 82°08′W	9	10	−18	10	−25
15	82°07′S 82°07′W	10	12	−23	8	−29
16	82°19′S 82°24′W	12	14	−19	10	−26
17	82°28′S 82°30′W	9	10	−23	10	−31
18	82°28′S 82°30′W	0	—	—	—	—
19	82°39′S 82°35′W	11	13	−15	5	−17
20	82°48′S 82°38′W	9	10	−16	5	−18
21	82°48′S 82°38′W	0	—	−15	27	−32
22	82°58′S 82°55′W	10	12	−10	8	−15
23	83°08′S 83°08′W	10	12	−13	8	−18
24	83°19′S 83°25′W	12	14	−14	15	−24
25	83°31′S 83°20′W	12	14	−17	15	−28
26	83°42′S 83°31′W	11	13	−18	12	−27
27	83°53′S 83°32′W	11	13	−18	20	−32
28	84°06′S 83°47′W	13	15	−14	6	−17

29	84°20'S 84°07'W	14	16	−13	8	−18
30	84°34'S 84°25'W	14	16	−15	4	−17
31	84°47'S 84°50'W	13	15	−19	10	−26
32	85°01'S 85°28'W	14	16	−15	4	−17
33	85°16'S 86°15'W	15	17	−15	4	−17
34	85°29'S 86°45'W	13	15	−17	10	−24
35	85°41'S 86°41'W	12	14	−16	5	−18
36	85°55'S 86°24'W	14	16	−19	5	−22
37	86°08'S 86°29'W	14	16	−18	3	−19
38	86°17'S 86°25'W	8	9	−16	2	−17
39	86°17'S 86°25'W	0	−	−16	2	−17
40	86°28'S 86°19'W	11	13	−15	1	−16
41	86°38'S 86°24'W	11	13	−18	3	−19
42	86°51'S 86°30'W	12	14	−21	4	−23
43	87°03'S 86°17'W	12	14	−24	5	−27
44	87°13'S 86°03'W	10	12	−24	8	−30
45	87°24'S 86°21'W	11	13	−25	8	−31
46	87°35'S 86°27'W	11	13	−24	3	−26
47	87°46'S 86°36'W	10	12	−25	9	−32
48	87°46'S 86°36'W	0	−	−25	10	−33
49	87°53'S 86°25'W	8	9	−26	15	−38
50	88°04'S 86°15'W	11	13	−21	6	−25
51	88°15'S 85°51'W	11	13	−22	5	−25
52	88°24'S 86°03'W	9	10	−24	5	−27
53	88°36'S 85°43'W	12	14	−26	6	−30
54	88°47'S 86°19'W	11	13	−27	7	−32
55	89°00'S 86°09'W	13	15	−28	3	−30
56	89°12'S 87°32'W	12	14	−27	1	−28
57	89°24'S 88°18'W	12	14	−28	6	−32
58	89°36'S 90°19'W	12	14	−24	6	−28
59	89°48'S 93°20'W	12	14	−28	6	−32
60	90°00'S	12	14	−34	22	−55
	Total	604	695			

Table of Our Weights

| | On departure | | | On arrival | | |
	kg	lb	stone	kg	lb	stone
Caroline	73.2	161	11st 7lb	62.3	137	9st 11lb
Ann	68.6	151	10st 11lb	59.1	130	9st 4lb
Pom	60.3	133	9st 7lb	53.2	117	8st 5lb
Zoë	58.3	128	9st 2lb	50.5	111	7st 13lb
Rosie	52.4	115	8st 3lb	43.6	96	6st 12lb

Appendix 6

Map of the Japanese Crevasses

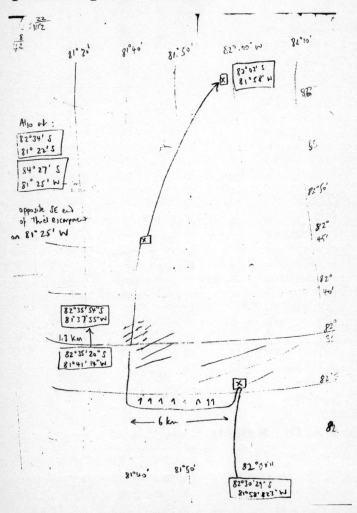

My handwritten map, taken from one shown to us by one of the pilots at Patriot Hills. It shows some crevasses to avoid.

Appendix 7

Map of the Thiel Mountains

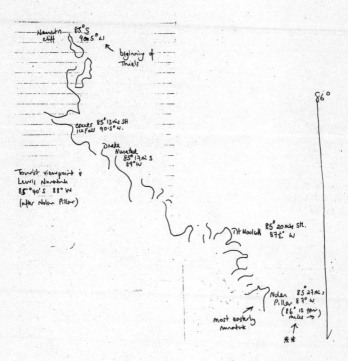

Pom's *Swallows and Amazons* map of the Thiel Mountains.

Appendix 8

Map of Daily Positions

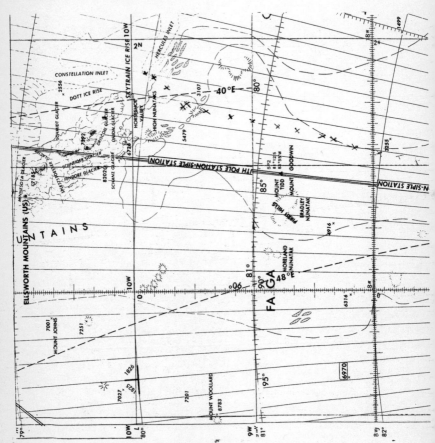

The chart we marked with crosses to show our positions each day.

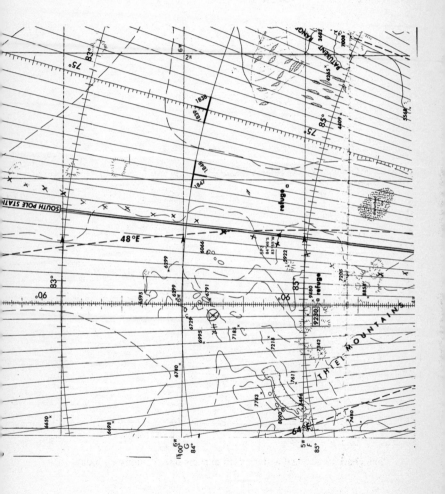

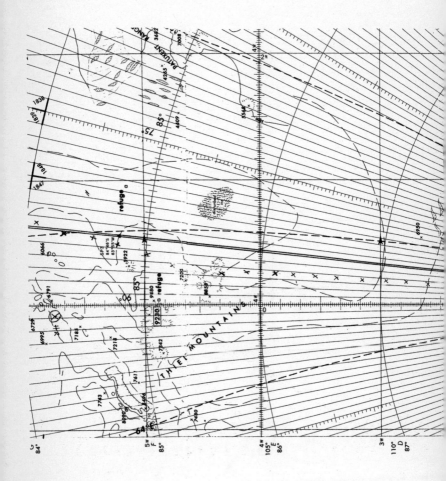

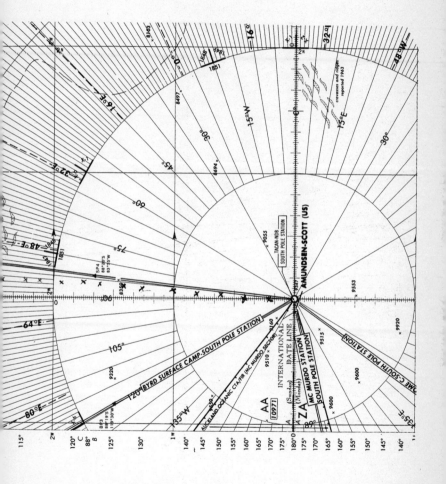